Notation Used in Identifying Exper
of Instructional Mater

Format Notation	Format Name	Identif...
BC	Base Control	Learner reads a 30-paragraph text only.
CR	Covert Responding	Learner reads text and then reads 30 multiple-choice test items, each with 3 response options. Learner is permitted and invited to respond covertly, but not overtly.
OR	Overt Responding	Learner reads text and then emits 30 overt responses to 30 multiple-choice test items, each with 3 response options.
AE	Auto-elucidative	Learner reads text and then emits responses to 30 multiple-choice test items, receiving in each case immediate feedback in the form of KCR (knowledge of correct response). Learner must emit a correct response before proceeding to a subsequent test item.
BRM-R	Branching Minus Remediation	Learner reads 30 small-step frames, each consisting of a paragraph of text plus the associated test item. On each frame, he emits a response and receives feedback in the form of KCR. Learner must emit a correct response before proceeding to a subsequent frame.
BRM/BRB	Branching	Learner reads 30 small-step frames as described above. On each frame he emits a response and receives feedback in the forms of both KCR and remediation (restatement of the item and emitted response, plus remedial text if the response is incorrect). Feedback was contained in paper envelopes which were torn open to reveal KCR and remediation. Learner must emit a correct response before proceeding to a subsequent frame.
BRB	Book-presented Branching	The notation BRB simply indicates that the BRM/BRB experimental format described above was used and considered to be a good simulation of branching programs in the software medium.
BRM	Machine-presented Branching	The notation BRM simply indicates that the times taken by the learners to complete the program were lessened by the amount of time required to obtain feedback from the BR experimental format. This correction was necessary in order for the BR format to better simulate a branching program teaching machine with its capability to provide instantaneous feedback.
BRM-F	Branching Minus Feedback	Learner reads the 30 small-step frames. As with a true branching program, he responds to each of the 30 test items, frame by frame. However, he receives no feedback as to the correctness of his responses.
BRM-OR	Branching Minus Overt Responding	Learner reads the 30 small-step frames. However, each of the 30 multiple-choice items has its correct answer conspicuously disclosed by an asterisk. No responses required or permitted.
AE-OR	Auto-elucidative Minus Overt Responding	Learner reads text and then simply reads the 30 multiple-choice items in the form of study questions, with each correct answer conspicuously disclosed by an asterisk. No responses required or permitted.

Programmed Instruction

The Century Psychology Series

PROGRAMMED INSTRUCTION

TECHNIQUES AND TRENDS

EDWARD F. O'DAY
San Diego State College
with
RAYMOND W. KULHAVY
WARREN ANDERSON
RONALD J. MALCZYNSKI

APPLETON-CENTURY-CROFTS
EDUCATIONAL DIVISION
MEREDITH CORPORATION

New York

7021-1

Library of Congress Card Number: 77-138657

PRINTED IN THE UNITED STATES OF AMERICA

390-67511-3

Preface

The several research studies reported in this book are based on data supplied over a two-year period by nearly three thousand learners from a state college, three separate junior colleges, and a military installation, all in San Diego County. Obviously, an investigation of this size, scope, and diversity could not have been performed without support from many sources.

San Diego State College provided the facilities, the majority of learners, and a one-semester research leave for the principal investigator. The San Diego State College Foundation made it possible for much of this research to be reported at the 1968 Convention of the National Society for Programmed Instruction in San Antonio, Texas. Also, a generous grant to the project was made by the San Diego Chapter of NSPI. The personnel of the host institutions at San Diego City College, Mesa College, Palomar College, and the U.S. Naval Training Center responded cooperatively to all reasonable requests. Most of all, the members of the team made the greatest contribution in the form of their effort and time. They donated their evenings, weekends, and holidays to get the job done.

Included among the studies reported are the master's theses of Messrs. Kulhavy and Anderson, and also of Mr. Dale O. Hukari, whose special contribution was the junior college study, and of Mr. John T. Orrelle, who analyzed some of the San Diego State College data.

Backstopping these researchers was a crew who assisted by proctoring, by classifying and assigning learners to the conditions, and by reducing and analyzing data. Noteworthy in this regard were: Robert Chabot, Bonner Phelps, John Roccaforte, Phyllis Russell, and Steve Sander. Many helpful editorial suggestions were made by Myfanway Glasso, of Non-linear Systems, Incorporated.

E. F. O'D.

Notes to the Reader

The reader's attention is called especially to reference materials, whose use begins with Chapter 4. Reference tables, printed on endpapers, show the six principles underlying all programmed instruction and the relationships among several programmed instruction formats. The left-hand table shows the configuration of principles making up each of the several formats. The right-hand table describes how the learner behaves on each format investigated in this research study.

Also for the reader's benefit, the practical implications of the book's research are condensed following the Subject Index in a section entitled Summary and Recommendations. This section can be clipped out along the dotted lines and used as a handy set of guidelines to assist programmers in creating appropriate instructional materials. While the recommendations themselves are concisely organized to facilitate reference, they are also keyed to specific chapters, so that the reader may refresh his memory on the detailed discussion leading to each recommendation.

Contents

Programmed Instruction

1

The Principles of Programmed Instruction - Mandatory and Optional

This book is about *programmed instruction*. Programmed instruction is referred to also as programmed learning, automated instruction, self-instruction, instructional technology, and teaching machines. The designation, *teaching machines,* actually refers to a narrower field than programmed instruction. Present-day programmed instruction is more often in book-presented form ("software"), than in machine-presented form ("hardware"). The designation, *instructional technology,* refers to a broader field than programmed instruction. Instructional technology embraces such areas as instructional radio and television, instructional films, and the earlier audio-visual techniques.

Producers of programmed instruction refer to themselves as *programmers* and to their products as *programs.* To be classified as programmed instruction (hereafter abbreviated PI), the instructional materials must have been developed in accordance with what are known as PI *principles.* However, programmers disagree as to what are, and what are not, the essential PI principles. Among the more frequently mentioned principles are the following.

PI Principles

Objective specification

The programmer identifies the terminal behaviors that the learner will be able to perform when he has completed the program. He describes intended outcomes rather than substantive content. He also indicates the conditions under which the terminal behaviors are to be manifested and states explicitly any restrictions to be imposed or resources to be provided. He specifies a standard for judging if, upon completion of the program, the learner's performance is acceptable. These criteria for objective specification are expounded at greater length by Mager (1962).

Empirical Testing

Empirical testing is used in program *development.* After a programmer has written his initial program draft, he tries it out on a pilot sample of learners from the target population. The program will consist of an instructional portion and a measurement portion. The instructional portion of most varieties of program will be divided into subunits referred to as *frames.* A frame will contain both some informational text and some form of test item.

The programmer examines the response records of the pilot sample of learners. From their responses, both on the instructional frames and on the posttest, he can identify the shortcomings of his initial draft and find clues to revamping the material. The programmer looks for frames or posttest items on which several people made errors. While such information tells him which concepts have not been adequately presented, he does not automatically rewrite the frames having high-error rates: the trouble might be that earlier concepts were not sufficiently consolidated. Frequently, all that is needed is more redundancy on those earlier concepts so they will be mastered completely before advancing to the higher-order concepts. Revised versions of a program are usually longer in terms of frames but shorter in terms of time. Thus, empirical testing is used as a guide to revision in program development.

As noted by O'Day (1968), conventional books are generally read and criticized by experts, not by naive students. Nonprogrammers have difficulty in appreciating the degree to which material that seems clear to an expert can be unclear to a novice. One must actually examine the responses made on frames in order to comprehend fully the variety of misinterpretations that can be placed upon one's best, first effort at communication. Fortunately, in programmed instruction, the responses of a tryout sample of learners provide evidence that permits the faulty sentences or paragraphs to be identified. Such a tight feedback loop to the author is simply not available from conventional books as they do not require learners to respond paragraph by paragraph.

Cohen (1962) furnishes a dramatic example of just how indispensable the empirical testing procedure is in refining instructional material. From the responses of actual students, he found that Plato's *Meno* required revision in order to eliminate overprompting and to add more redundancy and test frames.

Empirical testing is used also in program *validation.* When the program is thought to be ready for release, it is administered to yet another sample of learners from the target population. The posttest scores obtained on this last administration demonstrate that the learners do, in fact, attain the predetermined criterion level.

Self-pacing

The learner sets the rate at which he progresses through the program. He adjusts the pace to his own ability and motivation level and is free of external influences. The importance of individualized pacing can be seen by observing two learners who take the same amount of overall time on a program. Because of differences in background, experience, and prior knowledge, they may still differ markedly in the time each takes on any given frame. Working at his preferred rate, the learner can pause to deliberate if he is of a reflective nature, and yet the continual reinforcement provides him with incentive to push on.

Overt Responding

The learners are asked to respond frequently to explicit or implicit questions as they progress through the program. These responses may take several forms: supplying a word left blank in a sentence, supplying a numerical answer to a mathematical problem, choosing from several statements the one which best describes a concept, or identifying a particular element on a chart. The overt-response requirement of programmed instruction insures that the learner will become and remain attentive to the instructional material. Such active involvement increases the learner's motivation. Moreover, while not all learning theories hold the overt response to be essential, all would acknowledge that, for some skills, the overt response makes a contribution toward learning, particularly if it is reinforced by a reward of some kind and if the learning is to become resistant to extinction.

Responding is considered overt when the learner performs upon request some physical, as opposed to strictly mental, act. Otherwise, responding is considered to be covert. Apart from whatever contribution toward learning effectiveness the overt response makes when emitted on a completed program, its contribution toward program development is essential. In order to implement the principle of empirical testing, the programmer must have available for examination the response records of a sample of learners from the target population.

Immediate Feedback

Broadly interpreted, feedback is information fed back to the learner regarding which of two or more alternative answers to a test question is correct. Ordinarily, however, there is the implication that the learner will have just completed emitting an overt response before receiving the feedback. This implication accounts for why the principle is referred to more specifically as the *immediate*-feedback principle, suggesting that feedback is given immediately after a response. The narrower interpretation also requires the learner to emit a correct response before proceeding to new text or to a new test item. Feedback is interpreted by some programmers to mean providing the learner with *knowledge of correct response* (KCR), as just described, and interpreted by others to include both KCR and remediation. Remediation exhibits the following two features:

(a) the question and emitted response are restated before the indication of correctness or incorrectness is given, and
(b) additional remedial text is provided to the emitter of an incorrect response before returning him to the test item.

From the standpoint of communications theory, feedback is simply information communicated to the learner by the program. From the standpoint of psychological theory, feedback can also have the property of reinforcement. Reinforcement is the strengthening of the bond between a stimulus configuration and a response. It raises the probability that an immediately preceding response will recur under similar circumstances.

Small-Step Size

The body of material to be learned is analyzed into small units which can be easily learned one concept at a time. The entire body of material may be complicated and formidable, but when broken down into its smallest components, the increments from frame to frame become simple and easy.

Mandatory and Optional Principles

The research to be reported in later chapters focused on the last three principles: overt responding, immediate feedback, and small-step size. These are the principles about which there is the most controversy; they have the most effect on the appearance of the material to the reader and, in the eyes of the layman, set programmed instruction apart from conventional instruction.

There is little disagreement among programmers that the principles of objective specification and empirical testing are indispensable to PI. Instructional material is simply not programmed unless it is directed at evoking certain terminal behaviors in a target group of learners and unless it has been repeatedly tested upon the learners to insure that these behaviors were indeed evoked. Self-pacing was not investigated for a different reason: it is inherent in all self-instruction and has been for centuries. It does not belong to PI, it is simply a by-product of the fact that PI is self-instructional.

For the foregoing reasons, the principles of objective specification and empirical testing will hereafter be referred to as *mandatory* principles, as will the principle of self-pacing, although in a slightly different sense. In contrast, the principles of overt responding, immediate feedback, and small-step size will be referred to as *optional* principles.

Other Features of Programmed Instruction

Apart from the above stated principles of programmed instruction, there are a number of other features differentiating the PI techniques.

Sequence

If every learner follows the identical sequence, that is, if the frames are encountered in a single, prearranged order, the program is described as *linear.* On the other hand, if on most of the frames the particular response emitted by the learner determines which of several alternative frames he proceeds to next, the program is described as *branching.* If the learner emits the correct response on a branching program, he will be directed to the next frame in the correct answer sequence. On the other hand, if he emits an incorrect response, he will be directed to a remedial frame or to a sequence of remedial frames before being returned to the correct answer sequence. Some branching programs have provisions for *washing-back* or *looping-forward* on certain critical frames covering key points of information. To be washed-back is to be returned to a frame upstream from the frame on which the incorrect response was emitted. It essentially forces the learner to review a recent portion of the program. To be looped-forward is to be advanced downstream, skipping frames that would be redundant for those learners able to respond correctly on the critical frame.

A technique using small steps tends to use a linear sequence. Small steps are used by programmers who believe that errors are learned and that small steps help reduce errors. It follows that a technique having few errors would be linear, because it would have little need to branch.

Type of Response

Some programs have frames that use multiple-choice test items to elicit responses. The learner merely selects the answer he believes to be correct. These programs are referred to as *multiple-choice response* programs. Other programs have frames that require the learner to fill in an answer he believes to be correct, and these frames are analogous to the completion or short-answer type of test item. These programs are referred to as *constructed-response* programs. Branching programs tend to use multiple-choice responses while linear programs tend to use constructed responses.

Error Rate

Linear programmers insist on a low-error rate and require that no more than 5 to 10 percent of responses should be erroneous. Other programmers are less demanding, although they think that a low-error rate is good. The principal means for reducing error rates is to revise the program after empirically testing it on a sample of learners to locate high-error frames.

Prompting and Confirmation

Some programmers use a lot of prompting in the belief that the important thing is to evoke the correct response. Prompting can be *formal,* meaning that the cues suggest the form of the response. Formal prompts may do such things as indicate the number of letters in a word or indicate its initial letter. The most extreme type of a formal prompt gives rise to a mere copying response. Formal prompts are used largely by response-oriented programmers, and thus the prompts are rather strong cues which force out the correct response by "giving it away". Prompting can be *thematic,* meaning that the text material of the frame is worded so that the context makes a correct response highly probable. Thematic prompting can be accomplished by showing the learner a verbal analogy or referring him to an illustration which makes the correct response apparent. Or the frame may present a rule or principle and ask the learner to solve a problem which requires the use of the rule for its solution.

Some programmers use prompting rather sparingly. They rely more upon *confirmation,* that is, having the learner emit a response and then indicating to him whether or not it is correct. The degree of prompting used is related to the programmer's belief in the nature of learning. Some attach a lot of importance to the process of reinforcement. The research on this matter is, as it is on so many matters in programmed instruction, incomplete. However, the effectiveness of overt responding and confirmation is supported by a number of studies summarized by Holland (1965) and contested by a number of studies by Cook (1963). Cook maintains that:

> *(a)* Overt responding to programmed materials is unnecessary and sometimes less efficient than covert responding.
> *(b)* Reinforcement of a response can be less effective than complete prompting, i.e., fully indicating the correct response to the learner before he responds.

The foregoing features are the main characteristics that typify one or more PI techniques. When two techniques are characterized as similar, it will be because many of these features are shared, and when characterized as different, it will be because few of these features are shared.

2

The Contemporary Techniques of Programmed Instruction

The principal techniques of programmed instruction in widespread use today are:

(a) linear, constructed-response, or as it sometimes is called after its founder, the "Skinnerian"

The linear technique, as its name suggests, presents material in a fixed sequence. The preponderance of existing programs are in linear format. This is in part due to Skinner's having set forth a consistent, demonstrable rationale for his technique, backed up by an impressive number of laboratory studies showing that a wide variety of responses can be taught effectively to a wide variety of learners by the use of reinforcement. The popularity of the linear technique can be further explained by the pragmatic facts that the principal producers of programmed materials are publishers, that publishers produce books, and that books lend themselves more readily to a linear sequence than, for example, a branching sequence. The linear technique breaks content down into relatively small steps and presents it in frames. Typical frames contain a few sentences or a paragraph of information. Linear programs require the learner to emit a constructed response. This response is reinforced immediately by showing the learner the correct answer.

(b) branching[1]

[1] Readers should understand that the use of the term branching, in accordance with popular custom, includes both those programs which are machine-presented and those which are book-presented ("scrambled books"). Crowder (1960) prefers to label his techniques more specifically as *intrinsic*. By intrinsic, he means to indicate that the necessary program of alternative frame sequences is built into the program itself so that no external programming device, such

Branching programs derive their name from their ability to adapt to a learner by adding or deleting frames, effectively washing him back, or looping him forward. Subject matter is broken down into larger segments than in the linear technique. Each frame may contain several paragraphs. Further, the learner is required to respond to a multiple-choice test item at the foot of each frame. The purpose of the test item is not to teach, but to determine if the learner has "understood" the material correctly. If so, he continues in the correct response sequence. If not, he may be branched to a remedial frame, or sequence of frames, or returned to the original frame. Advocates of the branching technique contend that humans do not need to emit constructed responses in order to learn effectively. Most current computer-assisted-instruction presents the learner with branching programs. A principal reason for using computer-presented instructional material is that the computer can supply an extensive variety of alternatives to the learner as a consequence of his responses. The fast learner who makes nearly all correct responses on the critical frames continues in the correct answer sequence. The slow learner receives remedial instruction every time he makes an incorrect response.

(c) auto-elucidative[2]

Pressey and Kinzer (1964) recently claimed that a technique they call "auto-elucidative" is superior to linear in instructional effectiveness. They also maintained that the auto-elucidative technique is much less time-consuming, less redundant, and, therefore, less likely to bore the bright learner than is the linear technique. In addition, it is much more compatible with existing educational and training materials. The auto-elucidative technique consists of a large-step text, followed by multiple-choice items to which the learner responds on a custom-designed response card that supplies immediate feedback by telling him if his answer is correct. He continues responding to each item until he responds correctly.

Comparing the Techniques

Studies showing an overt response to be unnecessary in many applications, and studies showing prompting to be superior to confirmation, at least

---

as a computer, is required. Computer-assisted-instruction would be referred to as *extrinsic* by Crowder. In this book, both intrinsic and extrinsic programs are classified as branching.

[2] The inclusion of auto-elucidation among programmed instruction techniques will be contested by some instructional technologists. For example, Holland (1965) would not include the auto-elucidative technique, even by its earlier name "adjunct programming," since it does not consist of a "carefully arranged sequence of contingencies leading to the terminal performances which are the object of education." However, both Lumsdaine (1964, p. 385) and Schramm (1964) cite the dangers of prematurely rejecting from programmed instruction any teaching instrument which may happen to depart from the presently accepted guidelines in its internal structural features. The inclusion seems to be warranted because auto-elucidation utilizes the programmed instruction principles of self-pacing, empirical testing, overt responding, and immediate feedback. It is also self-instructional.

in initial learning, weaken the case for the reinforcement principle and the Skinnerian theoretical position generally. However, they do not necessarily discredit the linear technique, because this technique makes quite heavy use of thematic prompting. The branching and auto-elucidative techniques are based less on theory than on demonstrations of efficacy in the form of comparisons to nonprogrammed instructional materials. The auto-elucidative technique uses the confirmation process, but does not base such use upon the reinforcement principle. The branching technique uses light thematic prompting and is a blend of prompting and confirmation.

Figure 2.1 illustrates schematically the linear, branching, and auto-elucidative techniques. The linear technique uses the small-step principle, presenting a few sentences of text and eliciting a constructed response about the key point. Errors are seldom emitted. When they are, the learner returns to the frame and writes in the correct response he has just been shown.

The branching technique uses a medium-size step, presenting a paragraph or two of text and elicits a multiple-choice response dealing with the key point. Errors are not infrequent. When they occur, the learner is given remediation, which includes remedial text. In the simplest form of the branching technique, as represented in the illustration, the learner, when in error, is returned to the frame and selects another response. If he is incorrect again, he receives more remediation; if correct, he proceeds to the succeeding frame. The more complex sequencings of remedial materials to which the branching technique lends itself are not illustrated in Figure 2.1.

The auto-elucidative technique uses a large-size step, presenting upwards of a chapter of text, and then elicits responses to a number of multiple-choice questions designed to test if the learner has understood those points in the text which are most often not understood. The learner is provided immediate feedback about the correctness of his responses and continues to respond to each test item until he does so correctly.

The proponents of the branching and auto-elucidative techniques agree with each other and differ from supporters of the linear technique in that they assume learning can, and to a great degree does, occur in reading plain text.

Branching proponents, however, differ from auto-elucidative proponents in viewing the test item primarily as a measuring device. For them, it indicates which of the several available frames is most appropriate for the learner. Crowder (1962, p. 3) does not regard the test item "as necessarily playing an active part in the primary learning process." He bases the branching technique on "detecting and correcting errors because we think it both impractical and undesirable (*sic*) to attempt to eliminate errors. It is impractical because of the inevitable individual differences, both in ability and information, that will occur among students; undesirable because to eliminate errors we would have to present material in such small steps and ask such easy questions that we would not be serving our educational objectives."

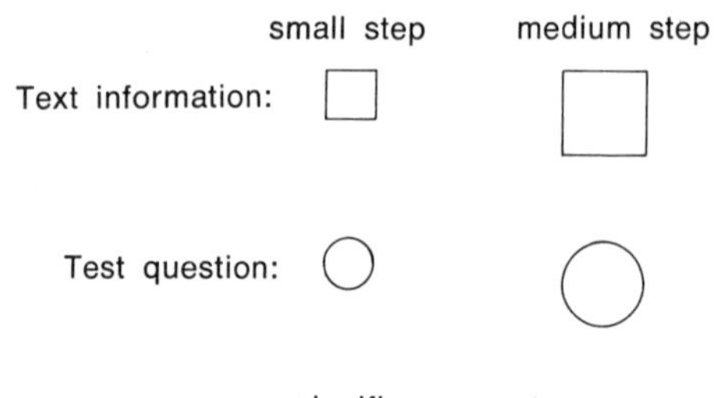

+ signifies correct response
– signifies incorrect response

LINEAR

BRANCHING

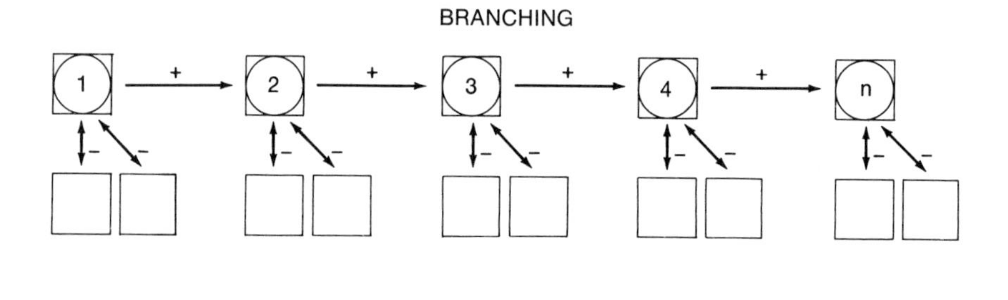

AUTO-ELUCIDATIVE

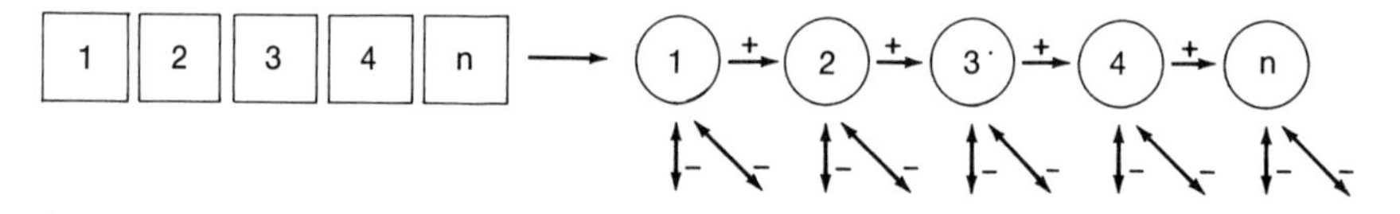

FIG. 2.1 A schematic illustration of the three most popular PI techniques.

Auto-elucidative proponents see the test item in a supplementary instructional role to the text. Like the branching proponents, they view the test item as a means for the learner to correct any erroneous understandings he may have acquired, but unlike the branching proponents, they do not supply remedial text.

Apart from their theoretical assets and limitations, the various programming techniques have advantages and disadvantages of a practical nature. Linear programs frequently appear too simple or banal to the learner when Skinner-oriented programmers adhere to the dictum of very low-error rate (5 to 10 percent). Redundancy leads to boredom. The problem, of course, is that the linear technique has no provision, once published, for tailoring the amount of repetition to the needs of the individual learner. Apart from the excessive repetitiveness of the typical linear program, its development is laborious, and its sheer bulk is large in relation to the scope of its content. We will never see an adequate portion of man's basic knowledge in programmed form unless we utilize techniques other than classical Skinnerian.

In the future, programs will become more adaptive to the learner, and consequently, the general field of programmed instruction will move in either, or both, of two directions. One direction will be toward computer-assisted-instruction, a medium which at present makes widespread use of branching programs as a vehicle. The other direction will retain the conventional medium of paper, but will convert to some more efficient technique, like the auto-elucidative, in order to avoid the shortcomings of the linear technique as it exists today. Efficacy of technique will, of course, eventually be found to vary with learner characteristics and instructional objectives.

The Pressey and Kinzer (1964) study claims superiority for the auto-elucidative technique over the linear. It is timely therefore to investigate the relative advantages of the auto-elucidative and branching techniques as they have not been compared heretofore. The present study had this comparison as a technological objective and therefore simulated the branching and auto-elucidative techniques as faithfully as possible in keeping with the scientific objective cited in the next chapter.

3

Toward a Technology of Instruction

What is new about programmed instruction? The principles? Not really, most of the principles were used by trainers and educators long before the field of programmed instruction became popular. Well then, what about the techniques? Yes, some of the techniques are new. To a large extent, we can think of these techniques as new configurations of old instructional principles. But the genuinely new aspect of programmed instruction is that it constitutes the leading edge of a new technology: *instructional technology*. A technology is the totality of the means employed to achieve a certain class of objectives. It is a communicable body of expertise concerning "how-to-do-it," or put more accurately, how to do it best in view of the particular givens of a situation. In practical terms, a technology is the means which enable a technologist to design, to plan, to build, to create, to do. It follows that the technologist must have known objectives. Moreover, he must know the strengths and weaknesses of alternate methods. He must know the appropriateness of a given technique to a given problem condition. And finally, if he gives recommendations, they must be based upon the particulars of the problem condition.

Some common examples of technologies are agriculture, engineering, and medicine. If you ask an agricultural agent to recommend a fertilizer, he will withhold advice until you tell him about your proposed crops, your previous crops, your drainage, your soil balance, and your water supply. If you ask an automotive engineer about the best car on the market, he will want to know if you are seeking performance, economy, durability, serviceability, safety, handling, or whatever. What about medicine? Does it qualify as a technology? If you think not, consider your reaction to the following situation. Suppose that you have recently been experiencing distressing physical symptoms. You visit your physician, and after hearing your recital of complaints, he tells you the following:

(a) keep regular hours and get plenty of rest,
(b) eat three light, wholesome meals each day; avoid condiments and saturated fats,
(c) forego tea, coffee, tobacco, and all forms of alcohol,
(d) exercise for an hour each day, work up a good sweat, but do not over-exert.

What's wrong with this advice? Nothing. For most people, following the above rules would be beneficial. However, you expect something more than these commonly known rules of hygiene from your private physician. You expect some specific prescription, something tailored to your specific disability.

Similarly, when you ask the instructional technologist to help you design an instructional instrument, you expect him to do something more than rattle off the following:

(a) have the learners overtly respond, frequently and often,
(b) provide the learners with immediate feedback,
(c) present additional information to the learner in small increments; let him take small steps.

This is not enough. You expect some informed recommendations regarding instructional procedures after an analysis of:

(a) the nature of the terminal behavior sought, and,
(b) the attributes of the learners: age level, grade level, pretest score, and other relevant factors.

Much of the research reported in this book is oriented toward instructional technology. Wherever that orientation prevailed, the purpose was to ascertain the most efficient instructional techniques for certain major types of learning tasks with learners having specific measured amounts of particular relevant attributes.

Because the research to be reported was initiated within an academic institution, the focus was upon a type of learning prevalent there: associative learning. When better taxonomies are developed for classifying types of learning, the learning tasks involved in our experimental materials (see Appendix A) may be characterized as association formation, involving, to a lesser extent, discrimination learning.[1] However, the selection of associative learning was not a mere arbitrary convenience. As discerned by Hilgard and

[1] For the designer of instructional materials, one of the more useful taxonomies developed to date is that of Gagné (1965). Eight types of learning are identified.

1. Signal learning: the classical conditioning of Pavlov, where a general, diffuse, and

Bower (1966, p. 559), a typical program teaches not just the correctly emitted responses but also the behaviors which led to the responses. They cite as an extreme example a hypothetical program calling for only *yes* and *no* responses. The implication of their observations for the present studies is that associative learning pervades many varieties of learning tasks.

On the other hand, with regard to learner attributes, we feel that we started with the attribute most significant for instructional technology and, fortunately, the one most easily measured. We refer, of course, to intelligence. More specifically defined, we focused on the learner's scholastic ability.

It is implicit from the foregoing observations that the findings regarding the relative efficiency of various techniques would not necessarily hold for all types of learning tasks. If the reader is interested in teaching military observers to identify quickly and accurately various types of enemy aircraft, he would borrow from studies of sensory-discrimination learning. If he is interested in teaching radiotelegraph operators to transmit Morse code, he would examine studies of motor-response learning. However, because the domain of associative learning is a large one, our findings, that show that the effectiveness of various instructional techniques is dependent upon the intelligence of the target learners, have implications for all instruction.

While the emphasis in this discussion has been on technology, it is not suggested that the scientific search for general PI principles be abandoned. It is suggested that many of the principles that, to date, have been identified, described, and popularized, do not generalize well. Furthermore, they have not yet been tested over a sufficiently widespread variety of learning tasks and learners. We cannot today write differential prescriptions for the most

---

emotional response is elicited involuntarily by some conditioned stimulus through temporal contiguity.

2. Stimulus-response learning: the instrumental conditioning of Skinner, where a precise response in the form of skeletal muscle movement is elicited by very specific stimuli or combinations of stimuli and where some of the stimuli are proprioceptive movements by the learner. Reinforcement is used to bring about discrimination in both stimuli and responses.
3. Chaining: the connecting together in a sequence of two or more previously learned stimulus-response bonds.
4. Verbal association: the learning of chains which are verbal, using stimuli and responses which are internal, such as language symbols.
5. Multiple discrimination: the learning of N different appropriate responses to as many different stimuli. Although the learning of each stimulus-response connection is Type 2 learning, the connections tend to interfere with each other's retention.
6. Concept learning: the learning of a common response to a class of stimuli.
7. Principle learning: the learning of a chain of two or more concepts.
8. Problem solving: learning whereby two or more previously acquired principles are somehow combined to produce a new capability that can be shown to depend upon a higher-order principle.

Gagné views this typology as provisional. However, because of the likelihood that instructional technology will give increasing recognition to the typology, it would be useful to describe the instructional materials of the present study in terms of Gagné's learning types. The mix of learning types, in decreasing order of importance, was 4, 5, 6, 7. Hereafter, for simplicity our materials will be described more succinctly by the generic classification *associative.*

efficient configurations of principles to be used in instructing various types of learners in various types of skills. And therefore, in setting up instructional programs, the state of the art is such that new formats, composed of different configurations of existing principles, should also be empirically tested for their relative effectiveness.

The results of several related studies are reported in this book. To keep them in perspective, it should be remembered that there were two broad, general objectives to the entire family of studies. One was scientific in nature: to identify and isolate the various fundamental principles of programmed instruction and to determine experimentally their effects upon learning, particularly their relative effects. The other general objective was technological in nature: to create and evaluate various formats of programmed instruction and to determine experimentally their efficiencies, particularly their relative efficiencies.

Whenever an ensuing discussion concerns the scientific objective, it will be based upon the fact that two formats differ by one principle or feature of PI. In this case, the focus will be upon a corresponding difference in either a posttest correct score or in an efficiency index composed of posttest gain per unit of program time. Whenever a discussion concerns the technological objective, it will be based upon the identity of one or more formats, and the focus will be upon a corresponding value of the efficiency index.

A researcher cannot be a loyal servant to two masters, one a science, the other a technology. Wherever a loyalty conflict occurred, technology was usually served first and science second. Why? Partially because when one attempts to combine the various PI principles into a number of configurations, each differing from some other configuration by some one principle, one soon discovers that other PI features not included in one's formal analysis will act as confounding variables. For example, if the responding principle is deleted from a format containing both the responding and feedback principles, the resulting format will be more heavily prompted. Another reason for serving technology before science is that cultism has gained a foothold in the field of programmed instruction. The result is that three techniques (linear, branching, and auto-elucidative) have nearly preempted the field without first having proven their efficiency against other possible techniques for all classes of tasks and learners.

4

Old and New Formats of Programmed Instruction

In all, nine experimental formats of instructional material were developed for this study. Before use, the material was written, empirically tested in a pilot study, and then revised. The first draft of the items used in the posttest and program were open-ended questions developed in accordance with the instructional objectives. The responses of the pilot study learners were used in forming the multiple-choice items of the posttest and in revising the text. The text and test items were administered to yet another sample of learners to insure that together they would not result in scores too near the chance or ceiling levels of performance. Of the nine experimental formats developed, two were simulations of popular PI techniques: branching and auto-elucidative.

The format simulating the branching technique was termed the branching format (BRM/BRB), and consisted of 30 frames, each comprised of a paragraph of text followed by a 3-response, multiple-choice, test item. The BRM/BRB format, including the directions, is reproduced in Appendix A. (In order to conserve space, the *remedial* [1] feedback has been provided only for frame 1, and the other 29 frames are printed several to a page.) Corresponding to each of the three alternative responses to the test item on frame 1, three envelopes, marked *a, b,* and *c* were available to the learner. He selected the envelope labeled with the response he believed to be correct, opened it, and received the KCR, plus remediation. If incorrect, he returned to the test item for another attempt. If correct, he proceeded to the text of a subsequent frame.

[1] The remedial text in this study was limited to suggestive cues.

The experimental BRM/BRB program, like the other eight formats, consisted of software. Because a certain amount of time was required to remove the feedback material from the 30 envelopes, a sample of learners was timed on just that operation. Their mean time was deducted from the mean time of learners instructed by the BRM/BRB format. The remainder was used as a reasonable estimate of the time required by a branching program in hardware form, because machine-presented branching programs furnish the feedback to the learner as soon as he pushed the correct button. The uncorrected mean program time was used as a reasonable estimate of the time required by a branching program in software form, because the time spent in tearing open the envelopes is approximately equivalent to the time spent in turning the pages of a "scrambled" book.[2]

Hereafter, the following notation will be used: BR*B* specifically indicates a simulated *book*-presented branching program, BR*M* specifically indicates a simulated *machine*-presented branching program. Both of these specific indicators are necessary only when the variable of interest is either program time or the efficiency index, posttest gain/program time. Because the ideal mode of presentation for a branching program is by machine, whenever subsequent reference is made to the branching format, the machine-presentation mode is meant unless book presentation is specifically indicated by word or symbol. Where the discussion pertains to both presentation modes, the notation BRM/BRB will be used.

The rationale for referring to the BRM/BRB format as branching was that it simulated the branching technique in its simplest form: the learner who emits an incorrect response is returned to the same frame for another attempt. In order to make the BRM/BRB format as good a simulator of the branching technique as the experimental considerations would permit, the feedback provided to the learner by the BRM/BRB format included not only KCR, but also remediation. No other format incorporated the feature of remediation.

The format simulating the auto-elucidative technique was termed the auto-elucidative (AE) format and consisted of the first 15 paragraphs of text followed by a corresponding 15 test items, then the second 15 paragraphs of text followed by another corresponding 15 items. The learner read the text, and then without reference to this text, he responded to the 15 test items on one of Pressey's "trainer-tester response cards." He repeated this procedure on the second half of the AE format. The instructions for the AE format along with the instructions for seven other formats are in Appendix B.

The response cards used with the AE format were the standard type recommended by Pressey for use with the auto-elucidative technique. The learner responds on these cards by erasing an ink-like material from the card to find if the answer he chose, *a, b,* or *c,* was correct. Since the response

2 Morse and Jones (1961) found the software version of a branching program to require about one-third more time than the corresponding hardware version.

card provided for three possible answers,[3] the test items used on the AE format had to have three possible answers, one correct answer and two distractors. Moreover, the test items used on the other formats had to be identical for purposes of experimental control. Thus, they too were limited to three options.

The feedback provided by the AE format, like that of the auto-elucidative technique it simulates, was only of the KCR type. The feedback provided by the BRM/BRB format, like that of the branching technique it simulates, included both KCR and remediation. Therefore, the BRM/BRB format differed from the AE in two ways: it incorporated feedback of the remedial type, and it incorporated the small-step principle. Thus, a comparison of the two formats tested the relative merits of the branching and auto-elucidative techniques, but did not test the merits of either the remediation feature or the small-step principle.

In order to test remediation and the small-step principle separately, a third format was devised. It consisted of the BRM/BRB instructional materials without the three answer envelopes. In their place, an auto-elucidative response card provided the learner with KCR. This third format was termed the "BRM minus remediation" (BRM-R). The instructions for the BRM-R format are in Appendix B. The appearance of the BRM-R frames remained identical to those of the BRM/BRB format. The BRM-R format was intermediate between the AE and BRM/BRB formats in terms of the features and principles of programmed instruction incorporated. A comparison of the BRM-R to the AE format tests the small-step principle, while a comparison of the BRM/BRB to the BRM-R format tests remediation.

Each of the nine experimental formats, including the three just described, incorporated all three of the mandatory PI principles, but differed from each other in which combination of the three optional principles they incorporated. The BRM/BRB and BRM-R formats used all three principles: overt responding, immediate feedback, and small step. The AE format used overt responding and immediate feedback, but omitted the small-step principle.

A fourth format used overt responding, but omitted the immediate-feed-back and small-step principles. Since the principle most apparent to the learner was that of overt responding, the format was termed overt responding (OR). The OR format outwardly simulated the conventional text plus workbook found in contemporary education, but the incorporation of the mandatory principles resulted in its being something more than that.

A fifth format used covert responding and, like the OR format, omitted the immediate-feedback and small-step principles. Because the principle most apparent to the learner was that of covert responding, the format was termed covert responding (CR). The CR format outwardly simulated that

[3] Other of Pressey's "trainer-tester response cards" have more response options, but their coding schemes confuse and annoy students.

type of conventional text which includes periodic "study questions" in the expository material, but the incorporation of the mandatory principles resulted in its being something more than that.

A sixth format omitted all three optional principles. Because this format used less PI principles than any other of the nine investigated, it was termed base control (BC). The BC format outwardly simulated the conventional text, but again, the incorporation of the mandatory principles resulted in its being something more.

The left-hand table on the endpapers shows these six experimental formats plus three others. Regarding, for the moment, just the six formats described above, note that they form a hierarchy in which a higher-order format incorporated all of the principles of a lower-order format plus one principle, or one feature of a principle, such as question-reading or remediation. Therefore, a comparison of the branching (BRM/BRB) and branching minus remediation (BRM-R) formats revealed the influence of remediation. A comparison of the BRM-R and auto-elucidative (AE) formats revealed the influence of the small-step principle. A comparison of the AE and overt-responding (OR) formats revealed the influence of the immediate-feedback principle. A comparison of the OR and covert-responding (CR) formats revealed the influence of the overt-responding principle. And a comparison of the CR and base control (BC) formats revealed the influence of question-reading.

The left-hand table on the endpapers also shows:

(a) A format, abbreviate BRM-F, which includes all the principles incorporated by the BRM/BRB format, except that of immediate feedback. The notation, *BRM-F* signifies BRM minus feedback.
(b) A format, abbreviated BRM-OR, which includes all the principles incorporated by the BRM/BRB format, except that of overt responding. The notation, *BRM-OR* signifies BRM minus overt responding.
(c) A format, abbreviated AE-OR, which includes all the principles incorporated by the AE format, except that of overt responding. The notation, *AE/OR* signifies AE minus overt responding.

The right-hand table on the endpapers summarizes the notation and names for all nine formats plus a capsule description of their identifying features. The instructions for all nine formats except the BRM/BRB are in Appendix B.

The BRM-R, BRM-F and BRM-OR formats were identical to the BRM/BRB with regard to text. The BRM-R and BRM-F were also identical to the BRM/BRB with regard to test items, except that they both dispensed with answer envelopes. In their place, the BRM-R format had the learner record his responses on the Pressey response cards, which provide KCR. The BRM-F format had the learner record his responses on conventional answer sheets, that, of course, do not provide KCR. The BRM-OR format was also identical to the BRM/BRB with regard to test items except that the correct answer was disclosed by an asterisk in front of it; no overt response was required or permitted. That is, the learner was permitted to read the questions and note the correct answer, but he was not allowed to cover up the asterisk and covertly respond. Technically speaking, formal prompting was provided; confirmation was prevented.

The other five formats lacked the small-step principle. Their text was identical to that of the four branching formats, but it was arranged differently. In the base control (BC) format, the text of the BRM/BRB frames was combined: each frame paragraph became a paragraph in a continuous exposition of 30 paragraphs. In the covert-responding (CR), overt-responding (OR), auto-elucidative (AE), and auto-elucidative minus overt-responding (AE-OR) formats, the exposition consisted of two sets of 15 paragraphs. Each set was followed by the 15 test items that had accompanied those 15 paragraphs in the BRM/BRB, BRM-R, BRM-F, and BRM-OR formats. The CR, OR, AE, and AE-OR formats were split into two halves in order to ascertain if learners would behave differently in reading the second half of the text, after having inspected or responded to questions on the first half without reference to the text paragraphs. This hypothesis was tested (and not sustained) by comparing performance on the first and second halves of a posttest. The AE format was identical to the OR, except that responses were recorded on Pressey's response cards instead of on conventional answer sheets. The AE format, like the OR, provided for overt responding, but unlike OR, it also provided for immediate feedback of a KCR nature. The CR format was identical to both the AE and OR, except that no answer sheets of any kind were provided. No overt response was required or permitted. The AE-OR format was identical to both the AE and OR with regard to text, and also with regard to test items, except that the correct answer was disclosed by an asterisk in front of it. No answer sheets of any kind were provided, and no overt response was required or permitted.

All groups read, word for word, the same expository text. In the BRM/BRB, BRM-R, BRM-F, and BRM-OR formats, one thirtieth of the text was presented, followed by a test item. In the CR, OR, AE, and AE-OR formats, one-half of the text was presented, followed by 15 test items. In the BC format, all the text was presented without test items.

The left-hand table on the endpapers shows that the overt-responding principle can be tested, not only by comparing the CR to the OR format, but also by comparing the AE-OR to the AE format, and by comparing the BRM-OR to the BRM-R format. The CR to OR comparison tests overt responding in the absence of feedback and small steps. The AE-OR to AE comparison tests overt responding in the presence of feedback and in the absence of small steps. The BRM-OR to BRM-R comparison tests overt responding in the presence of both feedback and small steps.

The left-hand table on the endpapers shows that the feedback principle can be tested by comparing the OR to AE format, because the AE format differs from the OR only by the presence of feedback (KCR type). Of the other principles of interest, all were either absent in both the OR and AE formats, as was the case, for example, with the small-step principle; or, they were present in both the OR and AE formats, as was the case, for example, with the overt-responding principle. The feedback principle can be further tested by comparing the BRM-F to the BRM-R format, if the principle is interpreted to include only KCR and not remediation. If the principle is interpreted to include both KCR and remediation, the feedback principle can be tested by comparing the BRM-F to the BRM format. In addition, the BRM-R to the BRM comparison provides a test of remediation unconfounded with KCR.

The left-hand table on the endpapers shows that the small-step principle can be tested in three ways: by comparing the AE to the BRM-R format, by comparing the OR to the BRM-F format, and by comparing the AE-OR to the BRM-OR format.

These several comparisons are not mere redundant replications of one another, but are, by design, tests of the effects of certain of the PI principles in the presence of various different configurations of other principles. Thus when these tests have different outcomes, they help reveal the possibility that the principles may interact with each other. For example, a given principle may facilitate the influence of some other principle; that is, the two may make a greater contribution to learning when acting in concert than the simple additive sum of their contributions when acting alone. But it is more probable that two principles acting in concert will make a lesser contribution to learning than the simple additive sum of their separate contributions; that is, each of the two principles may, to a great extent, accomplish what the other accomplishes. Therefore, since the increased yield from using both principles would be small compared to the increased cost, a decision to use one or the other may often result in better efficiency.

To illustrate, the comparison of the AE-OR to BRM-OR, like the comparison of OR to BRM-F, tests the small-step principle, but it does so in the presence of KCR. Therefore, if in the first comparison, the BRM-OR format were not to be significantly better than the AE-OR and if the BRM-F format were to be significantly better than the OR, it would suggest that KCR accomplishes much of what it accomplished by small-step size, because KCR is possessed by both formats in the first comparison but by neither format in the second.

While a technological aim of the study was to have as many as possible of the experimental formats be representative of popular PI techniques, the only two techniques which could be simulated were the branching and auto-elucidative. They both, unlike the linear technique, use multiple-choice items.

One may think of a linear frame as exemplifying small-step size and of an auto-elucidative "frame" as exemplifying large-step size. On this scale, the typical branching frame is of small- to medium-step size. In order to

5

The Relative Merit of the Optional Principles of Programmed Instruction

In Table 5.1 are the means and standard deviations of the six variables of interest. Initially attention will be focused upon:

(*a*) scholastic ability, as a classification variable, and
(*b*) posttest corrects and program time, as dependent variables.

Scholastic ability, as measured by a standardized test (the ACT), served two functions in this study. One, it separated the learners into high- and low-ability groups. The high group was comprised of approximately the highest octile, using twelfth-grade norms; the low group was comprised of approximately the second, third, and fourth highest octiles. There were about as many learners (N = 57) in the highest octile as in the next three octiles (N = 55) because a disproportionately higher number of the latter attend junior colleges in California. In its second function, scholastic ability formed a controlled, experimental parameter in the statistical analyses reported below.[1]

Posttest corrects, as a variable, was refined into another measure, more meaningful and easier to interpret. This measure was posttest gain. Posttest gain was computed by subtracting from the mean posttest corrects of each experimental group a simulated mean pretest corrects score. The pretest score was calculated from the posttest scores of yet another sample of learners not

[1] The learners were stratified into 15 levels of scholastic ability (ACT standard scores of 16 through 30), so that this systematic source of variance could be removed from the error term.

Table 5.1 Means and Standard Deviations of Variables Investigated Using Learners Who Were State College Students

		BC	CR	OR	AE	BRM-R	BRM	BRB	BRM-F	BRM-OR	AE-OR
Posttest corrects	M:	15.08	16.75	17.59	18.23	18.61	19.10	19.10	18.88	18.20	19.31
	SD:	4.15	4.27	4.39	4.44	4.13	3.94	3.94	4.00	3.82	3.76
Scholastic ability	M:	23.44	23.44	23.44	23.44	23.44	23.44	23.44	23.44	23.44	23.44
	SD:	3.39	3.39	3.39	3.39	3.39	3.39	3.39	3.39	3.39	3.39
Attitude	M:	10.39	nm[a]	9.72	10.04	nm	10.54	10.54	nm	nm	nm
	SD:	2.17	nm	2.12	2.23	nm	2.08	2.08	nm	nm	nm
Program time	M:	22.31	29.14	35.56	40.31	34.35	37.07	44.37	32.13	28.77	27.63
	SD:	5.89	6.10	6.96	6.10	6.91	6.84	6.84	5.90	5.90	5.64
Program items in error	M:	na[b]	na	10.47	10.54	4.33	3.25	3.25	3.31	na	na
	SD:	na	na	4.50	4.81	3.30	2.29	2.29	2.60	na	na
Program errors	M:	na	na	na	13.59	4.96	3.65	3.65	na	na	na
	SD:	na	na	na	6.42	4.34	2.66	2.66	na	na	na

[a] nm indicates variable not measured for that experimental group
[b] na indicates variable not applicable for that experimental group

exposed to the text. These learners were selected from the same student population after being matched for scholastic ability. The pretest mean for all learners was 11.94; for the octile 1 learners ($24 \leqq \text{ACT} \leqq 30$), it was 12.74; and for octiles 2, 3, and 4 learners ($16 \leqq \text{ACT} \leqq 23$), it was 11.05 Pretests were not actually administered to learners in the nine experimental groups, partly because of the limited time available per experimental session and partly because of the presensitizing effects of pretesting as reported by May and Lumsdaine (1958, ch. 7). While these effects might be desirable in an actual instructional effort, they produce unwanted complexity for experimental purposes.

Table 5.1 shows that the formats that incorporated the greater number of PI principles and features, such as the BRM/BRB, tended to have higher posttest corrects scores than those formats that incorporated the lesser number, such as the BC or OR. However, to correspond with the increases in the posttests corrects, there tended to be even greater proportional increases in the program times.

In order to arrive at a practical figure of merit for each of the nine formats, an index was formed from the ratio of posttest gain to program time. This ratio represented a learning yield per unit time cost. Posttest gain was used, instead of the raw posttest corrects, in order to have in the numerator a scale with a true, or absolute, zero. The usual assumption, that the test scores constitute an equal interval scale, was also made. The pilot study supported this assumption. The initial draft of the posttest was revised, on the basis of indices of difficulty and discrimination, to give rise to the final form of the posttest. Mean scores of every group were reasonably removed from both the chance and ceiling levels of test performance.

The Principle of Overt Responding

The principle of overt responding was tested by comparing the following formats:

(a) CR to OR	test of overt responding in the presence of the mandatory principles
(b) AE-OR to AE	test of overt responding in the presence of prompting in the form of KCR
(c) BRM-OR to BRM-R	test of overt responding in the presence of small steps and prompting in the form of KCR.

In all three comparisons, learners read the test items in the program in both formats. In the CR, AE-OR, and BRM-OR formats, the learner covertly responded. In the OR, AE, and BRM-R formats, the learner overtly responded.

In addition, a fourth comparison, BC to CR, tested the effects of being permitted to read the test items and respond covertly. A fifth comparison,

BC to OR, tested the effects of being permitted to read the test items and respond overtly. In the BC format, the learner read text, but not the test items.

Figure 5.1 shows the posttest gains, program times, and efficiency indices for the comparison BC to CR; Figure 5.2 shows these variables for the comparison CR to OR; Figure 5.3 for the comparison BC to OR; Figure 5.4 for the comparison AE-OR to AE; and Figure 5.5 for the comparison BRM-OR to BRM-R. For each variable, the data are portrayed separately for learners of higher ability (octile 1), undifferentiated ability (octiles 1 through 4), and lower ability (octiles 2 through 4).

Figure 5.1 shows that when the CR format was formed by adding to the configuration of principles comprising the BC format the features of permitting the learner to read the test questions and covertly respond, there was an increase in posttest gain, but also in program time. The increase in posttest gain appears greater for the low-ability learners than for the high. In contrast, the increase in program time appears greater for the high-ability learners than for the low. Correspondingly, the efficiency index, that is the ratio of posttest gain to program time, suggests that the CR format would be more efficient for low-ability learners and that neither format would have an advantage for high-ability learners. Statistically significant were the differences in posttest gain and in program time for all ability levels. None of the differences between efficiency indices were statistically significant.

Figure 5.2 shows that when the OR format was formed by adding the principle of overt responding to the configuration of principles comprising the CR format, the increase in posttest gain was modest, but the increase in program time was considerable. For both variables, the increase was greatest for the low-ability learners. Accordingly, the efficiency indices differed negligibly at all ability levels. Statistically significant were the differences between program times at all ability levels. None of the differences between the posttest gains nor between the efficiency indices were statistically significant.

Figure 5.3 shows that when the OR format was formed by adding to the configuration of principles comprising the BC format the features of permitting the learner to read the test questions and overtly respond, there was an appreciable increase in posttest gain and in program time. For both variables, the increase was greatest for the low-ability learners although the increase in program time was less dependent upon ability level than was the increase in posttest gain. Correspondingly, at the high-ability level the formats differed negligibly in efficiency; at the low-ability level, the OR format appeared to be more efficient than the BC. Statistically significant were the posttest gains and program times at all ability levels. None of the differences between the efficiency indices were significant.

Figure 5.4 shows that when the AE format was formed by adding the feature of overt responding to the configuration of principles comprising the AE-OR format, there seemed actually to be a decrement in posttest gain,

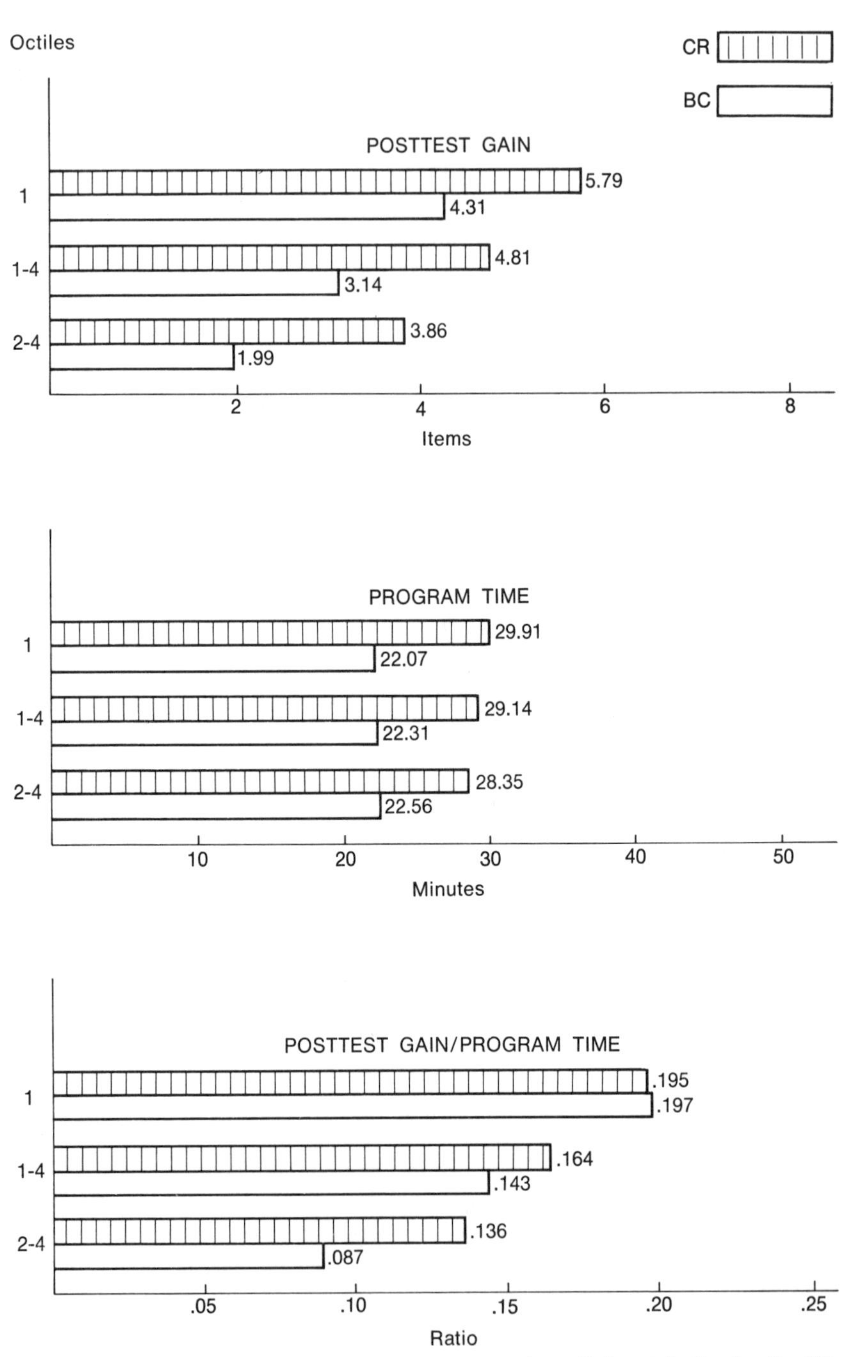

FIG. 5.1 Posttest gain, program time, and a learning efficiency index for the CR and BC formats presented to state college learners, differentiated and undifferentiated according to scholastic ability.

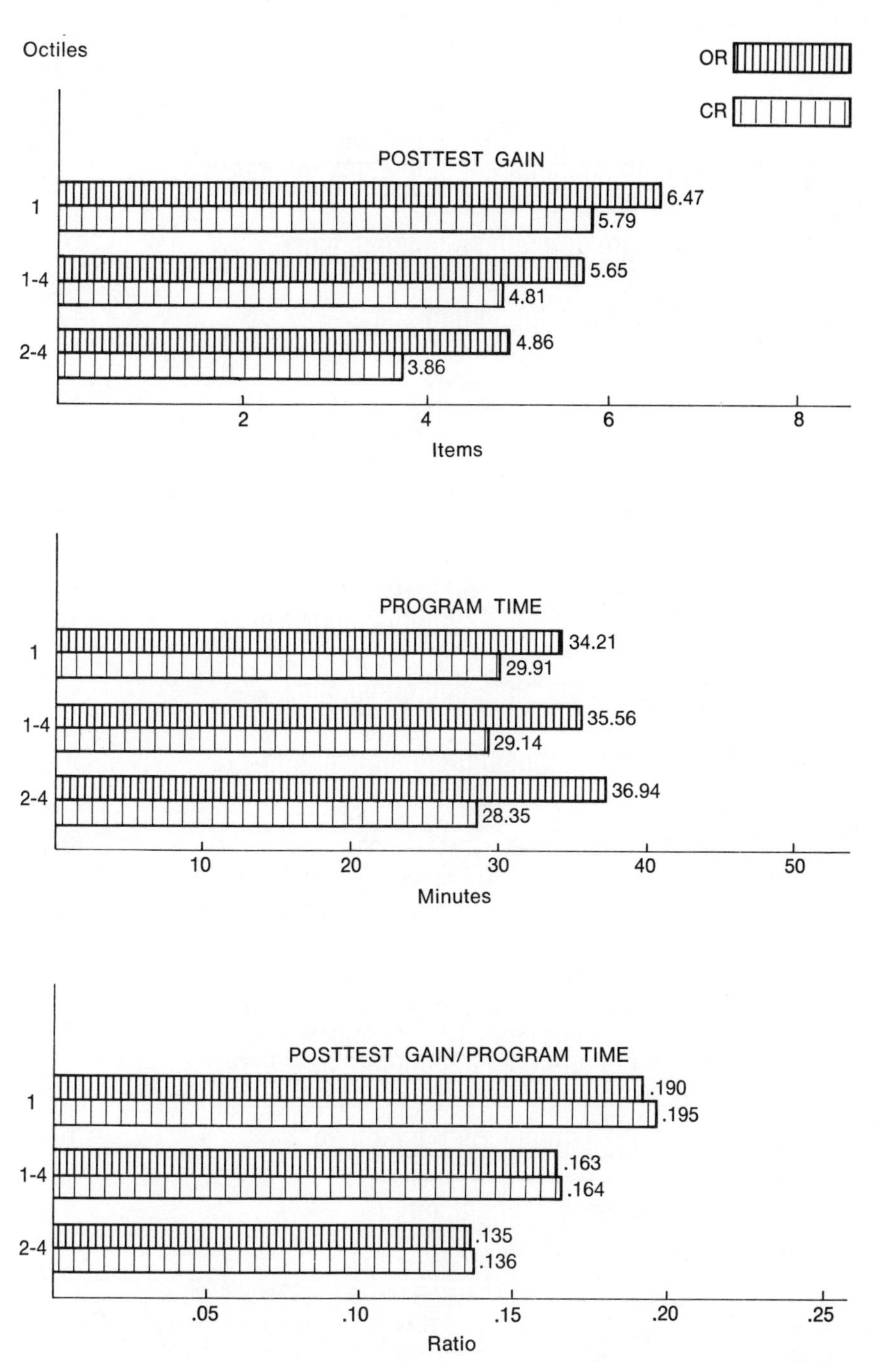

FIG. 5.2 Posttest gain, program time, and a learning efficiency index for the OR and CR formats presented to state college learners, differentiated and undifferentiated according to scholastic ability.

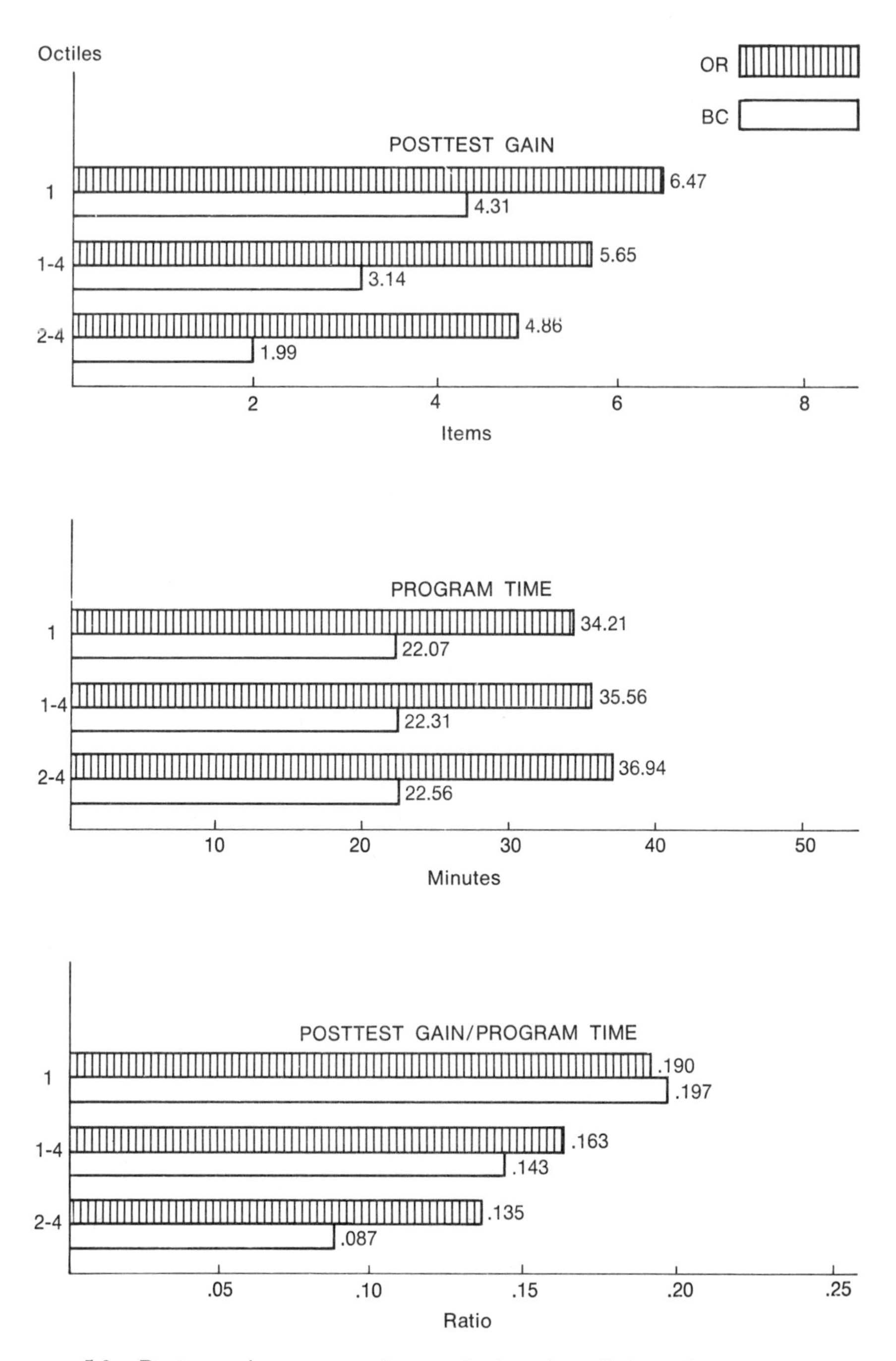

FIG. 5.3 Posttest gain, program time, and a learning efficiency index for the OR and BC formats presented to state college learners, differentiated and undifferentiated according to scholastic ability.

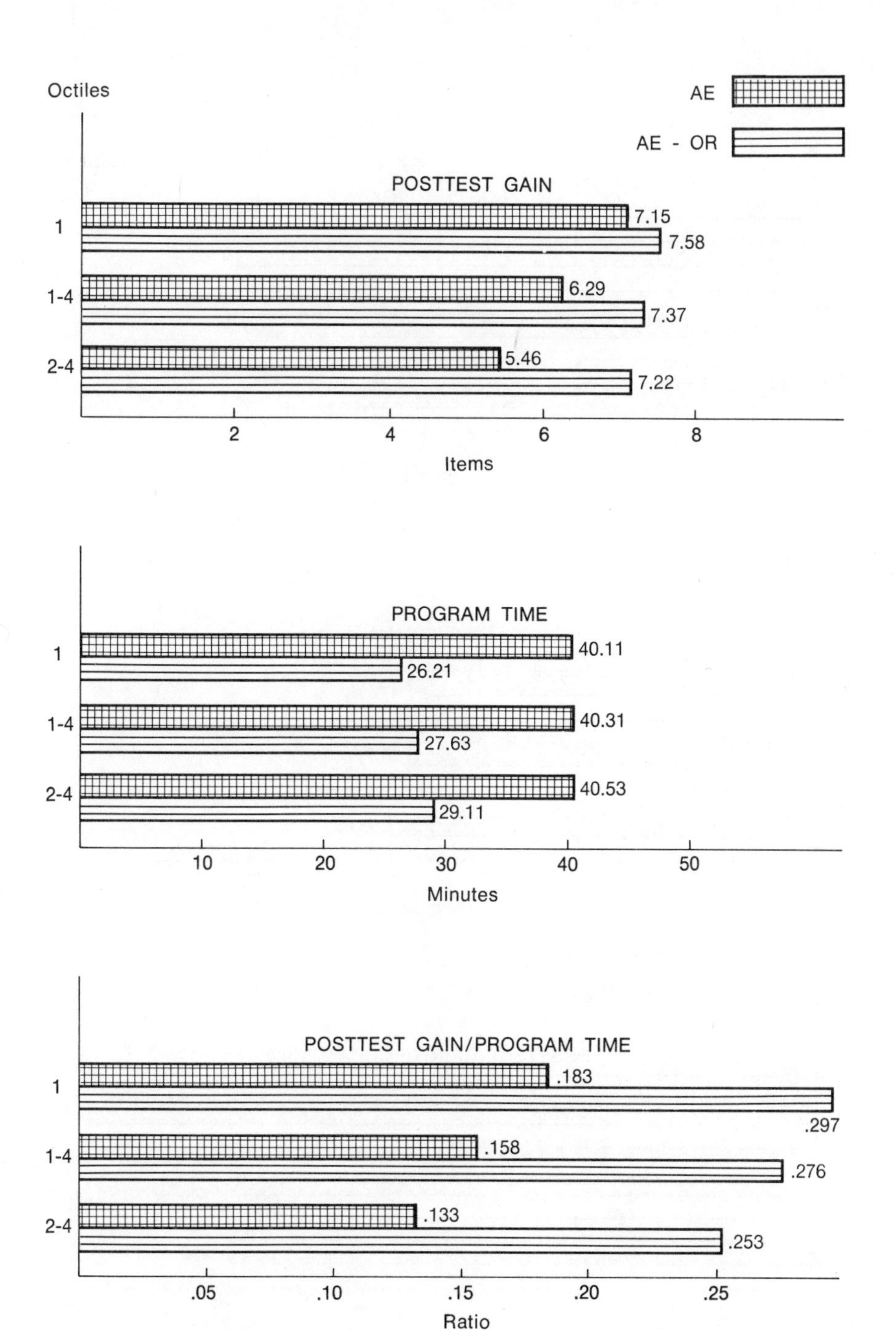

FIG. 5.4 Posttest gain, program time, and a learning efficiency index for the AE and AE-OR formats presented to state college learners, differentiated and undifferentiated according to scholastic ability.

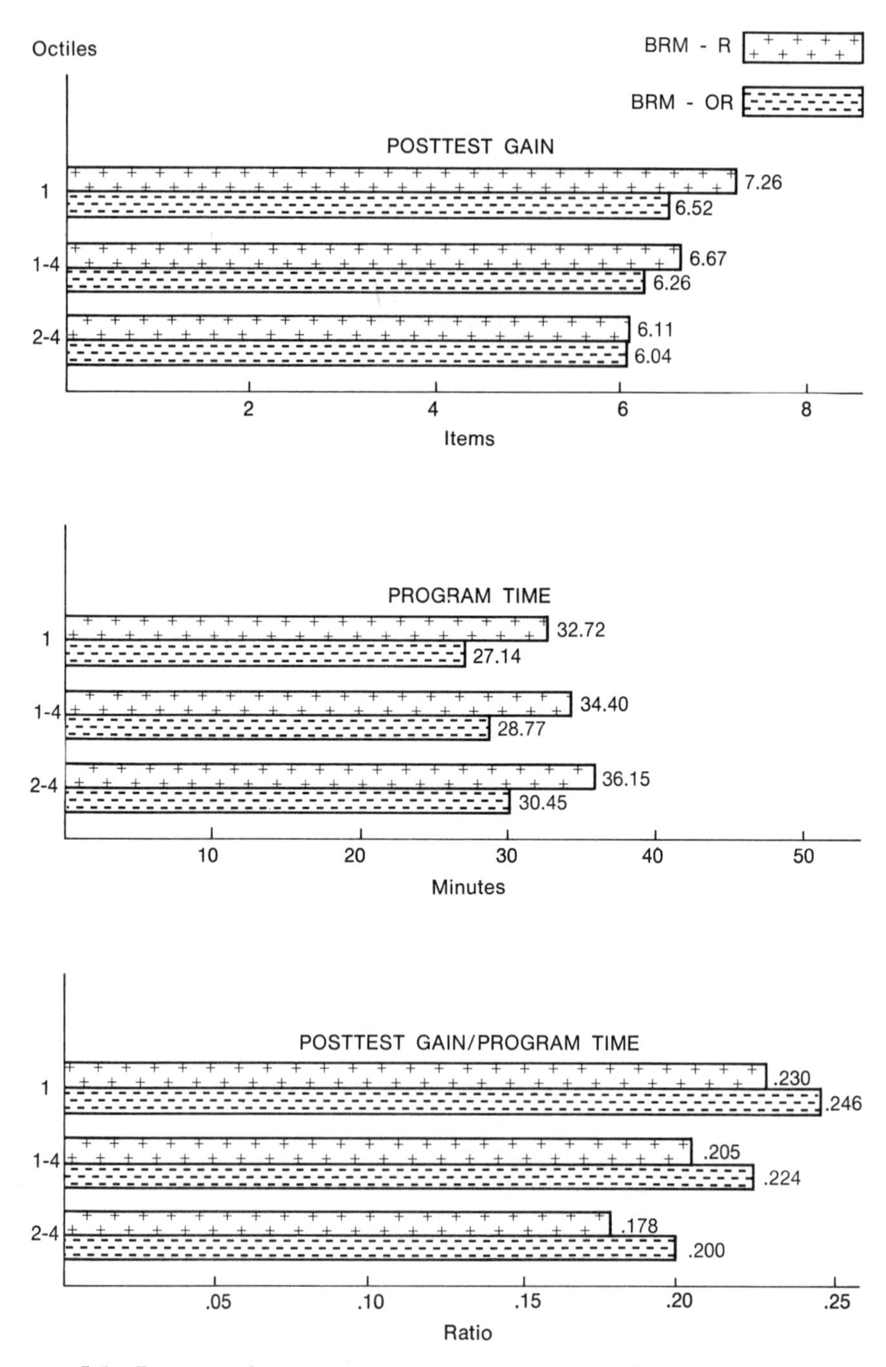

FIG. 5.5 Posttest gain, program time, and a learning efficiency index for the BRM-R and BRM-OR formats presented to state college learners, differentiated and undifferentiated according to scholastic ability.

particularly for the low-ability learners. There was, in addition, a large increase in program time across all ability levels. Accordingly, the efficiency index was much less for the AE format. While according to the formal analysis of PI principles made in Chapter 4, the AE format contains all the features of the AE-OR format plus the overt-responding principle, pragmatically the AE format exemplifies a confirmation procedure, while the AE-OR format exemplifies a formal-prompting procedure. Formal prompting is apparently superior both for the increased learning yield and decreased time cost where large-step size is used and no review of text material is permitted. The differences between posttest gains were statistically significant only for the learners of low and undifferentiated ability. On the other hand, the differences between program times and efficiency indices were significant at all ability levels.

Figure 5.5 shows that when the BRM-R format was formed by adding the features of overt responding to the configuration of principles comprising the BRM-OR format, there were modest increases in the posttest gains, but even greater increases in program times. Correspondingly, the efficiency indices seem somewhat less for the BRM-R format. None of the differences between posttest gains were statistically significant at any ability level. On the other hand, the differences between program times were significant at all ability levels, although not enough for the differences between efficiency indices to achieve significance at any ability level.

The Principle of Immediate Feedback

The principle of immediate feedback was tested by comparing the following formats:

(a) OR to AE	Test of KCR only
(b) BRM-F to BRM-R	Test of KCR only
(c) BRM-R to BRM	Test of remediation only
(d) BRM-F to BRM	Test of KCR plus remediation

Figure 5.6 shows the posttest gains, program times, and efficiency indices for the comparison OR to AE; Figure 5.7 shows these variables for the comparison BRM-F to BRM-R; while Figure 5.8 shows them for BRM-R to BRM; and Figure 5.9, for BRM-F to BRM.

Figure 5.6 shows that when the AE format was formed by adding the feature KCR to the configuration of principles comprising the OR format, there appeared to be a mild increase in posttest gain for learners at all ability levels. The increase in program time appeared to be greatest for the high-ability level and least for the low-ability level. The efficiency index differed little between formats. None of the differences between posttest gains, program times, and efficiency indices were statistically significant at any liability level.

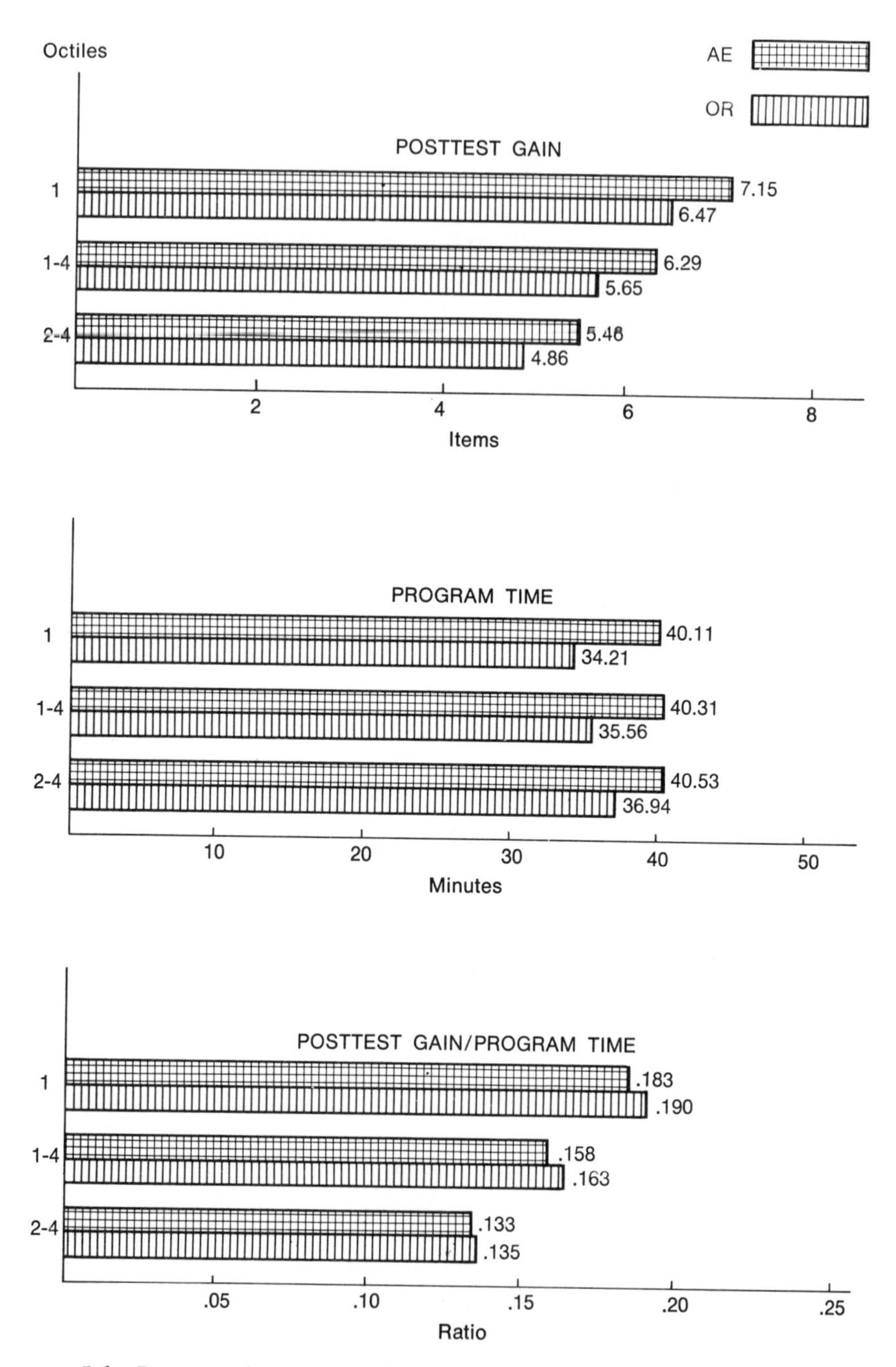

FIG. 5.6 Posttest gain, program time, and a learning efficiency index for the AE and OR formats presented to state college learners, differentiated and undifferentiated according to scholastic ability.

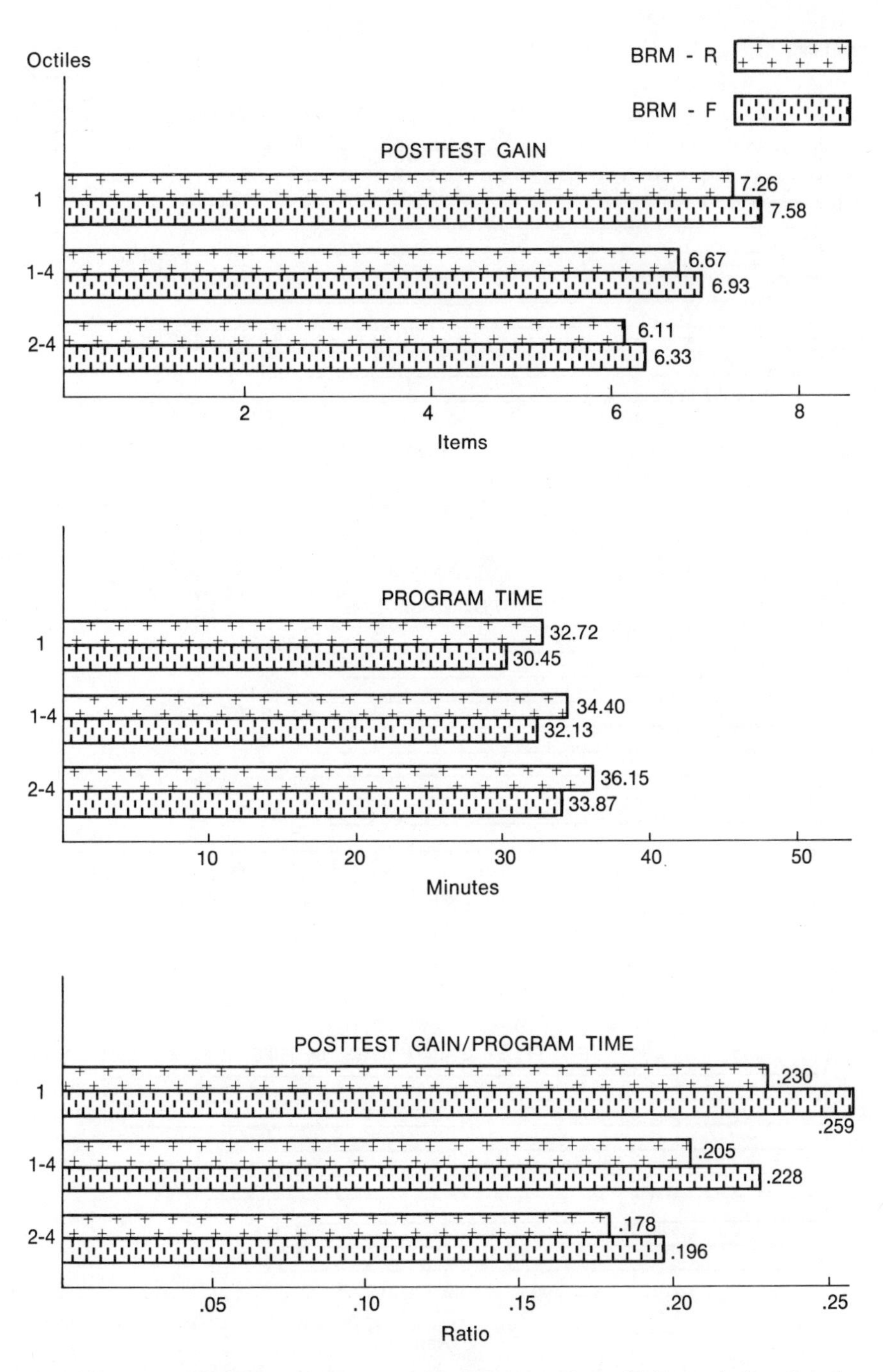

FIG. 5.7 Posttest gain, program time, and a learning efficiency index for the BRM-R and BRM-F formats presented to state college learners, differentiated and undifferentiated according to scholastic ability.

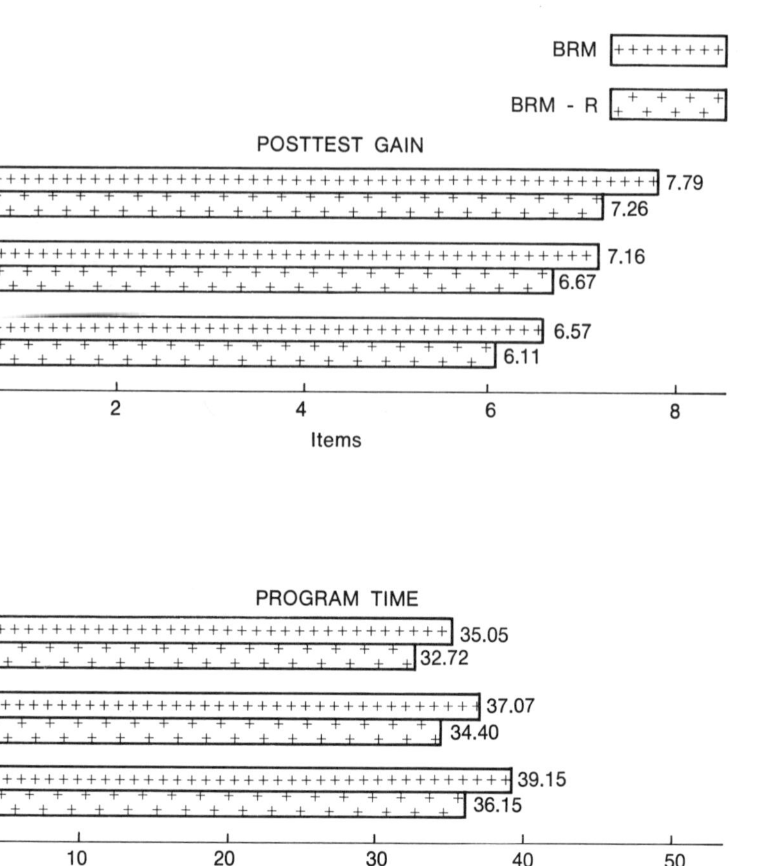

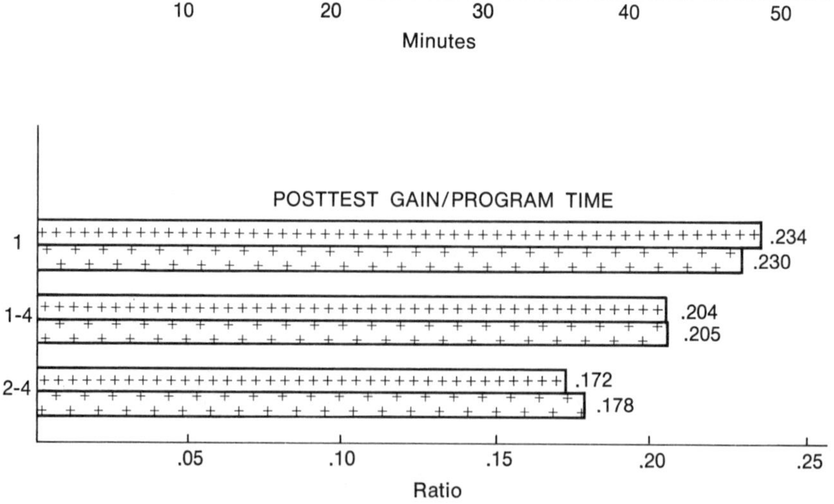

FIG. 5.8 Posttest gain, program time, and a learning efficiency index for the BRM and BRM-R formats presented to state college learners, differentiated and undifferentiated according to scholastic ability.

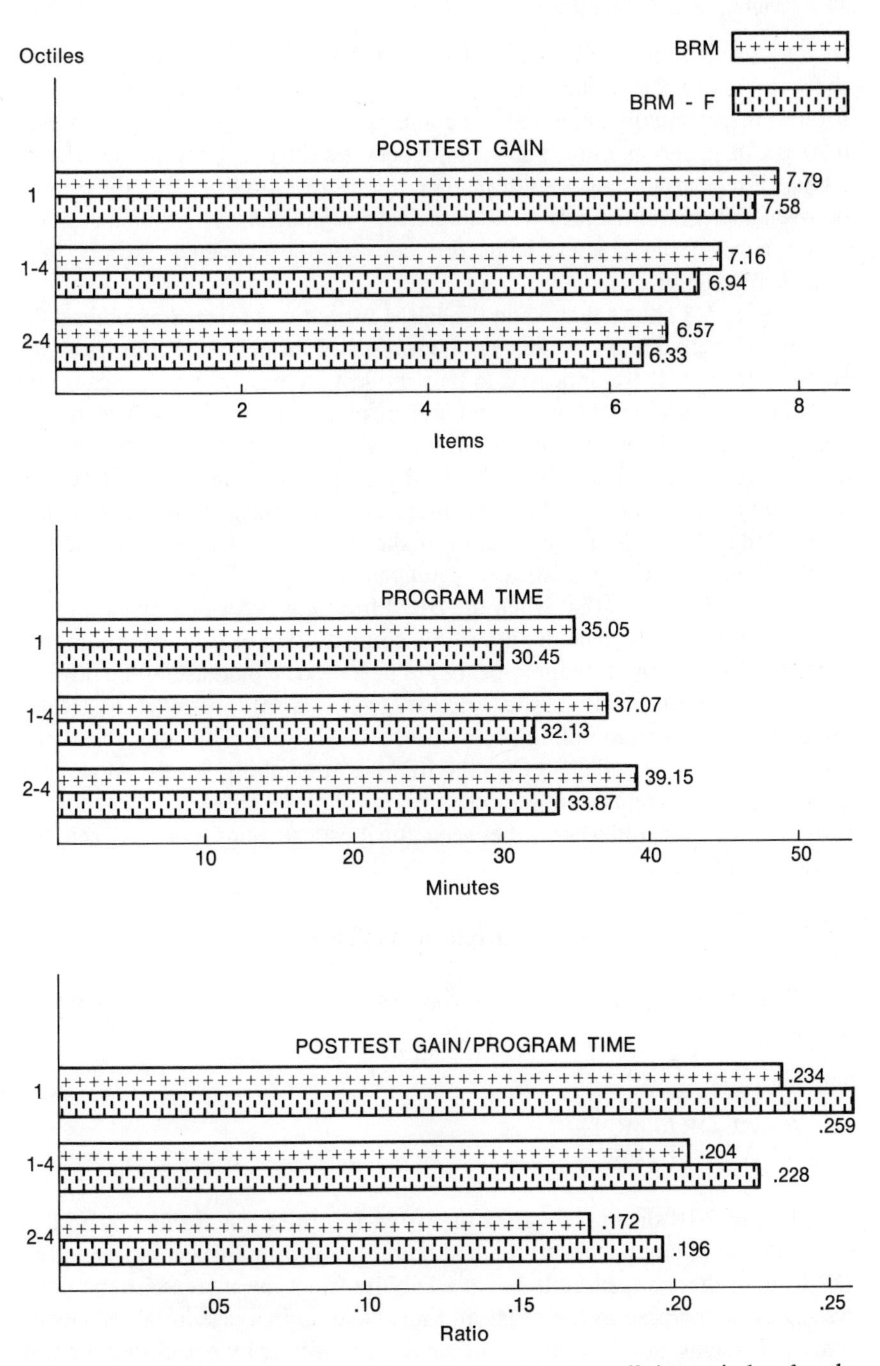

FIG. 5.9 Posttest gain, program time, and a learning efficiency index for the BRM and BRM-F formats presented to state college learners, differentiated and undifferentiated according to scholastic ability.

Figure 5.7 shows that when the BRM-R format was formed by adding the features of KCR to the configuration of principles comprising the BRM-F format, there actually appeared to be a mild decrease in posttest gain, a mild increase in program time, and a mild decrease in efficiency for all ability levels. For learners of undifferentiated and low ability, the differences between the program times were statistically significant. None of the differences between the posttest gains nor between the efficiency indices were statistically significant.

Figure 5.8 shows that when the BRM format was formed by adding the feature of remediation to the configuration of principles comprising the BRM-R format, there appeared to be a modest increase in posttest gain, but at the cost of a corresponding increase in program time. This held for all ability levels. The cost just about offset the yield so that the efficiency indices differed negligibly for all ability levels. For learners of undifferentiated and low ability, the differences between program times were statistically significant. None of the differences between the posttest gains nor between the efficiency indices were statistically significant.

Figure 5.9 shows that when the BRM format was formed by adding the features of KCR plus remediation to the configuration of principles comprising the BRM-F format, there appeared to be a modest increase in the posttest gain at all ability levels. However, there was a disproportionately greater increase in the corresponding program times, with the result that the BRM format appeared less efficient than the BRM-F at all ability levels. At all ability levels, the differences between the program times were statistically significant, but not the differences between the posttest gains nor between the efficiency indices.

The Principle of Small Steps

The principle of small steps was tested by comparing the following formats:

(a) OR to BRM-F
(b) AE-OR to BRM-OR
(c) AE to BRM-R

Figure 5.10 shows that when the BRM-F format was formed by adding the principle of small steps to the configuration of principles comprising the OR format, there appeared to be, at all ability levels, an increase in the posttest gains, a decrease in the program times, and an increase in the efficiency indices. It seems a format that uses thematic *prompting* by permitting the text to be reviewed after the test item is read, requires less time than a format that does not use such prompting. Thus, while it is generally true that the incorporation of an additional PI principle will increase the program time required

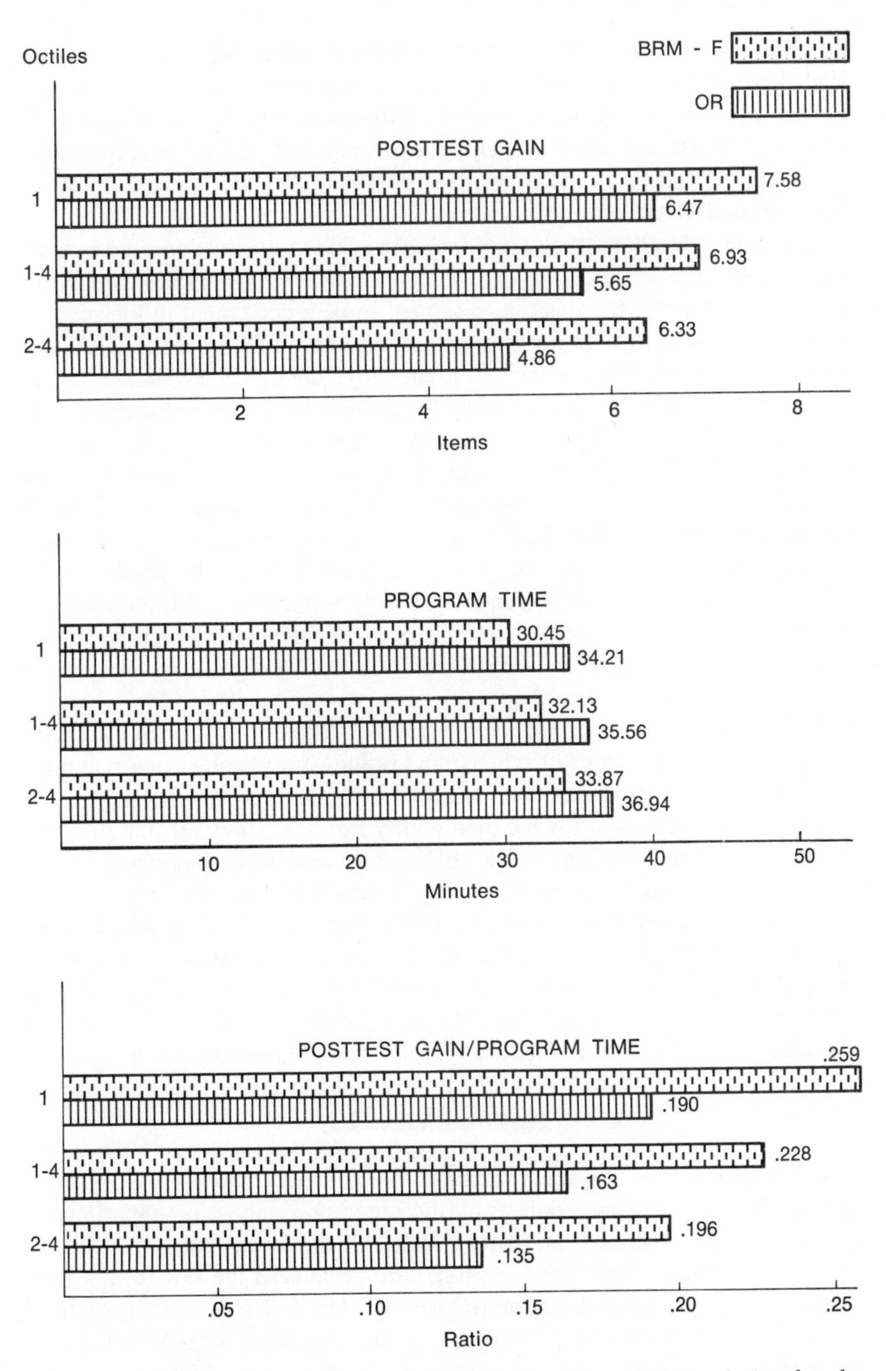

FIG. 5.10 Posttest gain, program time, and a learning efficiency index for the BRM-F and OR formats presented to state college learners, differentiated and undifferentiated according to scholastic ability.

by a format, it is not necessarily true in the case of the small-step principle. For all ability levels, the efficiency indices seemed greater for the BRM-F format. Statistically significant were the differences between the posttest gains at the undifferentiated ability level, the differences between the program times at all ability levels, and the differences between the efficiency indices at the high and undifferentiated ability levels.

Figure 5.11 shows that when the BRM-OR format was formed by adding the principle of small steps to the configuration of principles comprising the AE-OR format, there actually seemed to be a decrement in the posttest gains at all ability levels. Furthermore, the program times of the BRM-OR format seemed slightly greater. Consequently, the efficiency indices of the BRM-OR format all appeared to be far smaller than those of the AE-OR. Apparently, the use of formal prompting is beneficial to a large-step format, such as the AE-OR, where such prompting cannot adversely affect the reading of the text. But, for the purposes of associative learning, formal prompts can adversely affect the reading of the text and be detrimental to a small-step format, such as the BRM-OR. The differences between the posttest gains were significant at the undifferentiated ability level. None of the differences between the program times were statistically significant, although the differences between the efficiency indices were statistically significant for learners at all ability levels.

Figure 5.12 shows that when the BRM-R format was formed by adding the principle of small steps to the configuration of principles comprising the AE format, there appeared to be rather minor increases in posttest gain, the increase being negligible for the high-ability learners. However, the program times were appreciably less for the BRM-R format, indicating again that, if no formal prompting is present, adding in the small-step principle does not increase the cost in program time, but will ordinarily decrease it. At all ability levels, the efficiency indices for the BRM-R format were far greater than for the AE. None of the differences between posttest gains were statistically significant. However, the differences between the program times and between the efficiency indices were statistically significant at all ability levels.

The Other Variables

Let us consider the other variables in Table 5.1. The variable, attitude toward instructional materials, was measured for only four experimental groups: the BC, OR, AE, and BRM/BRB. Of the four groups, the learners expressed a significantly less favorable attitude toward the OR format than toward either the BRM-BRB or BC format. The OR format differed from both the BRM/BRB and BC formats in that the learners received a conventional test over the material following a reading of the text.

Of the formats where the variable, program items in error, was applicable, the formats incorporating the small-step principle (BRM/BRB,

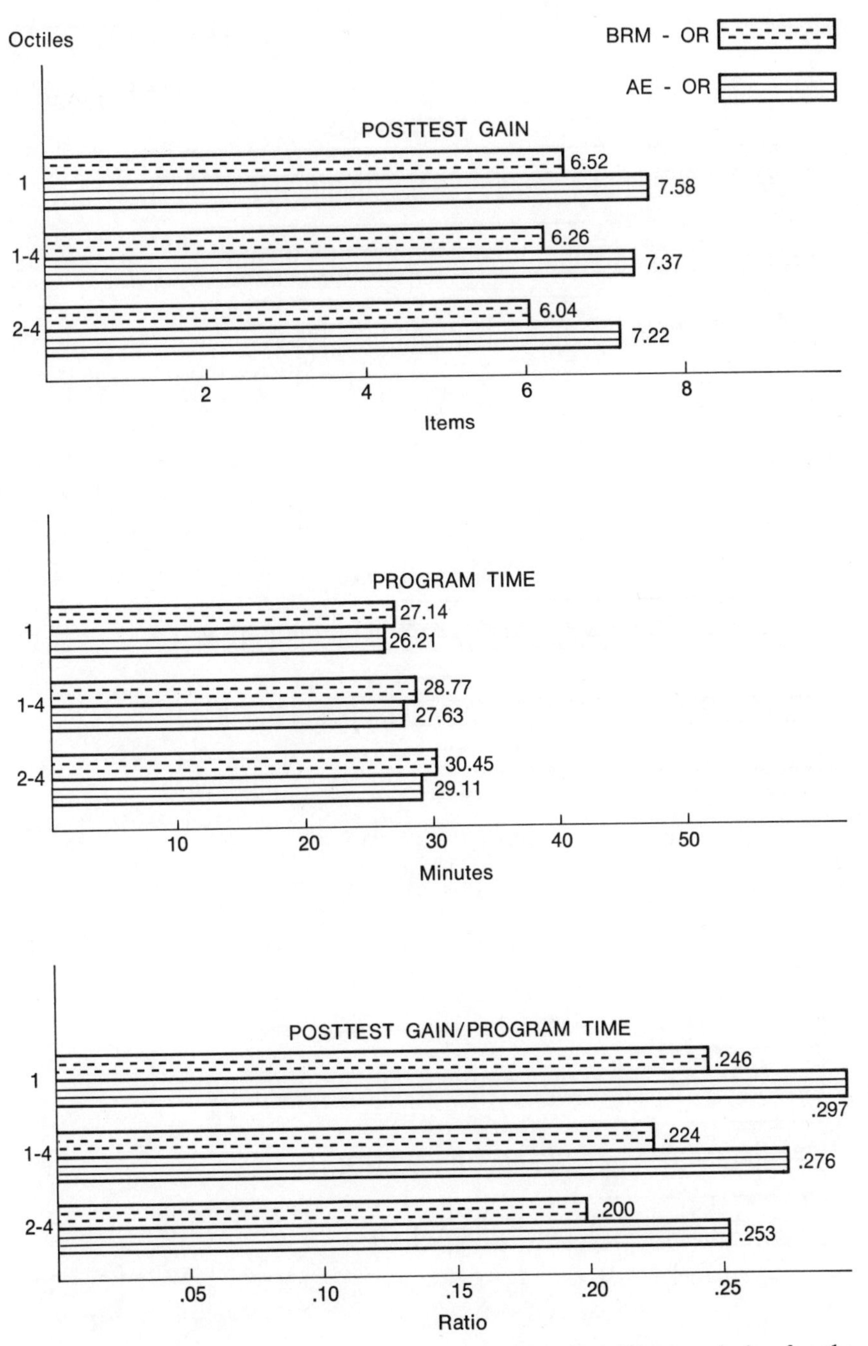

FIG. 5.11 Posttest gain, program time, and a learning efficiency index for the BRM-OR and AE-OR formats presented to state college learners, differentiated and undifferentiated according to scholastic ability.

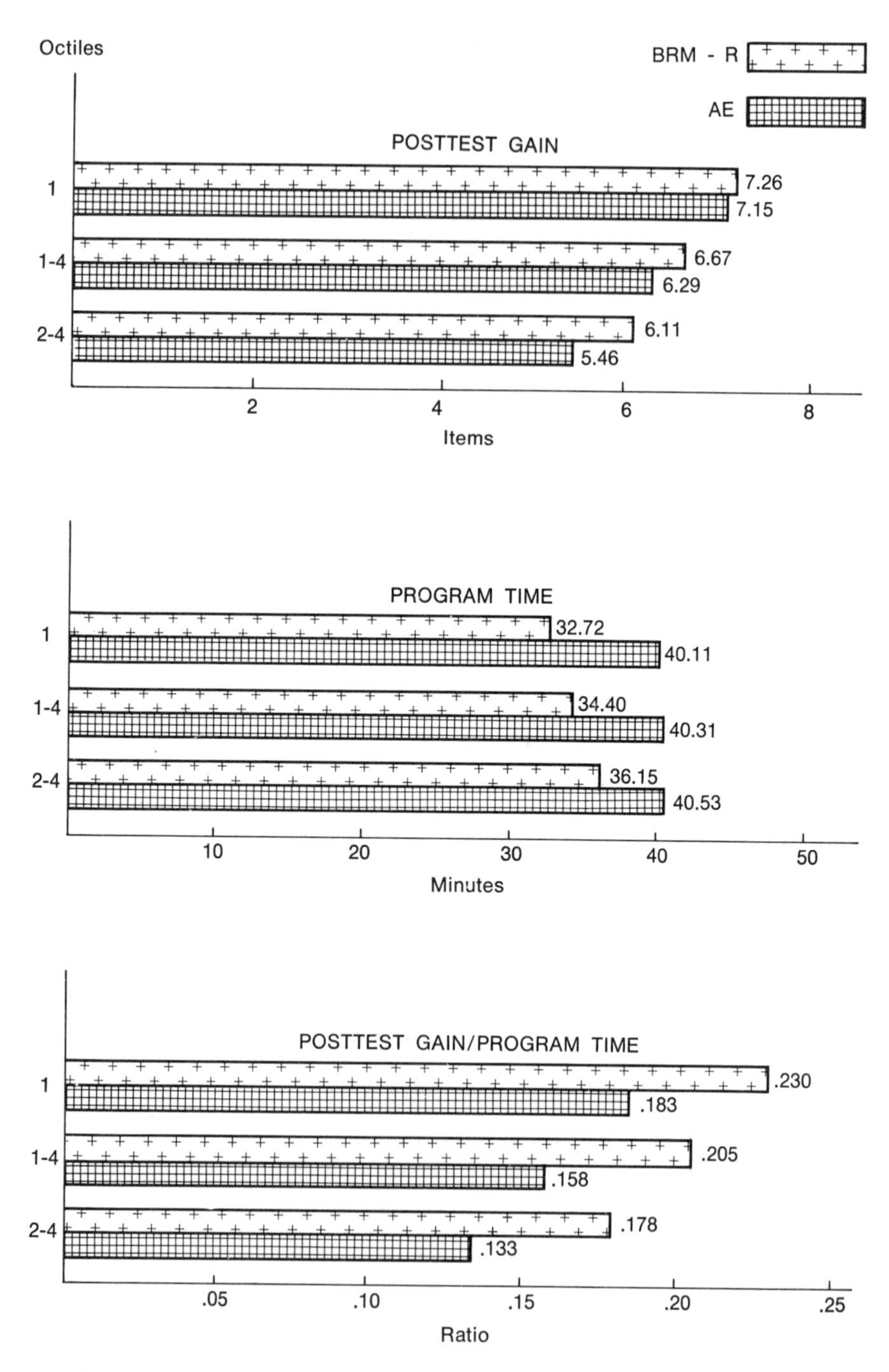

FIG. 5.12 Posttest gain, program time, and a learning efficiency index for the BRM-R and AE formats presented to state college learners, differentiated and undifferentiated according to scholastic ability.

BRM-R, and BRM-F) gave rise to significantly less program test items in error than did either of the large-step formats (OR and AE). Also of the formats where the variable, program errors, was applicable, the formats incorporating the small-step principle (BRM-BRB and BRM-R) gave rise to significantly fewer errors on the program test items than did the large-step format (AE). Of course, these findings were to be expected in view of the fact that only on the small-step formats were the learners able to examine at will the text material after inspecting a program test item.

Summary

As instructional formats include a greater number of the optional principles and features of programmed instruction, the learning yield tends to increase. However, the yield from any two or more features acting in combination will usually make a lesser contribution toward learning than would be expected from the separate contribution of each feature.

Program time tends also to increase where the added principles are overt responding and feedback (either KCR or remediation). In contrast, the program time tends to decrease:

(a) where the added principle is small steps, or
(b) where the added feature is to permit review of text prior to responding, or
(c) where confirmation is supplanted by prompting, either thematic or formal.

The most reliable thing one can say about overt responding is that it will increase program time considerably. Overt responding tends also to increase learning yield, but generally the increase is not commensurate with the increased cost in program time. Or putting it differently, it would seem that the increased time required could be used more profitably by having the learner read redundant text or by having him read and perhaps covertly respond to a greater number of study questions.

It is also true that the most reliable thing one can say about immediate feedback is that it will increase program time, although feedback is not as costly as overt responding. Both KCR, and to a lesser extent, remediation, seem to increase learning yield, but the increase is very modest. Either or both forms of feedback seem to contribute very little in programs having small steps, prompting, and the opportunity to review text after viewing a test item.

Unlike the other two optional principles, small steps typically result in less program time (assuming the absence of formal prompting). Small steps also tend to increase learning yield particularly for those learners of lower ability. From an efficiency standpoint, the savings in time may be a more important payoff of the small-step principle than the increase in learning yield.

In practice, the use of small steps automatically supplies thematic prompting and the opportunity to review text after viewing a test item. All of these confounded variables engender less errors and are thus desirable.

With reference to learner motivation, it appears that if the learner is asked to respond overtly, he should also be given immediate feedback, and the material should be presented in small steps.

6

Implications for Programmed Instruction Technology

The following formats simulated popular PI techniques:

(a) the BRM simulated the machine-presented branching technique,
(b) the BRB simulated the book-presented branching technique, and
(c) the AE simulated the auto-elucidative technique.

Figure 6.1 shows the posttest gains, program times, and efficiency indices for these three formats. The BRM format was identical to the BRB, except that the program times were corrected for the feedback delay interval imposed by the software simulation. According to the formal analysis in Chapter 4, both the BRM and BRB formats differed from the AE in that they furnished remediation and incorporated the small-step principle.

Figure 6.1 also shows that, when the BRM/BRB format(s) was formed by adding both the remediation feature and the small-step principle to the configuration of principles comprising the AE format, there appeared to be a modest increase in posttest gain, although this difference was not statistically significant at any ability level. The BRM format was free of the artifactual feedback delay imposed by the software simulation. Hence, the program times of the BRM format were significantly shorter than those of the AE format for both the high and undifferentiated ability levels. The efficiency indices of the BRM format were significantly greater than those of the AE format at all ability levels. In comparing the BRM to the BRB format, the BRM program times proved to be significantly shorter and the BRM efficiency indices significantly greater than those of the BRB at all ability levels.

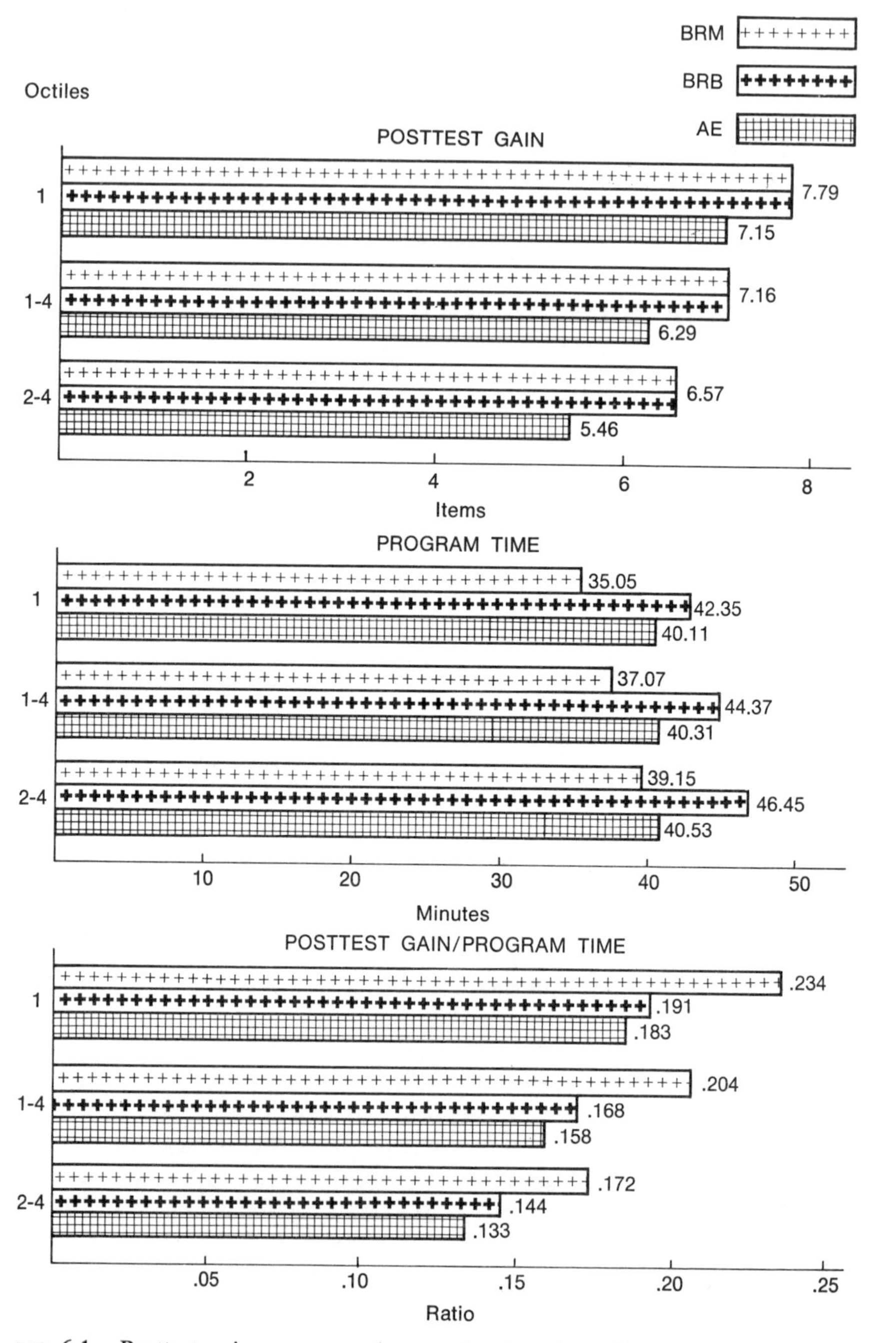

FIG. 6.1 Posttest gain, program time, and a learning efficiency index for the BRM, BRB, and AE formats presented to state college learners, differentiated and undifferentiated according to scholastic ability.

Comparing the BRB to the AE format, the AE program times proved significantly shorter at the undifferentiated and low ability levels, but none of the differences between efficiency indices were statistically significant.

Of the three popular PI techniques, the data supplied the least support for the auto-elucidative technique, since, in most comparisons, the yield in posttest gain per cost in program time was the poorest of all formats. In fact, for high-ability learners, the AE compared unfavorably to the BC, that resembled a mere conventional text. Of the two modes of presenting a branching program, the data indicate strongly that machine presentation is less wasteful of time and hence more efficient.

Figure 6.2 shows the efficiency indices of all the experimental formats. Appendix D contains three tables that show which indices differ significantly from each other. The most efficient format was the AE-OR. This format was simply large-step text followed by a series of test questions with the correct answer indicated.

Of the ten formats listed, three represent popular PI techniques. Collectively, these formats (the AE, BRB, and BRM) are of no more than intermediate efficiency. In fact, the AE and the BRB are comparable to those experimental formats (the BC, CR, and OR) incorporating fewer principles. Those experimental formats made of new configurations of PI principles appeared overall to be more efficient than those customary configurations corresponding to the widely accepted PI techniques of branching and auto-elucidation.

Let us assume a target population of learners having a scholastic ability equal to that of the top octile of twelfth graders. Figure 6.2 and the tables of Appendix D show that a machine-presented branching program would be a more appropriate instructional tool than a text plus an ordinary non-programmed workbook, an auto-elucidative program, or a book-presented branching program. Suppose however that no machine-presented branching program were available in the subject matter to be taught. The locations of the BC format in Figure 6.2 and in the tables of Appendix D suggest that a simple conventional text (if based upon sound instructional objectives and empirically tested, as was the BC format) might by itself be a more appropriate instructional tool than a book-presented branching program or an auto-elucidative program because both of the latter are more bulky and cumbersome.

Let us now assume a target population of learners having a scholastic ability equal to that of the top half of twelfth-graders. In these circumstances, the simple conventional text would no longer be recommended. Figure 6.2 and the tables of Appendix D show that a machine-presented branching program would be a more appropriate instructional tool than a simple conventional text, a text plus study questions, a text plus an ordinary non-programmed workbook, an auto-elucidative program, or a book-presented branching program.

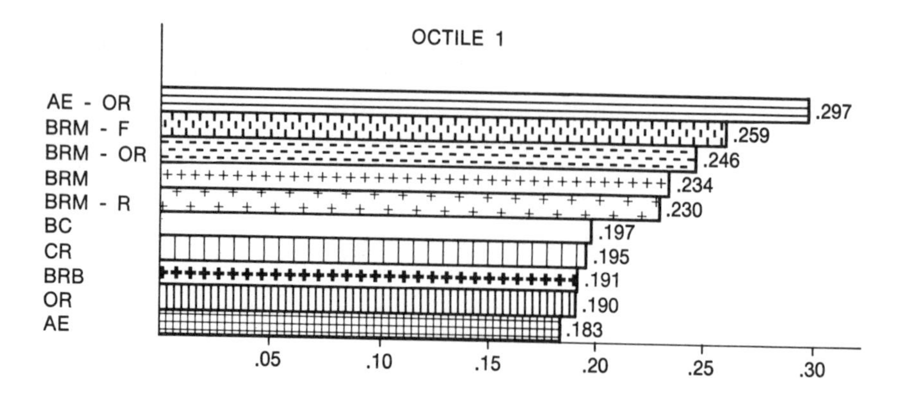

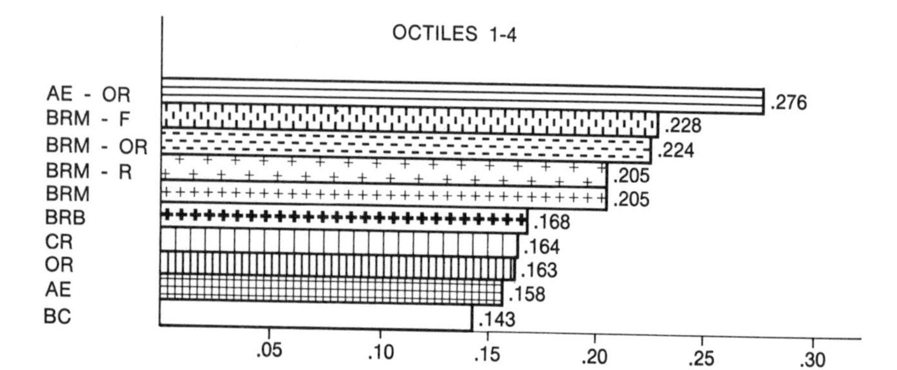

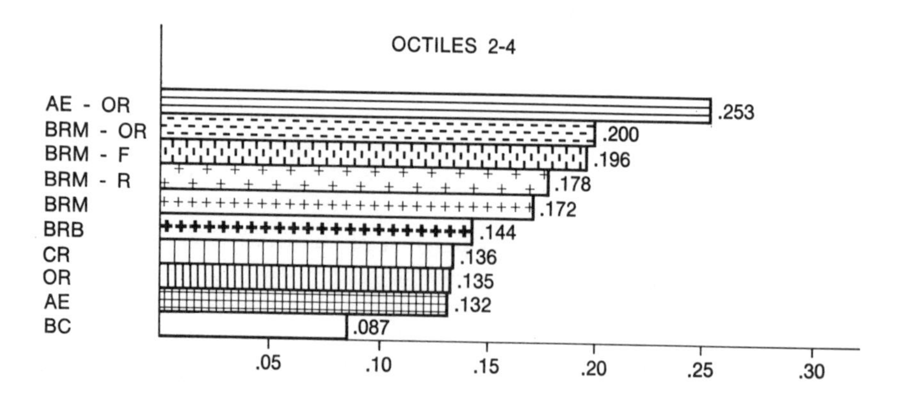

FIG. 6.2 Efficiency indices for the various formats presented to state college learners, differentiated and undifferentiated according to scholastic ability.

Obviously, the relative merit of a format and of the principles comprising it are very much determined by the intellective calibre of the learners. Consequently, the implications of this study cannot be generalized to include learners of less ability nor other subject matters having greater or lesser degrees of interconnectedness.

How Generalized are the Validities of the Optional Principles?

Responding

The principle of responding was tested by comparing the following formats:

(*a*) BC to OR
(*b*) BC to CR
(*c*) CR to OR
(*d*) AE-OR to AE
(*e*) BRM-OR to BRM-R

In the BC to OR comparison, responding was operationalized in the broad sense to include covert and overt responding. Moreover, in this comparison the OR group differed from the BC group, not only by responding in advance to the posttest items, but also by reading the items, an act that had some instructional value. For example, Rothkopf (1966) provides evidence that such questions following a text have facilitative effects that not only are specific to the subject matter of the question, but also generalize beyond it.

In the BC to CR comparison, question reading and covert responding were tested. In the CR to OR, AE-OR to AE, and BRM-OR to BRM-R comparisons, responding was operationalized in the narrower sense to include only overt responding.

The configurations of other principles present in each of the above five comparisons were:

(*a*) BC to OR	mandatory three
(*b*) BC to CR	mandatory three
(*c*) CR to OR	mandatory three (plus question reading)
(*d*) AE-OR to AE	mandatory three plus feedback
(*e*) BRM-OR to BRM-R	mandatory three plus feedback and small-step size

On posttest gain, the only statistically significant differences were: between the BC and CR formats and between the BC and OR formats for all ability groups, and between AE-OR and AE formats, for the learners in the undifferentiated and low ability groups, but in the reverse direction, that is, the AE-OR format showed more posttest gain than the AE, although the AE-OR format incorporated fewer principles.

In efficiency, the only statistically significant differences were: between the AE-OR and AE formats, in all ability groups, but in the reverse direction.

Thus, there was no support for the principle of overt responding. Covert responding, coupled with the reading of the test items, significantly enhanced posttest performance as shown by the BC to CR comparison. But adding overt responding, as in the CR to OR comparison, did not significantly improve posttest performance.

Another test of the overt-responding principle was made by comparing the AE-OR to the AE format. Except for the high-ability learners, more was learned from the format not incorporating the overt-responding principle. This negative payoff in posttest gain, coupled with the large and disproportionate cost in program time, signifies that the instructional technologist can no longer assume the ubiquitous merit of overt responding, particularly if the principle of feedback is also to be employed. Where both of the other two optional principles, feedback and small-step size, were present, as in the BRM-OR to BRM-R comparison, overt responding did not prove its merit with either dependent variable. The poor showing made by the overt-responding principle in this investigation is harmonious with the conclusion of Gates (1917) that overt responding makes less of a contribution in structured material such as was used here. On the other hand, Krumboltz and Weisman (1962) found the overt response to be more effective on delayed-retention tests, such as the one used in the present study, than on immediate-retention tests.

The comparison, AE-OR to AE, was designed as a test of the overt-responding principle, since according to the formal analysis in Chapter 4, the AE format differs from the AE-OR only in that the former incorporates the responding principle. However, as noted in Chapter 5, on both the postest gain and the efficiency index, the superior format was the one without the overt-responding principle incorporated. It does not seem probable, at these ability levels, that the overt response, *per se,* actually impairs learning. Rather, it appears than an analyis of a format in terms of its composition of the PI principles does not exhaustively describe all its relevant features. The superiority of the AE-OR format is probably due to its being favored by one or more of the other features of programmed instruction. A likely cause is the formal prompting that the learner receives from the AE-OR format but not from the AE format.

As noted earlier, the three comparisons, CR to OR, AE-OR to AE, and BRM-OR to BRM-R, are tests of the overt-responding principle. The BC to CR comparison is a test of covert responding plus question reading since the CR format differed from the BC, not only by having the learner emit covert responses, but also by having him read the questions. The BC to OR comparison is a test of overt responding plus question reading because the OR format differed from the BC, not only by having the learner emit overt responses, but also by having him read the questions. Because the OR was not statistically superior to the CR, nor the AE to the AE-OR, nor the BRM-R to the BRM-OR, these comparisons furnished no support for the principle of overt responding. What interpretation then should be placed upon the statistical superiority of the CR and OR formats over the BC in posttest gain at all ability levels? It appears that the reading of the questions accounted for the superiority of the CR format over the BC and also was sufficient to account for the superiority of the OR format over the BC.

Considering all five comparisons, the inclusion of overt responding did not improve posttest performance significantly, whether in the absence or presence of either feedback or small steps. The combination of responding and feedback did not seem superior to feedback alone. Perhaps this result was due to the fact that feedback without overt responding permits prompted covert responding; and, prompting is a PI feature of substantiated effectiveness. This interpretation is compatible with the following results: the learners receiving the BRM-OR format posttested lower than those receiving the BRM-R, but the learners receiving the AE-OR format posttested higher than those receiving the AE. Why the discrepancy? A possible explanation is that a branching program by its very nature is thematically prompted already. Removing the overt-response requirement weakens the format by preventing a prompted overt response from occuring. On the other hand, an auto-elucidative program by its very nature uses confirmation exclusively. Removing the requirement for an overt response strengthens the format by converting the responses from confirmed overt to prompted covert. In other words, trading an overt response for a covert response was a bargain when prompting was exchanged for confirmation. At least, this result seemed to be true on initial learning trials.

Other possible explanations for the AE-OR posttesting higher than the AE, while the BRM-OR posttested lower than the BRM-R are:

(a) On the AE-OR format, unlike the BRM-OR, the attention of the learner, in reading the text paragraphs, could not be adversely influenced by the subsequent reading of the test items.
(b) On the AE-OR format, unlike the BRM-OR, the paragraphs of text were not interspersed with the test items. Therefore, there was less opportunity for subsequent text reading to inhibit retroactively the learning acquired from reading and covertly responding to the test items.

Feedback

The principle of immediate feedback was tested by comparing the following formats:

(a) OR to AE
(b) BRM-F to BRM-R
(c) BRM-R to BRM
(d) BRM-F to BRM

In the OR to AE, and the BRM-F to BRM-R comparisons, only KCR was tested. In the BRM-R to BRM comparison, only remediation was tested. In the BRM-F to BRM comparison, the combined effects of KCR and remediation were tested.

The configurations of other principles present in each of the above four comparisons were:

(a) OR to AE	mandatory three plus overt responding
(b) BRM-F to BRM-R	mandatory three plus overt responding and small-step size
(c) BRM-R to BRM	mandatory three plus overt responding, small-step size and that portion of feedback comprised of KCR
(d) BRM-F to BRM	mandatory three plus overt responding and small-step size

On both posttest gain and efficiency, there were no statistically significant differences between formats. Thus, there was no support for the principle of immediate feedback, whether this principle is interpreted to mean KCR only, remediation only, or the combined effects of both. In contrast, Angell (1949) and Kaess and Zeaman (1960) found feedback to be effective on multiple-choice test items comparable to those used in the present study. However, the Angell study used a posttest consisting of items entirely different from those in the program, and the Kaess and Zeaman study posttested without appreciable delay. Thus, the results of neither study are in outright conflict with those of the present study. In view of the precipitous decline in memory during the first several days, studies not using a delayed posttest have doubtful implications for instructional practice. Nevertheless, the Kaess and Zeaman study seriously challenges the auto-elucidative technique or any technique that foregoes prompting for confirmation. They found that the emitting of an erroneous response to a multiple-choice item, even in the face of feedback, raises the probability of a subsequent error, particularly the identical error. In this regard, their findings are compatible with the small difference found between the posttest performances of the OR and AE groups in the present study, because the OR format requires an unprompted response and the AE adds only KCR.

The BRM-R format was identical to the BRM, except that it did not provide remediation to the learner. Although the remediation provided by the BRM format was only nominal, the lack of any significant difference between the BRM-R and BRM formats casts doubt upon the value of remediation. These results differ from those of Hirsch (1952) who found that remediation facilitated learning. However, these results agree substantially with those of Kaufman (1963), who found no significant differences between the posttest gain scores of groups of learners, who for each mistake on a correct response sequence frame either:

(a) received just KCR and were returned to the correct response sequence frame, or

(*b*) received one frame of remeditation and were returned to the correct response sequence frame, or
(*c*) received two frames of remediation and were returned to the correct response sequence frame.

Kaufman also found no significant differences in program time. The present study, using larger samples of learners, did find significant differences in program time: the undifferentiated and low ability learners took less time when given just KCR than when given KCR plus remediation.

The data for the BRB (book-presented branching) format were not cited in this context in the last chapter because of the previously stated opinion that paper is an inappropriate medium for branching type programs. This opinion was substantiated by the fact that the efficiency indices for the BRB format were significantly below those of the BRM-R format at the undifferentiated ability level.

The implications for instructional technology are, that for learners having scholastic abilities in the upper half of a twelfth-grade reference group and for associative learning tasks, a machine-presented branching program without remediation may often be as efficient as one with remediation. It might not teach as much content, but it might teach as much per unit time while not requiring as complicated a presentation apparatus. Moreover, a machine-presented branching program without remediation appeared more efficient than either a book-presented branching program with remediation or an auto-elucidative program.

Small Steps

The principle of small steps was tested by comparing the following formats. Also indicated are the configurations of other principles present in each of the three comparisons below:

(*a*) OR to BRM-F	mandatory three plus overt responding;
(*b*) AE-OR to BRM-OR	mandatory three plus that portion of feedback comprised by KCR; and
(*c*) AE to BRM-R	mandatory three plus overt responding and that portion of feedback comprised by KCR.

On posttest gain, the only statistically significant differences were at the undifferentiated ability level where sample size remained large. The BRM-F format was found superior to the OR, and the AE-OR was found superior to the BRM-OR. The small-step principle was incorporated by the superior format in the first comparison, but not in the second.

On efficiency, the statistically significant differences were:

(*a*) between the OR and BRM-F formats, for all ability groups;

(b) between the AE-OR and BRM-OR formats, for all ability groups, but in the reverse direction; and
(c) between the AE and BRM-R formats for all ability groups.

Thus, when overt responding was absent from the configuration of principles incorporated in a format (AE-OR), adding in the small-step principle detracted from the instructional effectiveness of the format (BRM-OR). As noted earlier, an analysis of a format in terms of its configuration of the PI principles still leaves great latitude for variation, and the presence of formal prompts in the AE-OR format probably played an important role that was not controlled by the research design.

Significant superiority for the format incorporating the small-step principle was attained in the other two comparisons on the efficiency index, where the shorter program times associated with small steps exerted its influence. Thus, the main support for the principle of small steps was indirect, more in the form of time savings than in direct learning yield. Only in the OR to BRM-F comparison did the format incorporating the small-step principle attain significant superiority on posttest gain. It would seem that whatever contribution small-step size makes toward learning effectiveness is not unique to it, because, in the presence of the additional principles of overt responding and immediate feedback, the inclusion of small-step size did not improve posttest performance significantly.

However, several features were confounded with step size in comparing the formats with and without small steps. For example, the AE differed from the BRM-R format, not only because the AE did not incorporate small steps, but also because the AE relied upon confirmation more heavily than did the BRM-R format, that possessed some thematic prompting. Stolurow and Lippert (1964) found that prompting is best for retention when there is little overlearning and confirmation is best when there is a great deal. The instructional materials used in this study contained very little redundancy and hence made for little overlearning. Therefore, this confounding feature would be expected to act in favor of the BRM-R format and in the same direction as the small-step principle so that its presence does not explain the apparent failure of the small-step principle to show its merit.

However, if an interpretation by Anderson (1967, p. 135) is correct, this particular confoundment is more troublesome. Anderson suggests that prompting leads to more rapid response learning because the learner can make the response without attending wholly to all aspects of the stimulus configuration. But he also suggests that prompting might be inferior to confirmation for associative learning. The materials used in the present study involved associative learning more than response learning. Therefore, if Anderson's interpretation is correct, an advantage would presumably lie with the OR and AE formats. This feature of the materials would then act to disfavor the thematically prompted BRM-F and BRM-R formats and thus act in the opposite direction from step size. Any format that is a reasonable simulation of the branching technique must have both a smaller-step size and relatively more prompting than any format that is a reasonable simulation of the auto-elucidative technique. Thus, the only way in which the inevitably confounded variables could operate in the same direction would be to use instructional materials directed at response learning rather than at associative learning. Hopefully, Anderson's recommendation that prompting not be used for associative learning may only be valid for formal prompting.

In comparing the OR to the BRM-F format and the AE to the BRM-R format, there is an even more troublesome feature confounded with step size. Table 5.1 discloses that inncorrect responses were emitted on only 3.31 of the test items by the BRM-F group and on only 4.33 by the BRM-R group, but they were emitted on 10.29 of the items by the OR group and on 10.54 by the AE group. Consequently, the BRM-F and BRM-R groups were disadvantaged by receiving less "actual corrective feedback" than did the OR and AE groups, because, according to Buss et al. (1956), feedback to the effect that a wrong response is wrong is superior to feedback to the effect that a right response is right. However, other PI research suggests that the BRM-F and BRM-R groups are advantaged by the lower-error rate. If the latter interpretation is the correct one, it would again be fortunate, from a research standpoint, that a confounding feature acts in the same direction as the small-step principle because its presence then would not explain the apparent failure of the small-step principle to show its merit.

It should be noted also that the relative advantages found among the various formats are dependent upon the amount of interrelationship among substantive points in the program text. These advantages may not hold for subject matter having less interconnectedness, less structure, and less dependence on sequence than did the topical material used in this study.

Also, the material was programmed "lean", and hence the posttest was moderately difficult. The results may not generalize to tests containing more redundancy. In fact, the conclusions of Hovland, Lumsdaine, and Sheffield (1949, ch. 9) suggest that both overt responding and feedback have had favorable and unfavorable circumstances in which to show their merit in the present study. A favorable circumstance was the high-difficulty level of the material. An unfavorable circumstance was the high-ability level of the learners. Thus, the results of these studies on state college learners may not generalize to target populations with less scholastic ability. Even within the top half of the ability spectrum, the relative efficiencies of the various experimental PI formats varied as a function of ability.

Another point is that all correct responses to the items on the posttest were evoked earlier on all formats, except the BC. Briggs et al. (1961) have found that a control group, such as the BC group in the present study, when exposed to plain expository text, learned more of the responses which, for a programmed instruction group, were deliberately not evoked. Thus, the advantages found in this investigation for any other format over the BC would perhaps diminish if the responses elicited had been less relevant to the correct responses on a posttest. That is, the other eight formats would probably not have led to such relatively high posttest scores if the posttest items had covered material that had been nonevoked, or misevoked, instead of confining itself as it did, to properly evoked material. This interpretation is supported by the results of Eigen and Margulies (1963) that, while based upon response learning as well as upon associative learning, showed overt responding to facilitate the learning of material at moderate and high difficulty levels, provided the responses were strictly relevant.

Silberman (1961), in summarizing recent research, finds that experiments with specific variables, such as small/large steps, prompting/confirmation, multiple-choice/constructed response, overt/covert response, branching/linear, and standard/self-pacing, are inconclusive when evaluated by criterion performance, but not so inconclusive when evaluated by program time. In contrast, he finds that field studies comparing programmed and nonprogrammed materials typically favor the former.

Silberman points out that this apparent conflict might be explained by:

(a) the "Hawthorne" or novelty effect favoring the newer programmed instruction techniques,
(b) inefficiencies of time utilization in some of the conventional groups that used fixed instruction periods (a point which seems to support the self-pacing principle), and
(c) the possibility that the instruction of the conventional groups was less criterion relevant.

The last explanation, if not a criticism of experimental control, supports the PI principles of objective specification and, tacitly, of empirical testing. It follows that these two principles should receive relatively more attention in experimental studies. Perhaps, due to their implicit merit, they have been subjected to less experimentation than other principles more easily operationalized.

The present study, like so many of those summarized by Silberman, fails to find generalized validity for overt responding, immediate feedback, and small-step size, all of which were considered cornerstones of programmed instruction only a few years ago. Each of these three principles can prove its merit under special conditions, particularly when it is not accompanied by one or both of the other two principles. But one or more of these three principles can often be omitted from an instructional format without a loss in efficiency and sometimes with a gain. An instructional technologist can therefore consider them optional principles and subject them to empirical tests in the course of program development, or he can rely upon the experience of others who have instructed similar learners in related tasks.

There are few formulated principles left to account for the superiority, in field study comparisons, of programmed over nonprogrammed materials, except objective specification and empirical testing. Pending evidence to the contrary, it would seem prudent to regard them still as mandatory principles. The self-pacing principle might also be still regarded, at least provisionally, as a mandatory principle. There is some evidence to indicate that self-pacing may not be essential, because speeded presentations of computer-assisted-instruction have sometimes proven more efficient. However, until the day that CAI becomes widespread in use, self-pacing will mean more specifically "pace-not-controlled-by-the-other-learners," and, because for many learners a class ordinarily proceeds too rapidly or too slowly, self-pacing is preferable.

On Measuring Instructional Efficiency

Whether in science or technology, when we speak of an index of efficiency, we refer specifically to a ratio of yield per cost. In instructional technology, both the yield and the cost may someday be expressed in dollar units. Even today, the cost of instruction in industry, in the military, and even in education can be accurately measured. The cost can be related to time so as to provide a dollars/hour measure. The yield, however, is not so easily measured. What is it worth to a company for a trainee to respond correctly to 94 test items on a 100-item examination covering two weeks of indoctrination? What is it worth to the Navy for a radioman to copy 60 words a minute of Morse Code? What is it worth to society for a student at a public, western college to earn a C in Introductory Psychology? In most instructional applications, whether training or education, true worth cannot be related to instructional output. Until the day when there is a breakthrough in cost accounting, the instructional technologist must limit himself to trying to identify or to develop a technique of instruction that is relatively efficient for a given application. Some have argued, because true worth cannot be related accurately to instruction output, that the efficiencies of various techniques are best measured by computing their costs in obtaining a standard amount of instructional output.

This method would apply to the present study as follows: a criterion level of learning to be accomplished would be fixed. We could, for example, designate that 90 percent of the posttest items must be responded to correctly. As each learner reached the criterion level of 27 of the 30 items correct, his program time would be measured. The technique upon which the learners achieved the lowest mean program time would be the most efficient.

In practice however, this method is more appropriate for experimental investigations using nonsense syllables than for those using meaningful educational materials. Without very frequent testing, this method is difficult to employ because it is difficult to ascertain exactly when the learner attains the criterion level. Moreover, if one tests periodically in order to measure amount learned, one inevitably introduces unwanted influences upon that amount, because learners do learn from test-taking. Furthermore, these unwanted influences would be greater for the slower learner because he would receive more testing before reaching the criterion level. And finally, immediate testing must be used rather than delayed testing. Delayed testing is more suitable for studies of techniques to be used in realistic training and educational settings, since trainers and educators are interested in achieving retention.

The unwanted teaching effects of the measurement attempts can be reduced by keeping the scope of the material to be learned large while keeping the length of the posttest brief, thus lessening the relative influence of the test upon the learner. However, most learner populations are only available for an hour or so of experimentation at any one time. Therefore, it seems that most studies, like the present one, must use a ratio of posttest gain to program time.

There are a couple of necessary precautions in using a ratio index. One must insure that the relationship between the numerator and denominator variables is essentially linear. But learning curves, such as the plot of post-

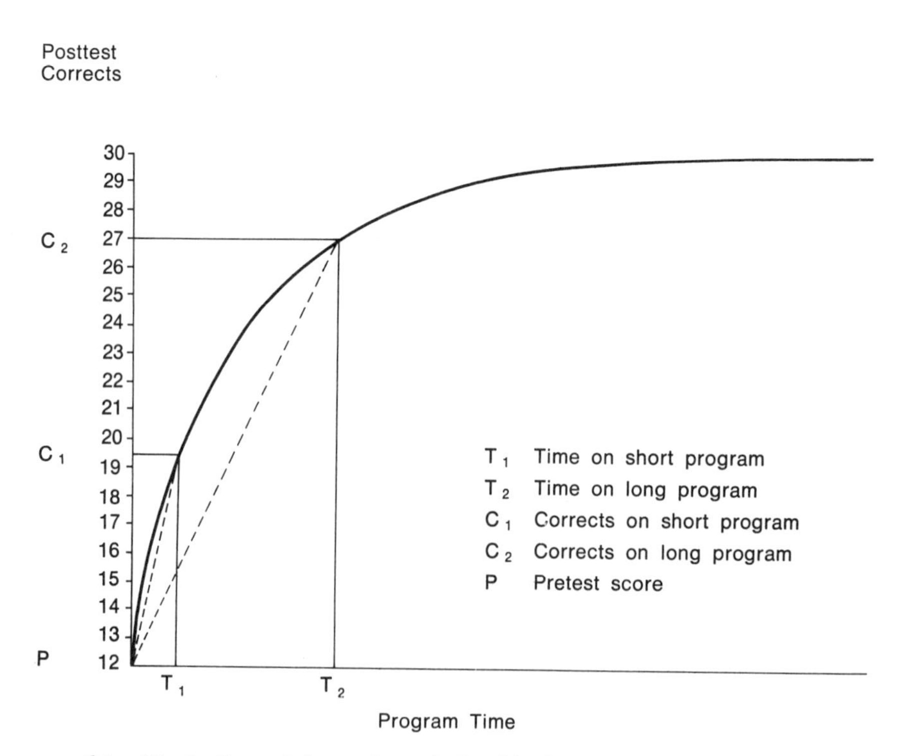

FIG. 6.3 Illustration of how the relationship between posttest corrects and program time approaches linearity when the time interval is kept sufficiently small.

test gain to program time, have a negatively accelerated slope to the plateau of complete success. It is also true, however, that if one takes a sufficiently small interval along the baseline, calibrated in program time, the disparity between the learning curve and a straight line becomes minor. This phenomenon is illustrated in Figure 6.3. Over a brief time span, T_1, the learning curve is closely approximated by a straight line. For a longer time span, T_2, the departure of the curve from a straight line is considerable. In the present series of studies, the statistical tests on each format revealed no significant departure from linearity.

Even if this disparity between the curve and a straight line is kept modest, there is another problem related to the foregoing one. Because the learning curve is negatively accelerated, the ratio, for a given learner or for a given sample of learners taking a given technique, declines as program time increases. One would therefore expect the ratio to disfavor a slow reader or a technique that requires a relatively long time to complete.

Some of the complexities are illustrated in Figure 6.4, containing two hypothetical learning curves. Curve E represents an arbitrarily chosen, effi-

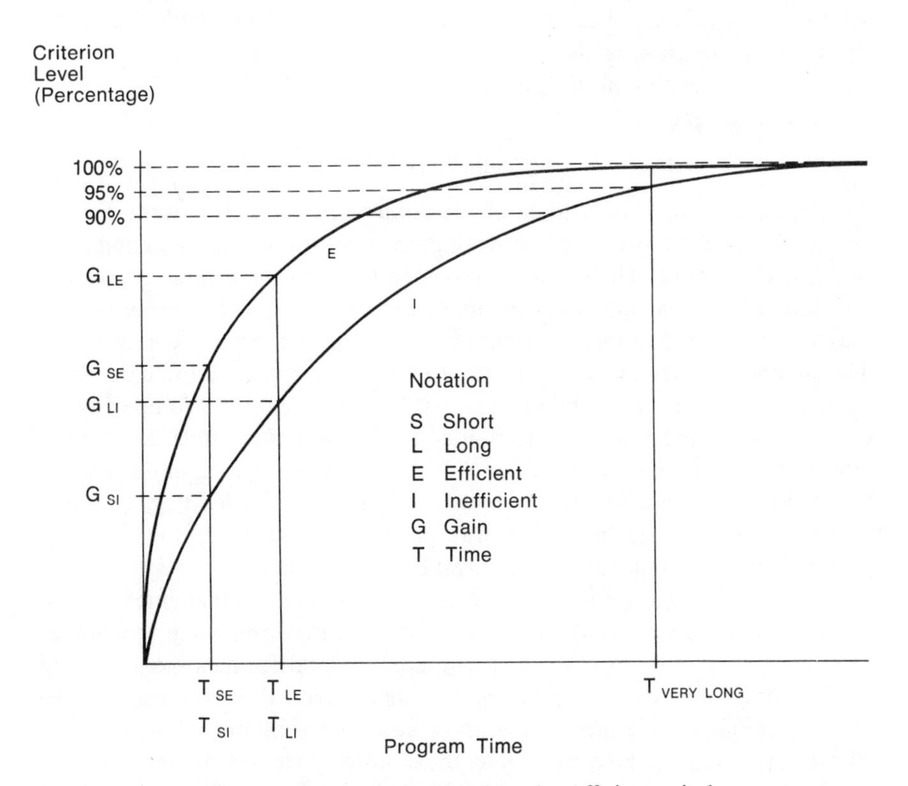

FIG. 6.4 Illustration of the defects of using the efficiency index to compare techniques differing markedly in program time.

cient curve. Curve I represents an arbitrarily chosen, inefficient curve. Let us assume that we have four techniques, which we will refer to as *short-efficient* (SE), *short-inefficient* (SI), *long-efficient* (LE), and *long-inefficient* (LI). On Figure 6.4, the two long techniques require twice the time of the two short techniques.

Consider for the moment the two inefficient techniques. Even though both techniques are, by definition, equally inefficient, the longer technique would appear to be relatively more inefficient: while the time doubled, the gain increased by a lesser amount. This phenomenon can be seen by comparing the two time scores (T_{SI}) and (T_{LI}) and by comparing the two gain scores (G_{SI}) and (G_{LI}). The penalizing effect is even more severe if we compare the two efficient techniques, long and short, because the curve of the efficient techniques is more negatively accelerated.

Further inadequacies of the efficiency index can be seen if we make a comparison between two "very long" techniques, one efficient and one inefficient. The apparent difference in efficiency is small. But it also can be seen from Figure 6.4 that the alternate method of fixing a criterion level of post-test corrects and measuring time is not a panacea either, because the level selected can markedly affect the apparent efficiency. The graph illustrates this shortcoming by drawing three different success criterion levels. The higher the criterion level chosen, the greater the time disparity shown between short and long techniques.

Summary

In these studies, only three of the popular PI techniques were directly tested: the machine-presented branching, the book-presented branching, and the auto-elucidative. The machine-presented branching was more efficient at all ability levels, than either of the other two techniques. The superiority over the book-presented branching technique was due to shorter program times. The superiority over the auto-elucidative technique appeared to be due both to shorter program times and to increased learning yield. In a comparison of the book-presented branching technique to the auto-elucidative, the former apparently yields more learning but also apparently requires more time so that there is no material improvement in instructional efficiency, although many instructional technologists will prefer the format having thematic prompts and low-error rate to the format relying upon confirmation.

All three of the popular PI techniques are of no more than intermediate efficiency. The auto-elucidative and book-presented branching techniques were comparable in efficiency to those experimental formats incorporating none or only one (overt responding) of the optional PI principles. Certain of the experimental formats made up of new configurations of the optional PI principles appeared, on the whole, to be more efficient than those customary configurations corresponding to the widely accepted PI techniques of branching and auto-elucidation.

However, among the more conventional techniques, the machine-presented branching program is recommended over a book-presented branching program, an auto-elucidative program, and a text plus an ordinary nonprogrammed workbook, if the learners are in the top octile of scholastic ability. It would also be recommended over a simple conventional text or a text plus study questions, if the learners are in the top half of scholastic ability.

If no machine-presented branching program is available in the subject matter to be taught and if the learners are in the top octile of college students, a simple conventional text could be written from instructional objectives and empirically tested, and then it could be recommended over either an auto-elucidative program or a book-presented branching program from the standpoint of instructional efficiency.

In the design of instructional formats, it is not possible to ignore the configurational effects of combining various of the PI principles and features into various patterns. This impossibility is partly due to the fact that the definitions of two of the optional principles, immediate feedback and small steps, relate tacitly to responding, if only covert responding. Broadly interpreted, feedback is information fed back to the learner regarding which of two or more alternate answers to a test question is correct. Ordinarily, however, there is the implication that the learner will have just completed emitting an overt response before receiving the feedback. This implication explains why the principle is referred to more specifically as the immediate-feedback principle, suggesting feedback immediately after a response. If, then, we were to delete the requirement of overt responding from a format, we could theoretically modify the format to call for just covert responding prior to feedback. But for research purposes, it is impossible to insure that the learner, having as much autonomy as he does with PI materials, will emit a covert response prior to feedback. When experimental controls are required, as in research, an experimental format with feedback and without overt responding becomes, as it did in the present studies, a format eliciting a formally prompted covert response. And thus we experimentally confound variables. If we are going to provide feedback, the decision to elicit overt responses is also the decision to use confirmation; the decision not to elicit overt responses is also the decision to use prompting. There is evidence that for many instructional objectives and for many learner populations, the advantages of prompted covert responses outweigh the advantages of confirmed overt responses. This recommendation is particularly useful in the earlier stages of learning and in cases where the learned material will later be repeated or built upon. Repetition and redundancy should accompany prompting because materials using prompting have been found inferior to materials using confirmation for consolidating learning and for insuring retention.

Small steps means that the program calls forth learning behavior in small increments. Correspondingly, the program presents information in small modules. But for there to be small modules, there must be small dividers to separate the modules. These dividers usually are explicit questions in the form of test items, but sometimes are implicit questions calling for at least a covert response. By implication then, responding and/or feedback will accompany small steps. The deletion of feedback from a format is simple to do and has straightforward consequences on the structure of the program. But, as noted above, the deletion of overt responding from a format converts a confirmed overt response into a (formally) prompted covert response.

Where small steps are present in the format, the interdependencies between PI features become even more complicated. The reason is that in small-step formats, the learner is permitted and encouraged to reread text prior to responding, whether overtly or covertly. Thus, all small-step formats are, to some degree, thematically prompted. So if overt responding is deleted from a small-step format, a thematically prompted overt response is converted into a formally prompted covert response. And the evidence is that for most instructional objectives, that is, those that include more than mere response learning, the advantages of thematic prompting outweigh the advantages of formal prompting.

The effects upon learning yield, of retaining the immediate-feedback principle and deleting the overt-responding principle, are generally favorable if the program is large step and unfavorable if the program is small step. Converting a confirmed overt response to a formally prompted covert response is appropriate for most instructional objectives. Converting a thematically prompted overt response to a formally prompted covert response is not appropriate for any known instructional objective. This is particularly true when it is recognized that formal prompts on small-step programs can actually distract attention from the text and thus degrade associative learning.

In view of the foregoing complexities, it is dangerous to make sweeping generalizations. However, a few conclusions do emerge from the thicket of interdependencies among the features of programmed instruction.

There are a minority of training and educational situations where the criterion of near-perfect performance must be attained. As examples of occupations where very few errors are tolerated consider the occupations of surgeons and diamond-cutters. To compare techniques for instructing such personnel, the instructional technologist should set the criterion of success as high as indicated and compare the times required by various instructional techniques to achieve the criterion. However, the vast preponderance of training and educational situations require only that instruction bring about substantial improvement. To compare techniques for instructing the bulk of the population, more use should be made of the efficiency index: posttest gain/program time. It must be recognized that the relationship between posttest gain and program time is nonlinear, in practical terms, only if an extremely high criterion of performance is adopted, so that the entire learning curve is used. Based upon pilot studies, research designers must anticipate the scores on both dimensions: posttest gain and program time. The plotted value for each technique investigated must fall upon the "reasonably flat" portion, i.e., the initial portion, of its negatively accelerated curve.

From an efficiency standpoint, the differences in time required by various instructional formats often plays a greater role than the differences in learning yields. For those who would discount the importance of time, it should be pointed out that, for many comparisons, the minor differences in learning yield lead to a situation where a format that required half as much time could cover twice as much scope if time were held constant.

Certain PI principles should be considered as mandatory. These are the principle of objective specification (or behavior analysis) and the principle of empirical testing. Also, included is the principle of self-pacing as long as self-pacing is interpreted to mean that the rate of progress through a program is mainly established by the individual learner, not by the entire class. But the principle of self-pacing should not rule out such refinements as:

(a) speeded presentations by computer, and,
(b) for frames having long latencies, such supplementary prompts as leading questions or analogies.

Wherever overt responding is used, it should be accompanied either by immediate feedback or, preferably, by small steps. That is to say, responses should always be either prompted, or confirmed, or both. For most instructional objectives, confirmation could be deleted more readily than prompting.

For most instructional applications which generally involve association learning and are introductory in level, pure confirmation is to be avoided except in the terminal stages of instruction and is used only for consolidation purposes. Thematic prompting is most desirable, but where it is difficult to incorporate, such as in large-step programs, formal prompting should be used.

Of the three optional PI principles, small steps is the riskiest to delete from a format. Those formats containing small steps are those which most reliably give acceptably large learning yields and acceptably small program times. The next riskiest principle to delete is the immediate-feedback principle. This is particularly true if either overt or covert responding is present and if small steps are absent. Effectively, this is tantamount to saying again that pure confirmation should be replaced by some form of prompting.

For learners having scholastic abilities in the upper half of a twelfth-grade reference group, and for associative learning tasks, a machine-presented branching program without remediation may often be as efficient as one with remediation. It might not teach as much content, but it might teach as much per unit time while not requiring as complicated a presentation apparatus. Moreover, a machine-presented branching program without remediation appears more efficient than either a book-presented branching program with remediation or an auto-elucidative program.

There exists gadgets and gimmicks that are designed to convert instructional material into programmed form, but that actually distract the learners attention from the software intelligence. Included among the gadgets are Pressey's "trainer-tester response cards", that, like some of the complicated response languages demanded of the learner by the more primitive CAI programs, require the learner to direct his attention away from the text. It is doubtful if the presumed benefits derived from any such gadget offset the negative consequences.

7

To Test or to Teach: That is the Question for Multiple-Choice Distractors

Branching programs have traditionally made frequent use of test items having more than two-response options, that is, more than one distractor. According to some learning theorists, e.g., Guthrie (1938, pp. 37 & 42) this practice would seem to be questionable; learners emitting erroneous responses learn those responses even when given immediate feedback disclosing that those responses were, in fact, erroneous. Also, in view of the results of studies, such as that by Kaess and Zeaman (1960), the use of more than one distractor would seem justifiable only in the presence of empirical evidence of its instructional merit. Keeping the distractors to a minimum can improve instructional efficiency in two ways: higher posttest gain and lower posttest time.

To test the instructional merit of test items with a minimum number of distractors, additional formats were created by modifying three of the existing experimental formats containing the small-step principle. The modified formats were the branching (BRM), the branching minus feedback (BRM-F), and the branching minus overt responding (BRM-OR). The instruction sheets for the two-response experimental formats are in Appendix E.

Each of these three formats contained 30 frames, each frame having its individual test item. Since each test item had two distractors, one was retained at random and one eliminated to create the frames for the three new formats. Below is a frame from the familiar branching (BRM) format with three responses. The newer two-response version (BRM_2) of the branching format is identical except that distractor *a* was eliminated and the other two responses relettered.

Color vision is not universal throughout the animal kingdom. Fish, bees, and birds have color vision, but most mammals do not. An exception to this rule are the primates, the order to which man belongs. Monkeys and the great apes possess various degrees of color vision, and the chimpanzee has a structural and perceptual visual system which is almost identical to that of man.

Regarding color vision which of the following is true?

(a) Most mammals see at least the primary colors.
(b) Primates have some color perception.
(c) Birds and bees are typically color blind.

This same example holds for the branching minus feedback formats in their three-response (BRM-F) and two-response (BRM-F_2) versions, because removing the feedback does not change the stimulus appearance of a frame.

This same example would also hold for the branching minus overt-responding formats in their three-response (BRM-OR) and two-response (BRM-OR_2) versions, except that the correct response had an asterisk (*) in front of it. To illustrate, the test item on the above frame in the BRM-OR_2 format appeared as follows.

Regarding color vision which of the following is true?

(a) Primates have some color perception.
(b) Birds and bees are typically color blind.

Table 7.1 contains the means and the standard deviations of all variables for all experimental formats, including the three new two-response versions. The program test items in error were significantly less on the BRM_2 format when compared to its three-response counterpart. Similarly, the items in error also were significantly less on the BRM-F_2 format compared to its three-response counterpart. (Actually, each of the two-overt-response formats had significantly less items in error than did any of the three-overt-response formats.) Thus, if the hypothesized adverse effects of program errors upon learning hold true, the posttest-gain scores for the BRM_2 should exceed those for the BRM, and those for the BRM-F_2 should exceed those for the BRM-F.

Figure 7.1 shows the posttest-gain scores of the three new groups of learners, 112 to each two-response format. In the top third of Figure 7.1 are the gain scores for the octile 1, or "high", group of 57 learners; in the bottom third of the figure are the gain scores for the octiles 2 through 4, or "low", group of 55 learners; and in the middle third of the figure are the scores for the entire undifferentiated group, consisting of all four top octiles. While the two-response formats seemed to be superior to their three-response counterparts for the lower ability learners, none of the differences attained statistical significance.

Figure 7.2 shows the program times. As would be anticipated, most of the significant differences were in favor of the two-response version being

Table 7.1 Means and Standard Deviations of Variables Investigated Using Learners Who Were State College Students

		BC	CR	OR	AE	BRM-R	BRM	BRB	BRM-F	BRM-OR	AE-OR	BRM_2	BRB_2	$BRM\text{-}F_2$	$BRM\text{-}OR_2$
Posttest corrects	M:	15.08	16.75	17.59	18.23	18.61	19.10	19.10	18.88	18.20	19.31	19.56	19.56	18.80	18.88
	SD:	4.15	4.27	4.39	4.44	4.13	3.94	3.94	4.00	3.82	3.76	3.83	3.83	3.75	4.39
Scholastic ability	M:	23.44	23.44	23.44	23.44	23.44	23.44	23.44	23.44	23.44	23.44	23.44	23.44	23.44	23.44
	SD:	3.39	3.39	3.39	3.39	3.39	3.39	3.39	3.39	3.39	3.39	3.39	3.39	3.39	3.39
Attitude	M:	10.39	nm[a]	9.72	10.04	nm	10.54	10.54	nm	nm	nm	nm	nm	nm	nm
	SD:	2.17	nm	2.12	2.23	nm	2.08	2.08	nm	nm	nm	nm	nm	nm	nm
Program time	M:	22.31	29.14	35.56	40.31	34.35	37.07	44.37	32.13	28.77	27.63	27.83	35.13	30.04	28.62
	SD:	5.89	6.10	6.96	6.10	6.91	6.84	6.84	5.90	5.90	5.64	6.42	6.42	5.94	6.65
Program items in error	M:	na[b]	na	10.47	10.54	4.33	3.25	3.25	3.31	na	na	1.61	1.61	1.97	na
	SD:	na	na	4.50	4.81	3.30	2.29	2.29	2.60	na	na	1.48	1.48	1.54	na
Program errors	M:	na	na	na	13.59	4.96	3.65	3.65	na	na	na	na	na	na	na
	SD:	na	na	na	6.42	4.34	2.66	2.66	na	na	na	na	na	na	na

[a] nm indicates variable not measured for that experimental group
[b] na indicates variable not applicable for that experimental group

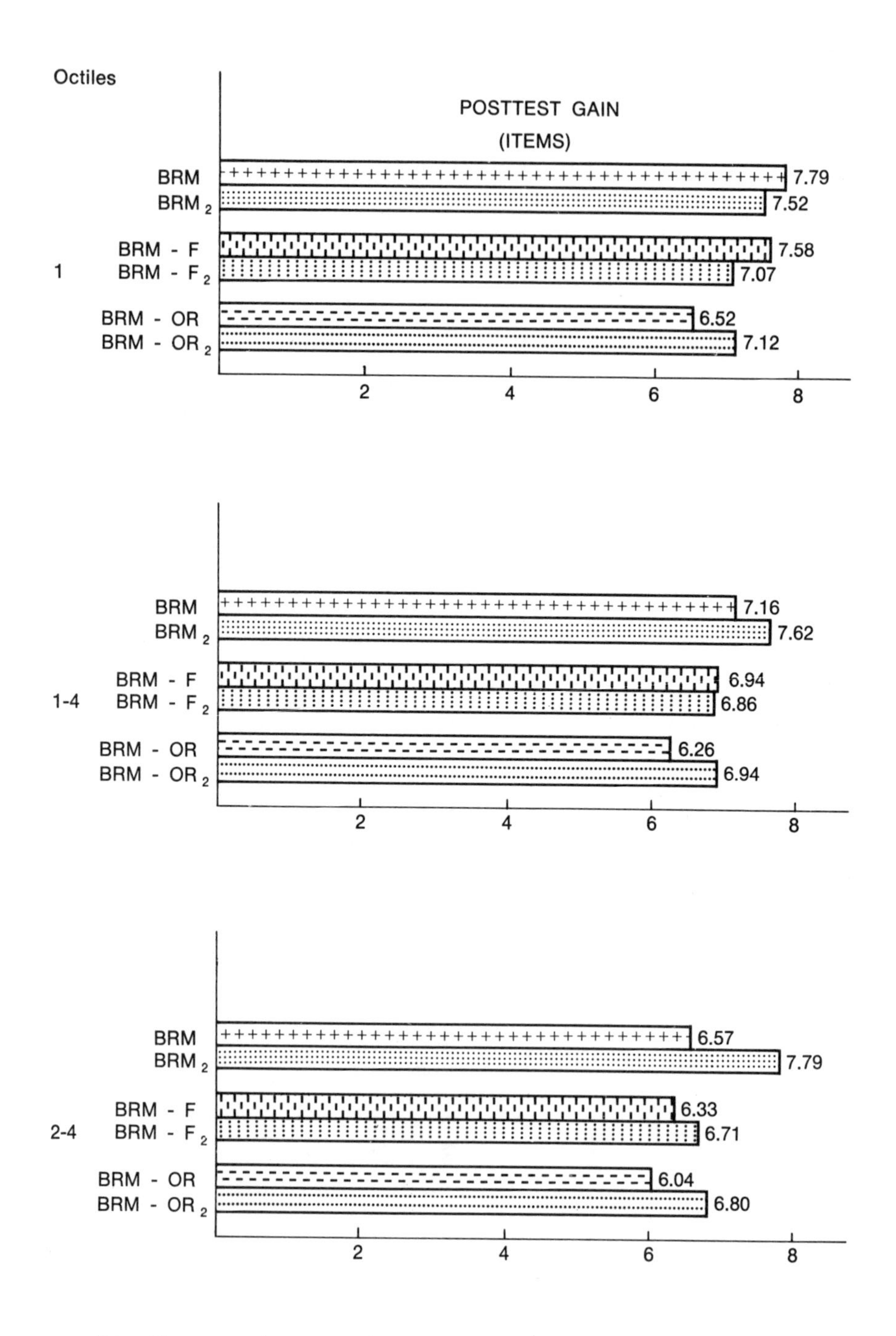

FIG. 7.1 Posttest gain scores for learners of high, undifferentiated, and low ability to three-response and to two-response versions of the formats: (machine-presented) branching; branching minus feedback; and branching minus overt responding.

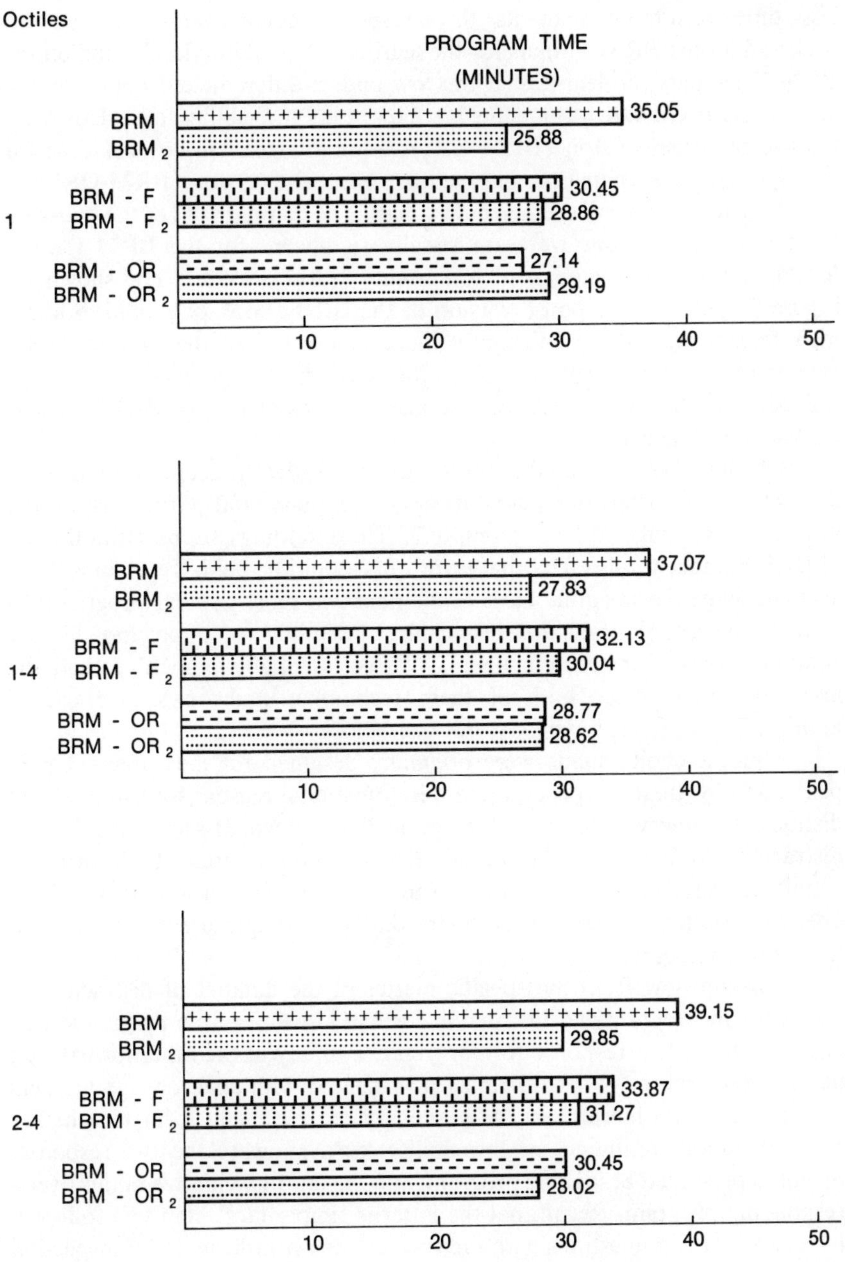

FIG. 7.2 Program times for learners of high, undifferentiated, and low ability to three-response and to two-response versions of the formats: (machine-presented) branching; branching minus feedback; and branching minus overt responding.

less time-consuming than its three-response counterpart. This pattern occurred on the BRM formats for the learners at all ability levels, and on the BRM-F formats for learners at the low and undifferentiated ability levels, and on the BRM-OR formats for learners at the low-ability level. However, the two-response version ($BRM\text{-}OR_2$) required significantly more time for the high-ability learners than did the three-response version (BRM-OR).

Figure 7.3 shows the efficiency indices. The comparisons of the two- and three-response versions were statistically significant for the BRM format, for high, undifferentiated, and low ability learners. While not shown on Figure 7.3, the two-response version of the BRB (book-presented, branching) format was also significantly more efficient than the three-response version at all ability levels. The only other statistically significant comparison was between the two- and three-response versions of the BRM-OR formats for low-ability learners.

On the whole, it would seem to be a good idea to keep the number of distractors low, particularly for low-ability learners, and particularly in the absence of formal, explicit, prompting. These findings support the dictum of B. F. Skinner to the effect that error rate should be held "very" low. They also challenge the scientific basis of the next two most popular programmed instruction techniques: the branching, including that portion of the computer-assisted-instruction field which is essentially branching, and the auto-elucidative, since both of these techniques make extensive use of multiple-choice items having several distractors.

Multiple-choice items were originally designed for measurement purposes; and for these purposes, there were functional reasons for using several distractors. However, for teaching applications, it would seem that the less distractors the better. Any technique that attempts to attain both purposes simultaneously is, of necessity, going to do a poor job in attaining at least one, if not both purposes. The auto-elucidative technique attempts to test and teach simultaneously.

Turning now from the specific matter of the number of distractors in test items in programmed instruction formats, to the simple pragmatic efficiency of these two-response formats relative to any of the other formats, let us consider Figure 7.4. All formats investigated with state college learners are arranged in a hierarchy. The seemingly most efficient formats, whether for high, undifferentiated, or low ability learners, were the two-response, machine-presented branching program, and the auto-elucidative minus overt-responding program. Recall that the latter is simply large-step text followed by a series of test questions with the correct answer indicated. An inspection of the significantly different efficiency indices of the various formats tabled in Appendix F reveals that for high, undifferentiated, or low ability learners, the BRM_2 and AE-OR formats were superior to either of the two popular programmed instruction techniques, the branching and the auto-elucidative.

Before concluding, however, that the AE-OR or any other formally prompted format is universally applicable, we must consider the type of

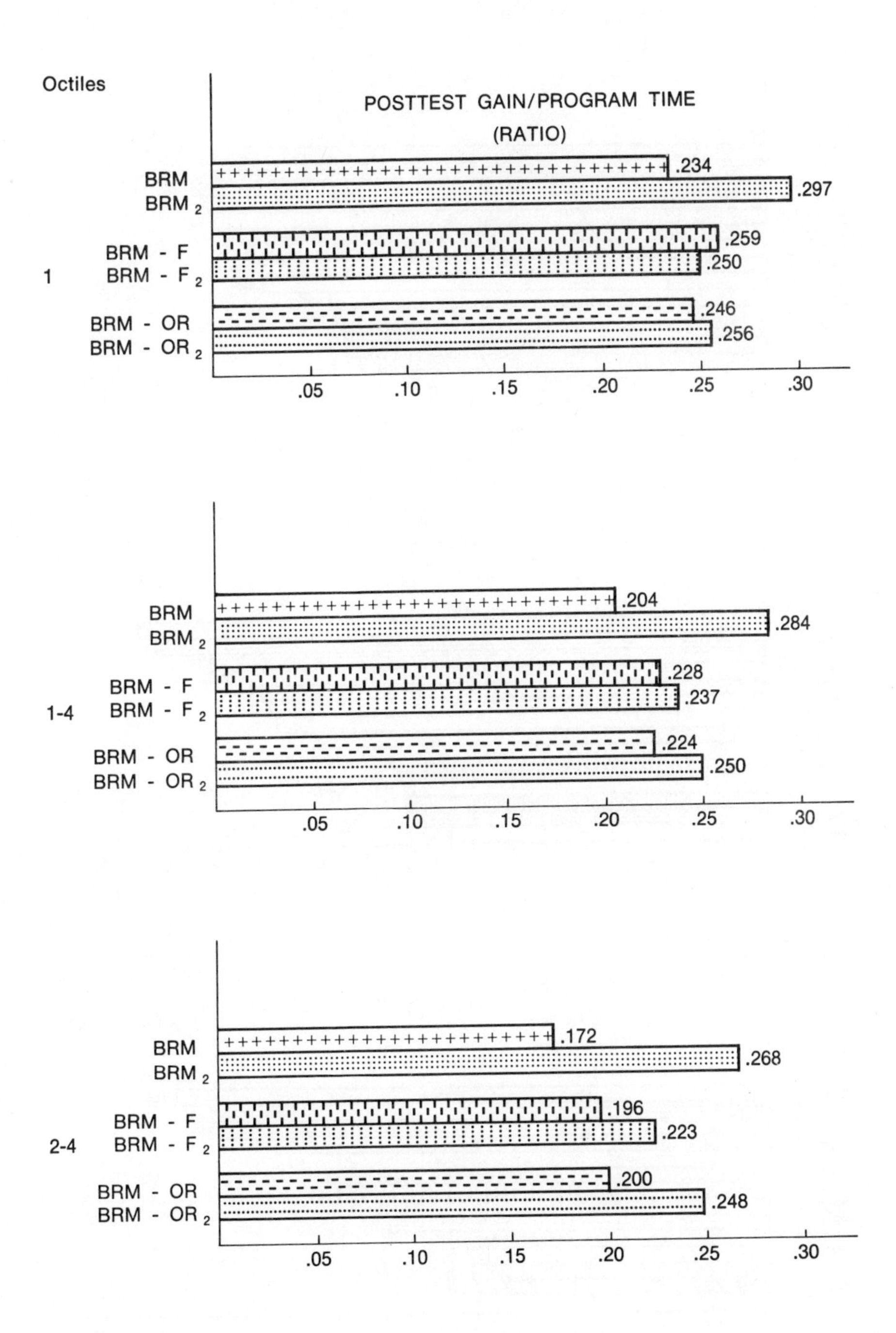

FIG. 7.3 Efficiency indices for learners of high, undifferentiated, and low ability to three-response and to two-response versions of the formats: (machine-presented) branching; branching minus feedback; and branching minus overt responding.

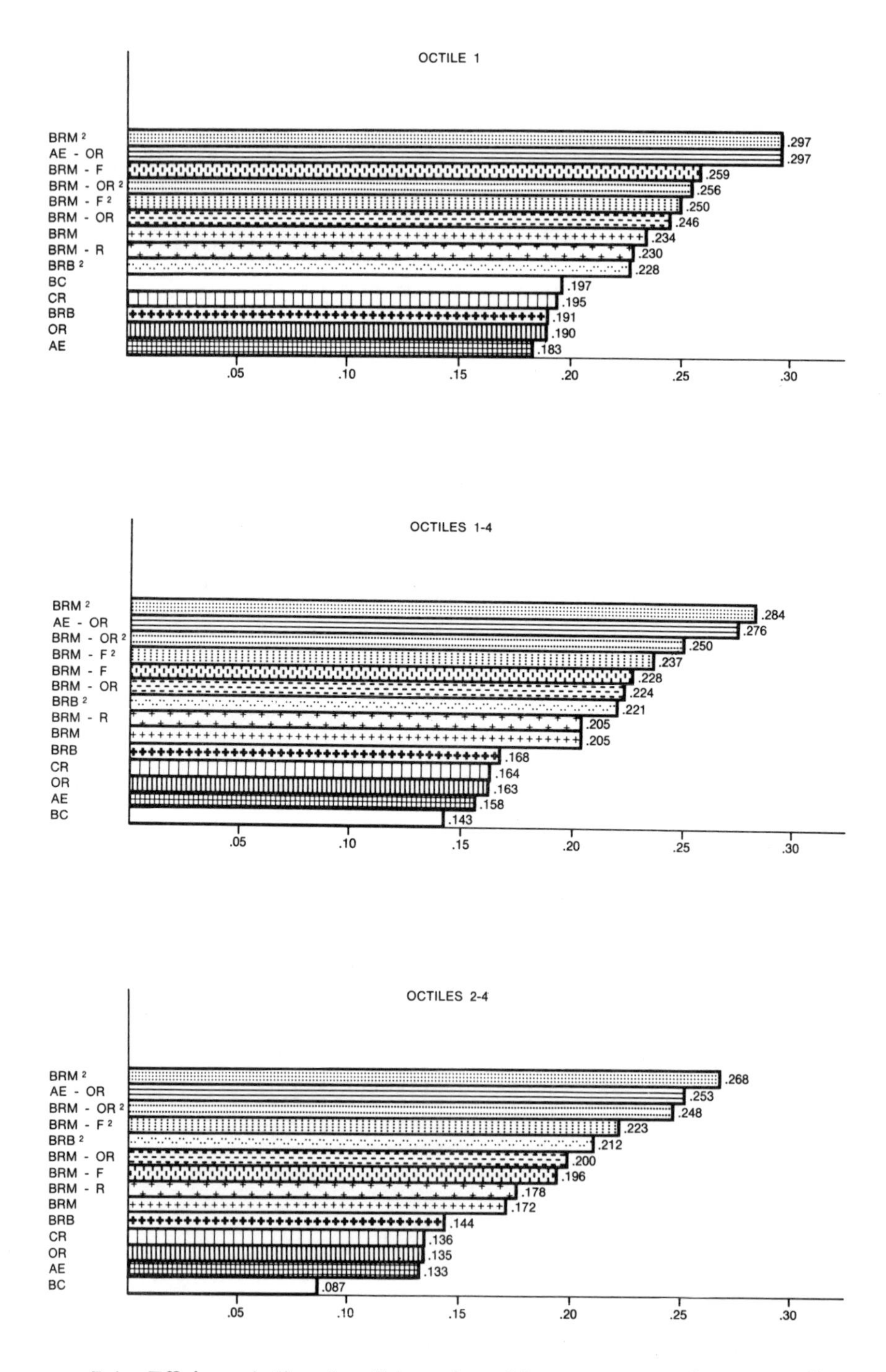

FIG. 7.4 Efficiency indices for all investigated formats presented to state college learners, differentiated and undifferentiated according to scholastic ability.

learning represented by the instructional objectives. The instructional materials used in the present study have the same items on the posttest as were used in the program. This restriction presents a problem when testing the merits of various formats for achieving certain instructional objectives, such as Gagné's Type 7 learning: the learning of principles. To test for the acquisition of principles, the posttest items should differ from those used in the program. To be sure that a learner has learned a principle and not just the particulars presented in a program, it is necessary to have him restate the principle in different terms than those that were taught him or to have him use the principle to solve a problem that he has not seen before. The difficulty just described becomes a serious problem in comparing formats with and without formal prompting. Those formats with formal prompting are much more susceptible to the charge that the learning is mere response learning and that this response learning only appears to be principle learning. We can acknowledge, however, that through careful frame construction, it is possible to use formal prompts for some of the learning types midway up Gagné's hierarchy. For example, let us consider a frame from a program on logarithms.

If $ab = c$, then $\log a + \log b = \log c$
$\log 2 \simeq .301$
$\log \mathit{10} = \mathit{1}$
$\log 5 \simeq .\text{---}$
(3 digits)

The learner emits the correct response, 699, and then sees that his response is correct. For the sake of illustration, let us grant that the feedback is reinforcing. However, what behavior is reinforced? Does the feedback reinforce the evaluation of log *5*, or does it reinforce the behaviors which enabled the learner to evaluate log *5*, i.e., the application of the law of logarithms at the top of the frame. It is difficult to answer this question because we will never observe a reinforcement taking place; so, let us pose a question that experienced programmers can answer. What would most learners learn from this frame, the simple association or the principle? Most learners will learn both to some degree; the thematic prompt at the top of the frame would predispose the learning of the principle. However, some learners might attend too strongly to the formal prompt at the bottom of the frame and be predisposed to learn only the simple association. It is for these reasons that some caution must be exercised in considering the formally prompted formats, including the AE-OR, for all instructional situations. If the instructional objectives include the teaching of principles, it would be well to heed this advice: we can only be sure that a learner understands a principle when he states it in different terms from those used to teach him. This advice leads to the following *caveat.* Where the learner is to be taught principles, formal prompting should be among the rarest programming tools employed.

8

Additional Relationships Between Formats and Learners

Table 8.1 contains the intercorrelations between all the variables, except the attitude scale, within each of the twelve experimental groups. Those values differing significantly from zero parameter values are indicated by numerals, as signified in the footnote to the table, using a two-tailed test in every instance. Those within-group correlations[1] that were significantly different from each other do not share a common underline.

Posttest corrects, a criterion of learning, and the scholastic ability measure shared a great deal of variance, the correlation coefficients being significant within each of the twelve groups. The CR and OR values were significantly greater than the BRM-OR_2 value. None of the other differences were significant. There appeared to be a trend for the correlation between ability and learning to decrease as the formats incorporated a greater number of PI principles. The presumed effects of ability upon learning seemed to be least for those formats incorporating the small-step principle, particularly those having only two response options. These results are compatible with the often heard opinion that programmed instruction reduces the disparity between the bright and the dull in performance on criteria of learning. However, because all the values differed significantly from zero, it is obvious that intellect was still manifesting itself to a significant extent in those formats that used most, or all, of the PI principles.

Program time was significantly correlated with posttest corrects only for the BC, CR, and BRM-OR_2 (positive values) and BRM-F (negative value) formats. However, many of these correlations differed significantly from each other. Perhaps, the most important implication of these results is

[1] Statistical tests were actually performed upon the z-transformations of the correlations.

that, for most of the formats, there was only a modest relationship between the amount of time spent by a learner on a program and how much he learned from the program.

The variables, program errors, and program items in error, are not applicable for those formats (BC, CR, AE-OR, BRM-OR and BRM-OR_2) that do not incorporate the overt-responding principle. In those groups to which they were applicable, they were significantly correlated, in a negative direction, with posttest corrects. Let us consider the correlations of those formats that contain the letters BRM in their notation. There are three PI features that distinguish these formats from the other two formats. The three features are: the small-step principle, thematic prompting, and opportunity afforded the learner to inspect the text after he has viewed a test item. These formats tended to have correlations with lesser absolute magnitudes than those of the other two formats. The result may be due, in part, to the attenuation of an intrinsically inverse relationship. This attenuation would be then simply a statistical artifact caused by the restriction in range of the program error variables. In Table 7.1 in the last chapter, note the reduced size of the standard deviations for the two program-error variables in all groups containing the letters BRM in their notation.

As expected, there tends to be an inverse relationship between scholastic ability and program time. The CR group was the sole exception. The correlations were significantly different from zero in all groups except the AE, BRM-OR_2, BC, and CR. The CR values differed significantly from all values except the AE, BRM-OR_2, and BC.

Scholastic ability was negatively correlated with both program-error variables in the seven groups where these latter variables are applicable. All values were statistically significant, except the BRM_2. Again, the values for the five formats having BRM in their notation could be attenuated due to the restricted range of the program-error variables. This would seem to be particularly true for those three small-step formats incorporating the feedback principle: the BRM, BRM_2, and BRM-R.

Program time was significantly correlated with both program-error variables for the BRM group, and the relationship was positive. Program time and program items in error were significantly correlated for the BRM-R group also. A reasonable interpretation of these correlations is that errors tended to make a learner proceed more slowly through a program having small steps and permitting review of a thematically prompted text, as was the case with all the formats containing the letter BRM in their notation.

Table 8.2 contains the intercorrelations between the attitude-scale scores and the other five variables. Attitude toward the instructional materials was significantly correlated with posttest corrects only in the OR group. None of the correlations differed significantly from each other.

Although not significant, the systematically negative correlations of low magnitude between scholastic ability and attitude suggest a slightly negative

Table 8.1 Product-Moment Correlation Coefficients Between Variables Within All Experimental Formats, Using Learners Who Were State College Students

Algebraically Low ← → Algebraically High

Between Posttest Corrects and Scholastic Ability

$BRM\text{-}OR_2$	$BRM\text{-}F_2$	BRM_2	BRM-F	AE-OR	BRM-OR	BRM	BRM-R	AE	BC	CR	OR
.203[1]	.297[3]	.314[3]	.314[3]	.322[4]	.358[5]	.422[6]	.425[6]	.485[6]	.488[6]	.392[6]	.401[6]

Between Posttest Corrects and Program Time

BRM-F	BRM	BRM-R	$BRM\text{-}F_2$	AE-OR	OR	AE	BRM-OR	BRM_2	BC	CR	$BRM\text{-}OR_2$
−.217[1]	−.158	−.139	.075	.095	.110	.126	.129	.174	.199[1]	.237[1]	.252[2]

Between Posttest Corrects and Program Items in Error

OR	AE	BRM-F	BRM-R	$BRM\text{-}F_2$	BRM_2	BRM
−.774[6]	−.663[6]	−.513[6]	−.440[6]	−.345[5]	−.321[4]	−.275[3]

Between Posttest Corrects and Program Errors

OR	AE	BRM-F	BRM-R	$BRM\text{-}F_2$	BRM_2	BRM
−.774[6]	−.687[6]	−.513[6]	−.414[6]	−.345[5]	−.321[4]	−.317[4]

Between Scholastic Ability and Program Time

BRM	AE-OR	BRM-R	BRM_2	$BRM\text{-}F_2$	BRM-OR	BRM-F	OR	AE	$BRM\text{-}OR_2$	BC	CR
−.326[4]	−.307[3]	−294[3]	−.290[3]	−.271[3]	−.268[2]	−.258[2]	−.193[1]	−.137	−.104	−.083	.126

Between Scholastic Ability and Program Items in Error

AE	OR	BRM-F	BRM-F_2	BRM	BRM-R	BRM_2
$-.513^6$	$-.473^6$	$-.427^6$	$-.343^5$	$-.290^3$	$-.260^2$	$-.152$

Between Scholastic Ability and Program Errors

AE	OR	BRM-F	BRM	BRM-F_2	BRM-R	BRM_2
$-.508^6$	$-.473^6$	$-.427^6$	$-.353^5$	$-.343^5$	$-.243^1$	$-.152$

Between Program Time and Program Items in Error

BRM_2	OR	AE	BRM-F_2	BRM-F	BRM-R	BRM
$-.129$	$-.093$	$-.040$	$-.029$	.067	$.200^1$	$.302^3$

Between Program Time and Program Errors

BRM_2	OR	AE	BRM-F_2	BRM-F	BRM-R	BRM
$-.129$	$-.093$	$-.050$	$-.029$	.067	.186	$.328^4$

Between Program Items in Error and Program Errors

BRM	AE	BRM-R	OR	BRM-F	BRM_2	BRM-F_2
$.971^6$	$.972^6$	$.976^6$	1.000^6	1.000^6	1.000^6	1.000^6

Note. Coefficients not sharing a common underline are significantly different at the .05 level.
Superscripts indicate how significantly coefficients differ from zero.

^{1} indicates .05 significance level
^{2} indicates .01 significance level
^{3} indicates .005 significance level
^{4} indicates .001 significance level
^{5} indicates .0005 significance level
^{6} indicates .0001 significance level

Table 8.2 Product-Moment Correlation Coefficients between the Attitude Scale Scores and the other Five Variables within Four Formats Using Learners Who Were State College Students

Algebraically Low	Between Attitude and Posttest Corrects		Algebraically High
BRM	AE	BC	OR
−.010	.124	.190	.220[1]
	Between Attitude and Scholastic Ability		
BRM	BC	OR	AE
−.083	−.073	−.071	−.010
	Between Attitude and Program Time		
BRM	AE	BC	OR
−.039	.012	.100	.325[4]
	Between Attitude and Program Items in Error		
	AE	OR	BRM
	−.236[1]	−.224[1]	−.224[1]
	Between Attitude and Program Errors		
	OR	BRM	AE
	−.224[1]	−.222[1]	−.214[1]

Note. Coefficients not sharing a common underline are significantly different at the .05 level. Superscripts indicate how significantly coefficients differ from zero.

[1] indicates .05 significance level
[2] indicates .01 significance level
[3] indicates .005 significance level
[4] indicates .001 significance level
[5] indicates .0005 significance level
[6] indicates .0001 significance level

relationship. If indeed a negative parameter value were to exist, its interpretation would be in doubt insofar as the various experimental formats are concerned, because the negative relationship holds for the BC group also. Consequently, a mildly negative correlation between scholastic ability and attitude toward serving in experiments is suggested.

The correlation between attitude and program time was significant only for the OR group. In that case, it was a positive relationship and significantly more positive than the value in the AE and BRM groups. One possible interpretation is that the time a learner spends on a program is influenced more by attitude on the OR format than by attitude on those formats (AE or

BRM) that either are novel to his experience or provide feedback. Novelty or feedback would serve to correct any initial negativism and thus prevent undue haste.

Attitude was negatively correlated with both program-error variables. All of the correlations differed significantly from zero, and negligibly from each other. Because the attitude scale was administered following the program, a negative attitude might have been engendered in the subjects by the number of errors they made on the program. It is more probable, however, that the negative correlations reflect an increase in errors due to initially oppositional attitudes where present. This latter interpretation is preferred because the correlation of the OR format is almost identical to those of the AE and BRM formats, in spite of the fact that the OR format gives no feedback to the learner regarding the correctness of his responses. It would appear that, if errors induced a negative attitude, the OR correlation would be less negative than the AE correlation because the AE format indicates when an error has been made. It would also appear that the BRM correlation would differ from the OR and AE correlations because the errors emitted on the BRM format were significantly fewer than those on either of the other two formats.

The means of the posttest and the means of the program times of the twelve formats shown in Table 7.1 in the last chapter correlate +.347. This correlation indicates that, to some extent, as additional principles were incorporated, the yield in posttest gain cost additional program time. On the other hand, the correlations of posttest corrects and program time within groups were low, indicating that the scores on the posttest, for any given format, were only modestly affected by the time spent by the learners with the instructional materials.

Figures 8.1, 8.2, and 8.3 show the regression equations and regression lines within each of the twelve experimental groups. All the regression lines were fairly close to horizontal; the slope for the BRM, BRB, BRM-R and BRM-F groups being slightly negative and those for other groups being slightly positive. It would appear that the positive slopes reflected a familiar relationship: the more time spent studying, the more learned. The negative slopes all occurred on formats having both overt responding and small steps. It seemed that on these formats, which permit the learner to inspect the text after he has viewed a test item, the more difficulty he experienced in responding to the items, the slower he read the text, or the more he reread the text. The relative flatness of all the slopes, and the nearness to being parallel of the positive slope lines on the one hand, and the negative slope lines on the other, reinforce the above interpretation: for a given format, individual differences in program time have only a mild influence on posttest corrects.

The foregoing regression equations and the efficiency index all assume linearity of regression. To test for significant departures from linear regression, posttest corrects on program time, an *eta* coefficient was computed

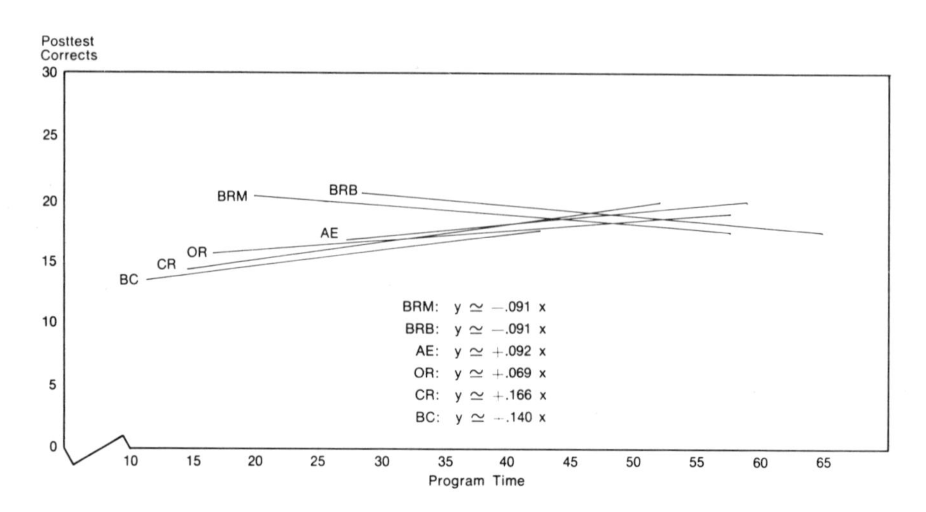

FIG. 8.1 Regression lines, posttest corrects on program time, within each experimental group of state college students, for formats BRM, BRB, AE, OR, CR, and BC.

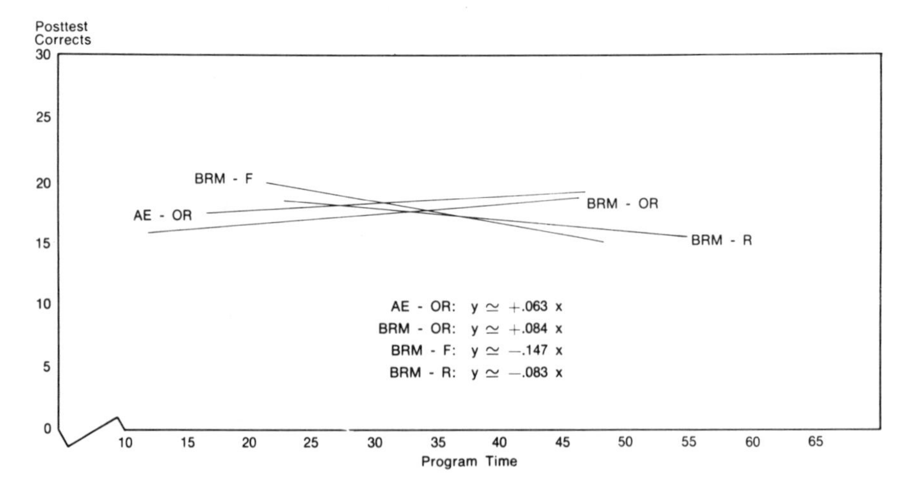

FIG. 8.2 Regression lines, posttest corrects on program time, within each experimental group of state college students for formats BRM-R, BRM-F, BRM-OR, and AE-OR.

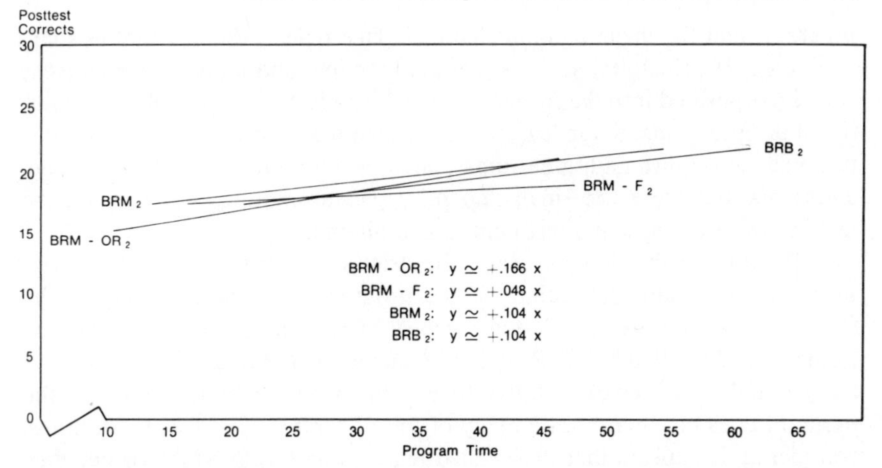

FIG. 8.3 Regression lines, posttest corrects on program time, within each experimental group of state college students, for formats BRM_2, BRB_2, $BRM\text{-}F_2$, and $BRM\text{-}OR_2$.

within each group. Below are the values of *eta* and Pearson *r* for each group. In none of the twelve groups were the departures from linearity significant.

	BC	CR	OR	AE	BRM[a]	BRM-R	BRM-F	BRM-OR	AE-OR	BRM_2[b]	$BRM\text{-}F_2$	$BRM\text{-}OR_2$
eta	.243	.295	.189	.194	.250	.214	.226	.200	.247	.190	.130	.297
r	+.199	+.237	+.110	+.126	−.158	−.139	−.217	+.129	+.095	+.174	+.075	+.252

[a] BRB values identical to BRM
[b] BRB_2 values identical to BRM_2

Summary

Scholastic ability and learning were appreciably correlated within any format, but this relationship held particularly true within those formats incorporating the lesser number of PI principles. The lowest positive correlations were found within those formats incorporating the small-step principle, prompting, and permitting review of text after a test item was read. The very lowest correlations were found within those small-step formats having only two response options. It appeared that the more PI principles and features employed, the less was learning dependent upon ability, although never was ability found to be unrelated to amount of material learned.

Within most of the formats, the amount of time spent by the learners did not influence greatly the amount learned. However, between formats, there was an appreciable correlation between the mean times spent on the programs and the mean amounts learned. This reflects the fact that as some additional PI principles, such as overt responding and immediate feedback, were incorporated into the formats, the yields in learning generally cost additional program time. Some features of programmed instruction, however, did not seem to require additional time penalties, but could actually save time. These features were the small-step principle, prompting, and keeping the number of distractors in a test item to a minimum.

Relative to the duller learner, the brighter learner typically takes less time on a program, particularly if the program incorporates many of the following PI features: small steps, review of text, prompting (thematic or formal), and feedback (KCR and/or remediation). Moreover, the brighter learner makes less errors relative to the duller learner, particularly, if the program does not incorporate many of the PI features just listed. All things considered, it appears that these listed features have a two-fold virtue: they enable the brighter learner to move along through the program faster, and they lead the duller learner to make less errors. Part of the explanation for the two-fold relationship is that errors tend to make the learner proceed more slowly through a program when these particular features are present. This explanation is supported by the finding that the correlations between program time and program errors are more positive in those formats where the above-mentioned features are present.

Program errors typically impair the learning desired, but they can be reduced by using small steps and prompting. Where poor attitudes or low motivation toward learning are present, it would be well to use instructional formats having novelty in their appearance. It would also seem desirable for the format to furnish feedback to the learner so that he becomes aware of the erroneous understandings he is likely to form if his approach to the materials is superficial and casual. Such awareness should occur as soon as possible, and thus, small steps seem advantageous. These recommendations are supported by the finding that the correlation between attitude and program time was significantly greater for the OR format than for the AE and BRM. A likely explanation is that the length of time spent on the OR format by the learner was influenced more by his attitude. The OR format, unlike the AE and BRM formats, had no novelty or feedback provisions to counteract the undue haste with which a learner would proceed through the program if he had a poor attitude. Poor attitudes or low motivation toward learning resulted in appreciably more errors on all formats studied. This relationship held true on large-step programs where error rate was relatively high for all learners and on small-step programs where error rate was relatively low. It is important therefore, that the instructional materials presented to poorly motivated learners should incorporate immediate feedback and small steps, particularly if overt responding is required, so that the error rate does not become enormous.

9

Response Elicitation, Miselicitation, and Nonelicitation and their Interrelationships with Attention and Program Noise

Let us consider a conventional book and a small-step program both containing the identical paragraphs of text. The program, of course, permits the learner to review the text before responding to the test item. The book does not even elicit any overt responses. Now let us assume that the program is imperfectly written, and while for some paragraphs of the text, it properly elicits a relevant response, for other paragraphs of the text:

(a) it either fails to elicit any response, or
(b) it elicits an irrelevant response, i.e., a response that can be given by the learner without his having full comprehension of the information.

In either case, we would expect the program to teach those latter paragraphs less well than does the book. Whatever else a small-step program accomplishes by requiring overt responses from the learner, it certainly focuses his attention more heavily upon that portion of the text paragraph referred to by the test items and correspondingly tends to divert his attention from the balance of the text paragraph. To some extent, the program creates for the learner a situation similar to a treasure hunt whereby he searches out the information he needs in order to respond correctly. Furthermore, the degrading effects of improper elicitation are intensified if the text contains considerable irrelevant or surplus information (program noise).

A study by Briggs et al. (1951), found that a conventional book was superior to a small-step program when the program used a stimulus context or elicited responses, either of which differed materially from those associated with the posttest. The Briggs study was concerned primarily with the matter of transfer of learning from program to posttest. However, if we accept the PI axiom that the posttest should measure the desired behavioral objectives, there is no problem of transfer, and the critical question becomes the following: once a program elicits some of the responses relevant to the posttest, what are the effects of not eliciting all of the relevant responses?

The present study sought to affirm the degrading effects of nonelicitation and miselicitation in a context of proper elicitation, using multiple-choice responses (in contrast to Briggs' use of constructed responses). Also, the study sought to ascertain the nature of the degrading effects. If the effects are more pronounced in a small-step program which permits review of the text before responding than they are on a large-step program which does not permit review, the result supports the interpretation that attention is being misdirected. On the other hand, if the effects are comparable in the small-step and large-step programs, the result supports the interpretation that consolidation of learning is somehow being impaired.

Procedure

Modifications were made in four existing formats, two of them, the OR and AE, being large-step, and the other two, the BRM-R and BRM being small-step. The original thirty test items used in each of these formats were separated into three groups, labeled α, β, and γ. The ten α items were retained unchanged so that they continued to properly elicit responses relevant to ten of the posttest items. The ten β items were deleted from the programmed materials so as to "nonelicit" responses relevant to another ten of the posttest items. The ten γ items were degraded so as to elicit ten irrelevant responses and thus miselicit responses relevant to another ten of the posttest items. The degraded γ items were directed at relatively trivial information contained in the corresponding ten text paragraphs. A correct response to a degraded γ item could stem from a low-order conceptualization. This condition was at best necessary, but never sufficient to the presence of the higher-order conceptualization upon which the original γ test item was based. Below is an example of a text paragraph with its original properly eliciting γ test item and then with its degraded, miseliciting counterpart.

Text paragraph

Waves of light entering the eye are refracted by the eye's internal structures, but most importantly by the lens. The phenomenon of refraction occurs whenever there is a change in the density of the media through which the light passes. As light rays pass through a surface, from a less dense to a more dense medium – as is the case when light passes from the aqueous humour to the lens – the rays, in effect, bend or refract toward a line perpendicular to the surface at the point of crossing. The degree of the refraction phenomenon depends upon the angle at which the light enters the lens, which, in turn, depends upon the degree of curvature of the front lens surface. (See Fig. 4.)

Properly eliciting γ test item

When a light ray passes from the aqueous humour to the lens it will refract

(*a*) toward a line perpendicular to the surface at the point of crossing.
(*b*) toward a line tangent to the surface at the point of crossing.
(*c*) away from a line perpendicular to the surface at the point of crossing.

Miseliciting γ test item

Light rays bend or refract:

(*a*) at a surface of the lens.
(*b*) behind the vitreous humour.
(*c*) within the aqueous humour.

The text and the posttest remained unchanged between the original and modified OR, AE, BRM-R, and BRM formats. Also, the ten test items in the α group remained unchanged between the original and modified OR, AE, BRM-R, and BRM formats. However, the ten test items in the β group changed from properly eliciting to noneliciting, and the ten test items in the γ group changed from properly eliciting to miseliciting.

Table 9.1 shows how the three groups of test items were changed from their original forms in the OR, AE, BRM-R, and BRM formats to their modified forms. Also, the familiar BC (base control) format is included as a reference group. The BC group is important because it serves as a simulated conventional book, and as such, enables a comparison to be made between the effects of noneliciting a response in a program (as by the modified β items) and in a book (as by the BC format). The key difference between the two types of nonelicitation is that in a program a nonelicited response occurs in a context of elicited responses, whereas, in a conventional book this is not the case.

It is apparent from Table 9.1 that the present study utilizes the data of the five familiar formats, BC, OR, AE, BRM-R, and BRM, along with the new data from the modifications of the OR, AE, BRM-R, and BRM formats. Of the nine, only on the two BRM-R and the two BRM formats, original and modified, is it possible for the learner to review the text material associated with a test item before responding to the item. In contrast, on an OR or AE format the learner cannot return to the associated paragraph of text after seeing a test item.

While all of the differences of interest pertain to the instructional materials, all of the results reported below are comparisons of posttest performances. Each group (α, β, and γ) of ten items was earlier matched for posttest

Table 9.1 Original and Modified Forms of the α, β, and γ: Test Items in the Program

	Test Items in Original Form				
	BC	OR1	AE1	BRM-R1	BRM1
α	NE	E	E	E	E
β	NE	E	E	E	E
γ	NE	E	E	E	E
	Test Items in Modified Form				
		OR2	AE2	BRM-R2	BRM2
α		E	E	E	E
β		NE	NE	NE	NE
γ		ME	ME	ME	ME

numeral 1 indicates original form
numeral 2 indicates modified form
E indicates properly elicited
NE indicates nonelicited
ME indicates miselicited

difficulty on the basis of the research reported previously. Each group had comparable means (proportion-passing index, .6) and standard deviations. The learners were state college students, matched in scholastic ability. There were 80 learners in each of the nine format groups.

Results and Discussion

Below are the results of 56 analyses of variance that compare various combinations of the experimental formats (BC, OR1, AE1, BRM-R1, BRM1, OR2, AE2, BRM-R2, and BRM2) and item types (α, β, and γ). In each comparison, the mean value of the posttest corrects score predicted to be greater was placed on the left side of the inequality sign. In only four comparisons did the mean value predicted to be greater turn out to be smaller. Comparisons significant at the .05 level were underlined once; comparisons significant at the .01 level or beyond were underlined twice.

Beneficial Effects of Proper Elicitation

The first eight comparisons[1] were simple tests of the beneficial effects of proper elicitation by "modified" α items, *versus* nonelicitation by modified β items (top row), and *versus* miselicitation by modified γ items (bottom row). Of the eight comparisons, there were two for each modified format.

[1] Only in these eight comparisons was a repeated measures design appropriate. Such an analysis resulted in the significant differences indicated.

(without KCR)	*(with KCR)*	*(with KCR)*	*(with KCR)*
(without small-step)	*(without small-step)*	*(with small-step)*	*(with small-step)*
OR2α> *OR2*β	*AE2*α> *AE2*β	*BRM-R2*α> *BRM-R2*β	*BRM2*α> *BRM2*β
OR2α> *OR2*γ	*AE2*α> *AE2*γ	*BRM2*α> *BRM-R2*γ	*BRM-R2*α> *BRM2*γ

Ten paragraphs of text properly elicited were superior to the same ten paragraphs, either nonelicited or miselicited, as long as KCR was supplied to the learner on elicited and miselicited responses. The results supported the practice of proper elicitation in the presence of KCR. Proper elicitation did not prove its worth on the OR2 format, that does not provide KCR.

Degrading Effects of Improper Elicitation

The degrading effects of improper elicitation upon attention were tested by the following comparisons of modified formats. In contrast to the AE and OR formats, only on the BRM-R and BRM formats can the learner's attention to the text be affected by the nature of the test item. In their modified form, proper elicitation took place only on the α items. Therefore, it was predicted that these ten items on the modified BRM-R and BRM formats would direct the learner's attention to the more relevant portions of the text, and thus the BRM-R and BRM format posttest scores would exceed those of the modified AE and OR formats. On the other hand, because, in their modified forms improper elicitation took place on both the β and γ items, it was predicted that on the modified BRM-R and BRM formats the learner's attention would be directed away from the more relevant portions of the text and thus the BRM-R and BRM format posttest scores would be less than those of the modified AE and OR formats.

α	β	γ
(proper elicitation)	*(nonelicitation)*	*(miselicitation)*
(BRM-R2 > AE2)[2]	*AE2 > BRM-R2*	*(AE2 > BRM-R2)*[2]
(BRM2 > AE2)[2]	*AE2 > BRM2*	*AE2 > BRM2*
BRM-R2 > OR2	*OR2 > BRM-R2*	*(OR2 > BRM-R2)*[2]
BRM2 > OR2	*OR2 > BRM2*	*OR2 > BRM2*

In the α column, there was a suggestion that proper elicitation had beneficial effects upon attention where small steps were present, but that these effects were not essential as long as KCR was present, as it was on the AE format. On the AE format, the learner eventually had to emit a correct response before proceeding to a subsequent test item.

In the β column, there was evidence that failure to elicit responses to ten paragraphs of text where responses were elicited to other paragraphs had

[2] Of all comparisons in this chapter, these are the only ones in which there was a reversal in the direction of predicted greater mean value.

unfavorable effects upon attention and, as a result, lead to unfavorable consequences upon learning in a small-step program where remediation was used.

In the γ column, the evidence was inconclusive, but by way of contrast to the β column, there were suggestions that eliciting even trivial responses to ten paragraphs of text, where responses were elicited to other paragraphs, was helpful in preventing inattentiveness in a small-step program.

The Degrading Effects of Program Noise

The α items, in their modified form, followed not only their appropriate paragraph of text but followed also a superfluous paragraph which, in fact, was the paragraph corresponding to the non-elicited γ items. (The temporal precedence of the relevant and irrelevant paragraphs, incidentally, was balanced.) The degrading effects of this irrelevant information (program noise) in the text were tested by the following four comparisons of original to modified forms of the α items.

(without KCR)	*(with KCR)*	*(with KCR)*	*(with KCR)*
(without small steps)	*(without small steps)*	*(with small steps)*	*(with small steps)*
$OR1\alpha > OR2\alpha$	$AE1\alpha > AE2\alpha$	$BRM\text{-}R1\alpha > BRM\text{-}R2\alpha$	$BRM\text{-}1\alpha > BRM2\alpha$

The results show that ten properly elicited frames of text, relatively noise-free, were superior to those same frames, relatively noisy, on the OR format only. Of the four formats, OR, AE, BRM-R, and BRM, only the OR lacked KCR. It would seem that program noise, even with proper elicitation, was degrading in the absence of KCR. The relationship between program noise and KCR was further clarified by the additional comparisons below. The first four comparisons show that ten frames, relatively noise-free and properly elicited, were superior to those same "frames" within a completely nonelicited book and that the superiority was greater where KCR was present for the elicited response.

$OR1\alpha > BC\alpha$ $\quad AE1\alpha > BC\alpha$ $\quad BRM\text{-}R1\alpha > BC\alpha$ $\quad BRM1\alpha > BC\alpha$

The last four comparisons show that only when KCR was present did the ten frames, relatively noisy and properly elicited, have an advantage over those same frames within a completely nonelicited book.

$OR2\alpha > BC\alpha$ $\quad AE2\alpha > BC\alpha$ $\quad BRM\text{-}R2\alpha > BC\alpha$ $\quad BRM2\alpha > BC\alpha$

A possible interpretation of all twelve comparisons is that program noise degrades instructional effectiveness, particularly, in the absence of KCR.

The Degrading Effects of Nonelicitation and Miselicitation

Of the four formats, OR, AE, BRM-R, and BRM, only the latter two present a test item together with its associated paragraph of text so as to make it possible for the learner to review the text paragraph before responding. The changes made in the β and γ items, from their original to their modified forms, were hypothesized to have degrading effects upon learning. These degrading effects can be classified into those effects upon text reading behavior and all other effects. The effects upon text-reading behavior, that is, upon the learner's attention would operate only in the case of the modified formats BRM-R2 and BRM2. The other effects would operate in the cases of all four modified formats, the OR2, AE2, BRM-R2 and BRM2. Thus, whether for β items or for γ items, a modified format would be expected to be inferior to an original format. Because, in the case of the modified formats, BRM-R2 and BRM2, the degrading effects include those of misdirected attention, these two modified formats should be particularly inferior.

Nonelicitation

The degrading effects of nonelicitation of responses to the β items in the modified formats were tested by the following four comparisons of original to modified formats, showing that ten frames with properly elicited responses were superior to those same frames nonelicited in a program in which other frames were elicited.

$\underline{\underline{OR1\beta > OR2\beta}}$ $\underline{\underline{AE1\beta > AE2\beta}}$ $\underline{\underline{BRM\text{-}R1\beta > BRM\text{-}R2\beta}}$ $\underline{\underline{BRM1\beta > BRM2\beta}}$

The foregoing comparisons were supported by four other comparisons showing that ten frames with properly elicited responses were superior to those same frames nonelicited in a completely nonelicited book:

$\underline{\underline{OR1\beta > BC\beta}}$ $\underline{\underline{AE1\beta > BC\beta}}$ $\underline{\underline{BRM\text{-}R1\beta > BC\beta}}$ $\underline{\underline{BRM1\beta > BC\beta}}$

Four other comparisons suggested that ten frames, nonelicited in a completely nonelicited book, were superior to those same frames nonelicited in a program having other frames properly elicited, where review of text was permitted and where remediation was given:

$BC\beta > OR2\beta$ $BC\beta > AE2\beta$ $BC\beta > BRM\text{-}R2\beta$ $\underline{BC\beta > BRM2\beta}$

The implication of all twelve comparisons is that nonelicitation of responses degrades learning effectiveness, especially, where elicitation occurs elsewhere in a program and particularly, if remediation is given.

Miselicitation

The degrading effects of miselicitation of responses to the γ items in the modified formats were tested by the following four comparisons of original to modified formats. They show that the ten frames with properly elicited responses were superior to those same frames with miselicited responses.

$OR1\gamma > OR2\gamma$ $AE1\gamma > AE2\gamma$ $BRM\text{-}R1\gamma > BRM\text{-}R2\gamma$ $BRM1\gamma > BRM2\gamma$

The foregoing comparisons were supported by four other comparisons showing that ten frames with properly elicited responses were superior to those same frames nonelicited in a completely nonelicited book.

$OR1\gamma > BC\gamma$ $AE1\gamma > BC\gamma$ $BRM\text{-}R1\gamma > BC\gamma$ $BRM1\gamma > BC\gamma$

Four other comparisons suggested that ten frames, nonelicited in a completely nonelicited book were superior to those same frames miselicited in a program having other frames properly elicited, where review of the text is permitted, and where remediation is given.

$BC\gamma > OR2\gamma$ $BC\gamma > AE2\gamma$ $BC\gamma > BRM\text{-}R2\gamma$ $BC\gamma > BRM2\gamma$

The implication of all twelve comparisons is that miselicitation of responses degrades learning effectiveness, especially, where proper elicitation occurs elsewhere in a program and particularly, if remediation is given.

The last significant comparison, BCγ to BRM2γ, must be qualified. Of all the 56 analyses of variance performed in this study, it was the only one having a statistically significant interaction of learner ability with main treatment effects. For the entire undifferentiated sample of learners, posttest performance for the ten frames within a completely nonelicited book was superior to that for the same frames with miselicitating test items in the branching format. When the learners were differentiated into higher and lower ability groups, the higher ability group's performance agreed with that of the undifferentiated group, but the lower ability group's performance was higher for the ten frames with miseliciting test items than for the same frames within a completely nonelicited book. This interactional effect was found only when comparing the BC (straight text) format to the BRM2 format, not to the AE2 or OR2 formats. The phenomenon would seem to be attentional in nature. It would appear that higher ability learners typically derive the higher-order concepts from a straight reading of a paragraph and are only misdirected by trivial questions. Lower ability learners, on the other hand, benefit from even a trivial question. Lower ability, it will be recalled, is used here in strictly a relativistic sense to refer to the second, third, and fourth highest octiles of high-school graduates. The relationships discussed above are illustrated in Figure 9.1.

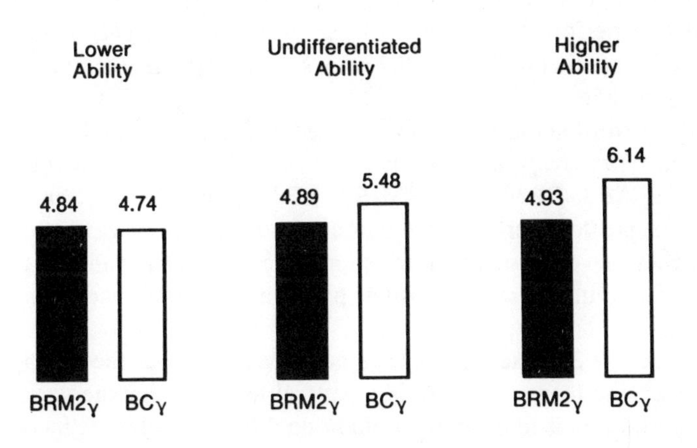

FIG. 9.1 Mean posttest corrects to ten paragraphs of information and their corresponding γ test items as a function of learner ability.

Recapitulation and Overview

The decrement in posttest performance due to the modification made in the ten α items on the program formats (OR, AE, BRM-R, and BRM) is assignable to program noise (superfluous and irrelevant information). The decrement was greatest for the OR format (no KCR) and least for the AE. However, none of the four formats had their mean posttest scores driven down below the mean posttest score of the BC format, signifying that the beneficial effects of overt, relevant responses more than offset the harmful effects of program noise.

The decrement in posttest performance due to the modification made in the ten β items on the four program formats is assignable to nonelicitation of relevant responses. The decrement was greatest for the BRM format and least for the OR. All of the four formats had their mean posttest scores driven down below the mean posttest score of the BC format, signifying that partial nonelicitation in a context of proper elicitation was more harmful than total nonelicitation.

The decrement in posttest performance due to the modification made in the γ items on the four program formats is assignable to miselicitation of relevant responses. The decrement was greatest for the BRM format and least for the BRM-R. All of the four formats had their mean posttest scores driven down below the mean posttest score of the BC format, signifying that partial miselicitation in the context of proper elicitation was more harmful than total nonelicitation.

Learner Variability

It is often asserted that programmed instructional material reduces the variability of performance between learners, whether bright or dull, highly motivated or apathetic. Figures 9.2 and 9.3 support this assertion, but this support is qualified.

First, a word about the data illustrated in Figures 9.2 and 9.3. For each of the item types (α, β, and γ) and for each of the nine formats (BC, OR1, OR2, AE1, AE2, BRM-R1, BRM-R2, BRM1, and BRM2), an index[3] of variation in posttest performance among the 80 learners was computed on the particular ten-item scores in question. The greater the value of the index the more variability there is in posttest performance within one of the twenty-seven groups.

In Figure 9.2, these indices have been averaged over the item types for each of the nine formats. There is a general tendency for the variability in posttest performance to decrease as additional PI principles are incorporated

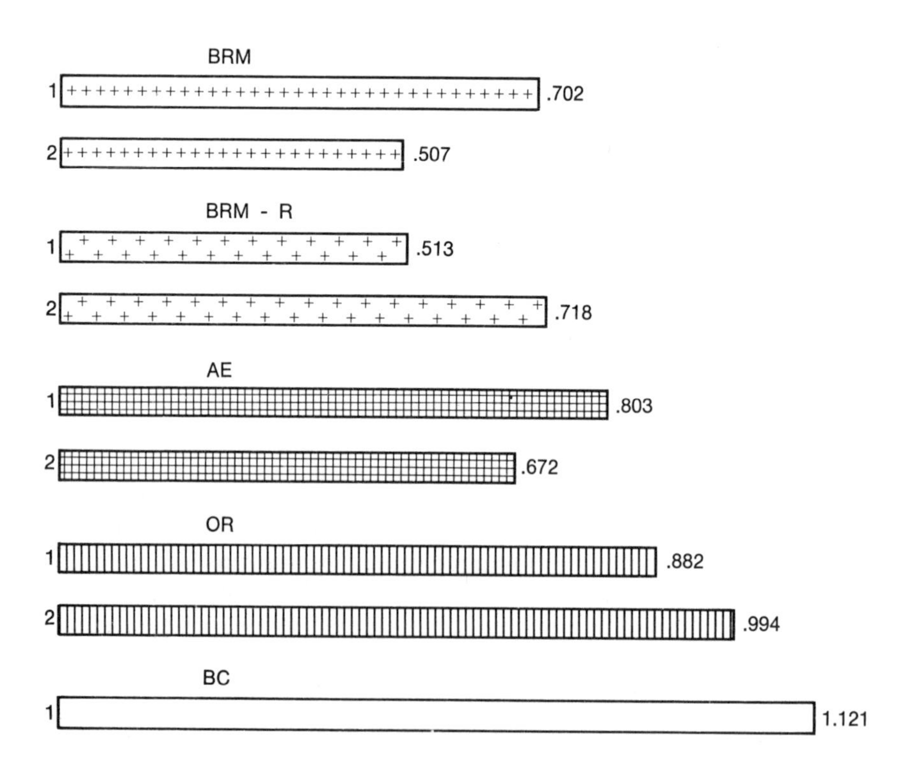

FIG. 9.2 Mean within-group variances of the posttest corrects for the several program formats, averaged over the α, β, and γ item types.

[3] The index was the unbiased estimate of the population variance within ability levels.

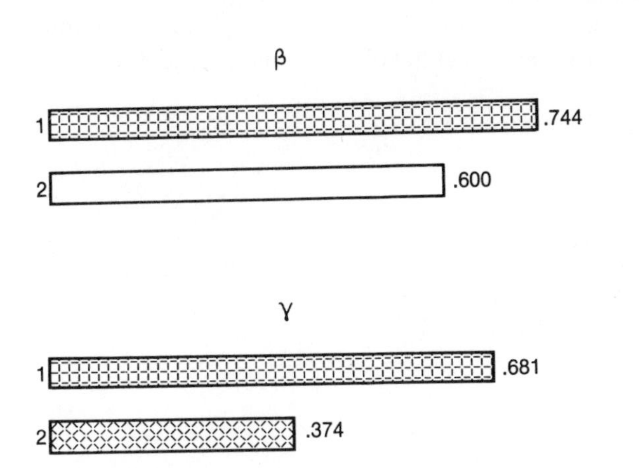

FIG. 9.3 Mean within-group variences of the posttest corrects for the three item-types, averaged over the original (1) and modified (2) versions of the OR, AE, BRM-R, and BRM formats.

into the formats. The most variation occurred on the BC format, the least on the BRM. However, except for the OR and BRM-R formats, the modified (degraded) versions of the formats led to less variation in posttest performance than did the original versions.

The data in Figure 9.2 can be interpreted to mean that the variability in performance between learners is reduced by some, but not all, of the features of programmed instruction. Incorporation of the principles of responding, feedback, and small-step size resulted in less learner variability. But, in the cases of the AE and BRM formats, the modified (degraded) formats also resulted in less learner variability than did the original versions.

In Figure 9.3, the indices have been averaged over each of the four formats OR1, AE1, BRM-R1, and BRM1, and over each of the four formats OR2, AE2, BRM-R2, and BRM2 for each item type. There is a general tendency for the variability in posttest performance to increase:

(a) as the β items change from noneliciting on the modified format to properly eliciting on the original format, and
(b) as the γ items change from miseliciting on the modified format to properly eliciting on the original format.

There is an opposing tendency for variability in posttest performance to decrease as the paragraphs of text accompanying the α items change from relatively noisy, on the modified format, to relatively noise-free on the original format. All three of these changes were statistically significant at the .01 level.

The data in Figure 9.3 can again be interpreted to mean that the variability in performance between learners is reduced by some, but not all, of the features of programmed instruction. Noise-free frames led to less learner variability than did noisy frames. However, nonelicitation or mis-elicitation also resulted in less learner variability than did proper elicitation.

10

Efficient for Whom? A Comparison of Formats on Junior College Students

From the foregoing studies using learners from the California State College System, it is clear that the relative merit of a format and of the principles comprising it is much determined by the intellective calibre of the learners. One purpose of the study reported in this chapter was to extend the range of scholastic ability of the learner population downward into the bottom half of the distribution in order to determine the relative merit of formats and principles for instructing learners in the fifth, sixth, and seventh highest octiles. A second purpose was to repeat some parts of the earlier investigation upon other samples of learners approximately equivalent in scholastic ability (insofar as this could be accomplished through matching learners on test scores) but differing along various nonintellective dimensions: motivation, aspiration level, socio-economic level, ethnic affiliation, and the other psychological and demographic dimensions.

In California, all high school graduates are eligible for the junior colleges. Thus, junior college (JC) students constitute a more heterogenous learner population than do state college (SC) students. As shown in Figure 10.1, the JC population included learners in octiles 2 through 4 (ACT scores ranging from 16 to 23, using twelfth-grader norms) and learners in octiles 5 through 7 (ACT scores ranging from 6 to 15). In contrast, the SC population included learners in octile 1 (ACT scores ranging from 24 to 30) and learners in octiles 2 through 4.

The comparison of the lower ability and the higher ability JC groups was aimed at revealing the effects of intellective factors. The comparison of the higher ability JC group to the lower ability SC group, matched as they

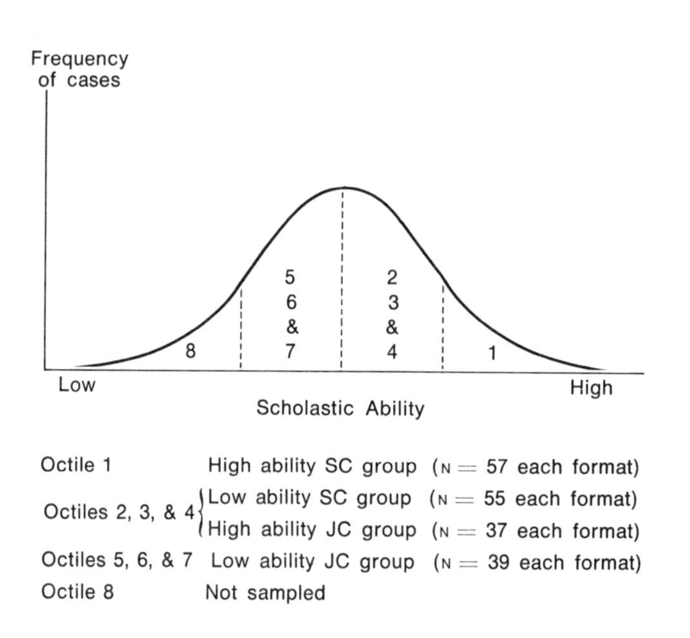

FIG. 10.1 ACT score distribution illustrating the overlap and nonoverlap of the SC and JC populations.

were on test scores, was aimed at revealing the effects of nonintellective factors.

Because the total number (N = 380) of JC learners was insufficient to obtain a minimum number in each of the experimental formats, the only formats tested were the BC, OR, AE, and BRM/BRB. These formats were chosen because they formed a hierarchy, differing from each other by a PI principle, and because they included all the formats (AE, BRB, and BRM) simulating popular PI techniques.

Because the input level of information concerning the subject matter of the program was expected to differ from that of the SC population, the simulated pretest was readministered to a group of JC learners matched to the other four JC groups. The number of items correctly responded to by the JC and the SC pretest samples were:

	JC	SC
ACT 24 - 30		12.74
ACT 16 - 30		11.94
ACT 16 - 23	11.19	11.05
ACT 6 - 23	10.82	
ACT 6 - 15	10.46	

Although the higher ability JC learners were equivalent to the lower ability SC learners on their total ACT scores, they were not assumed to be as high in scholastic ability. One reason is that admission to the state colleges is based on a combined measure of ACT scores and high school grade point average. An obtained low ACT score can, therefore, be balanced by a high performance in high school. However, admission to the junior colleges is open to anyone with a high school diploma. Thus, a low test score on the ACT (such as a 16 or 17) is more likely to be an underestimate of the scholastic ability of a state college student than it would be of a junior college student. For example, to enter a state college with an ACT score of 16 (percentile rank $\simeq$ 50), a student must have had very close to a *B* average in high school.

In addition to the above considerations, the only JC learners available for study had been preselected on the basis of their low scores on the English portion of the ACT. All learners had scores at the 60th percentile or lower in this category. Thus, those JC learners who were equated with the SC learners on their total (composite) ACT scores were actually a little inferior in reading comprehension, English facility and vocabulary, and correspondingly a little superior perhaps in their natural science information level. This information is compatible with the fact that the JC pretest sample at the second, third, and fourth octiles scored slightly higher than their counterparts in the SC sample.

While scholastic ability undoubtedly influences format efficiency a great deal, it is not the sole influence. W. J. Carr (1962, p. 70) agrees, and suggests more specifically that PI may be particularly well suited for learners with a high level of anxiety or a low level of aspiration.

A comparison of the low SC and the high JC learners, matched as they were on their test scores, should reveal the influence of all factors other than scholastic ability. Included among these other sources of influence was a difference in sexual composition. The SC sample was 45 percent male, while the JC sample was 61 percent male. Also, it should be pointed out that the conditions under which the JC learners operated could not be made identical to those under which the SC learners operated, and the conditions might have induced less motivation.

Table 10.1 shows the means and standard deviations of the several variables investigated. The variable, scholastic ability, again served the two functions it served in the studies of SC learners. The ACT scores were used to separate learners into high- and low-ability groups, and within these groups, the ACT scores stratified the learners in order that the statistical analysis would be more sensitive to true differences between formats. Table 10.1, like Table 5.1, is organized to compare differences between experimental formats, and thus it holds constant the institutional affiliation and ability level. Because the comparison of formats within one institutional setting was a prime goal of all the studies, the JC learners, like the SC learners, were matched perfectly on ability test scores from one experimental format to another.

Table 10.1 Means and Standard Deviations of Variables Investigated, Using Learners Who Were Junior College Students

		Experimental Formats				
		BC	OR	AE	BRM	BRB
Posttest corrects	M:	12.68	12.46	14.36	15.49	15.49
	SD:	3.39	3.88	3.92	3.41	3.41
Scholastic ability	M:	15.09	15.12	15.11	15.07	15.07
	SD:	3.94	3.89	3.97	3.96	3.96
Program time	M:	19.51	31.63	37.96	41.24	48.54
	SD:	4.39	6.41	7.37	9.60	9.60
Program items in error	M:	na[a]	15.53	15.50	5.91	5.91
	SD:	na	3.96	3.45	3.34	3.34
Program errors	M:	na	na	22.11	7.04	7.04
	SD:	na	na	5.98	4.38	4.38

[a]na indicates variable is not applicable for that experimental group.

Tables 10.2 through 10.7 are organized differently. The organization of Tables 10.2, 10.4, and 10.6 holds constant the institutional affiliation and experimental format and compares the results between ability levels. The organization of Tables 10.3, 10.5, and 10.7 holds constant the ability level and experimental format and compares the results between institutional affiliation. It was a simple matter to match learners on the variables, institutional affiliation and experimental format. It was not so simple to match learners on such a finely calibrated scale as ACT scores. The matching that was accomplished in ability level within an institution, such as the state college system or the junior college system, did not generalize across institutions. In order to match learners on ability level across institutions some learners from the SC sample and some from the JC sample had to be discarded. For this reason, the mean values listed in Tables 10.3, 10.5, and 10.7 are not identical to those in Tables 10.2, 10.4, and 10.6. The shrinkage in sample size was as follows in octiles 2 through 4:

(*a*) from 37 to 23 for JC learners
(*b*) from 55 to 23 for SC learners

Of the various differences between JC and SC learners, one of the most striking is the greater number of errors made by the JC learners in every format. But Tables 10.2 and 10.3, which compare the performance of the JC

Table 10.2 Program Items in Error and Program Errors Made by Learners in State College and Junior College Samples: Comparison of Effects of Intellective Factors

	SC Octiles			JC Octiles	
	1	2-4		2-4	5-7
Program items in error			BRM/BRB		
	2.68	3.84		4.76	7.00
			AE		
	8.30	12.84		14.54	16.41
			OR		
	9.05	11.95		14.68	16.33
Program errors			BRM/BRB		
	2.84	4.49		5.43	8.56
			AE		
	10.61	16.64		20.57	23.56

Note. Means not sharing a common underline are significantly different at the .05 level.

Table 10.3 Program Items in Error and Program Errors Made by Learners in State College and Junior College Samples: Comparison of Effects of Nonintellective Factors

	Octiles 2-4		
	SC		JC
Program items in error		BRM/BRB	
	4.39		4.35
		AE	
	13.83		14.39
		OR	
	13.35		14.17
Program errors		BRM/BRB	
	5.30		5.13
		AE	
	17.87		20.22

Note. Means not sharing a common underline are significantly different at the .05 level.

Table 10.4 Program Times for the State College and Junior College Samples: Comparison of Effects of Intellective Factors

	SC Octiles			JC Octiles	
	1	2-4		2-4	5-7
BRM	35.05	39.16		39.40	42.98
BRB	42.35	46.46		46.70	50.28
AE	40.11	40.53		38.03	37.90
OR	34.21	36.96		30.70	32.51
BC	22.07	22.56		19.62	19.41

Note. Means not sharing a common underline are significantly different at the .05 level.

Table 10.5 Program Times for the State College and Junior College Samples: Comparison of Effects of Nonintellective Factors

	Octiles 2-4	
	SC	JC
BRM	39.53	40.74
BRB	46.83	48.04
AE	40.30	39.43
OR	37.87	30.78
BC	23.22	18.91

Note. Means not sharing a common underline are significantly different at the .05 level.

Table 10.6 Posttest Corrects for the State College and Junior College Samples: Comparison of Effects of Intellective Factors

SC Octiles 1	SC Octiles 2-4		JC Octiles 2-4	JC Octiles 5-7
		BRM/BRB		
20.53	17.62		16.40	14.62
		AE		
19.90	16.55		15.65	13.13
		OR		
19.21	15.91		13.38	11.59
		BC		
17.05	13.04		13.49	11.92

Note. Means not sharing a common underline are significantly different at the .05 level.

Table 10.7 Posttest Corrects for the State College and Junior College Samples: Comparison of Effects of Nonintellective Factors

Octiles 2-4 SC		Octiles 2-4 JC
	BRM/BRB	
17.17		16.48
	AE	
15.48		14.87
	OR	
15.44		13.22
	BC	
12.78		13.44

Note. Means not sharing a common underline are significantly different at the .05 level.

and SC learners on the two program-error variables, show that the increased error rate of the JC learners is due primarily to intellective rather than non-intellective factors. The organization of Table 10.2 permits a study of the effects of intellective factors upon error behavior. The organization of Table 10.3 permits a study of the effects of nonintellective factors upon error behavior.

Table 10.2 shows that on both error variables the differences between the SC learners in octile 1 and those in octiles 2 through 4 were statistically significant for all three formats, OR, AE, and BRM/BRB. The differences between the JC learners in octiles 2 through 4 and those in octiles 5 through 7 were also significant for the AE and BRM/BRB formats, but not the OR. Thus, there was abundant evidence that intellective factors influenced error behavior.

Table 10.4 shows that on program time, the differences between the SC learners in octile 1 and those in octiles 2 through 4 were statistically significant only for the OR and BRM/BRB formats. None of the differences between the JC learners in octiles 2 through 4 and those in octiles 5 through 7 were statistically significant. Thus, there was evidence that intellective factors influenced program time for SC learners on some formats. Table 10.5 shows that the differences between the SC and JC learners in octiles 2 through 4 were statistically significant on the BC and OR formats. Thus, there was evidence that nonintellective factors influenced program time on those formats lacking immediate feedback. Because the SC and JC learners in Table 10.5 were matched on ability-test scores, it would appear that the JC learners are disposed to proceed at too rapid a pace unless slowed down by evidence, in the form of feedback, of their failure to comprehend the instructional material.

Table 10.6 shows that on posttest corrects, all of the differences between the SC learners in octile 1 and those in octiles 2 through 4 were statistically significant. Similarly, all of the differences between the JC learners in octiles 2 through 4 and those in octiles 5 through 7 were statistically significant. Thus, there was evidence that intellective factors exerted a widespread influence upon posttest corrects. Table 10.7 shows that the differences between the SC and JC learners in octiles 2 through 4 were statistically significant on only the OR format. Thus, there was evidence that nonintellective factors exerted a more selective influence upon posttest corrects.

As noted in Chapter 6, the relative efficiencies of the experimental formats changed depending upon the scholastic ability of the SC learner group. For the octile 1 (high ability) SC group, the efficiencies, from best to worst, were as listed in the left-hand column below. For the octiles 2 through 4 (low ability) SC group, the efficiencies, from best to worst, were as listed in the right-hand column.

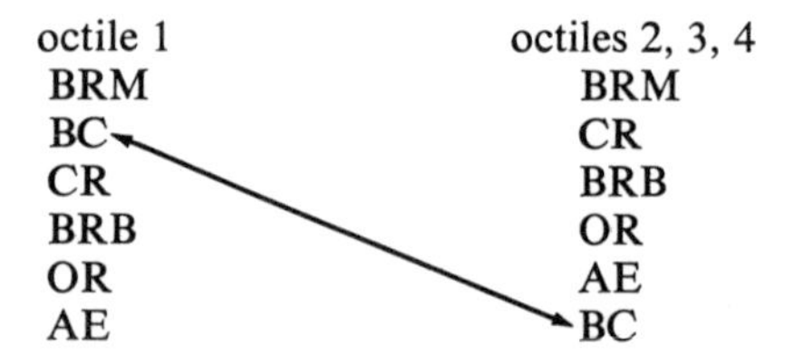

While not all the inversions in rank are of statistical significance, the drop of the base control format, from rather efficient for learners in octile 1, to very inefficient for the learners in octiles 2 through 4, clearly indicates that the efficiency of a format must be empirically tested upon the target population of learners. Figure 10.2 summarizes the results for three SC ability groups on the BRM/BRB, AE, OR, and BC formats.

In a similar manner, Figure 10.3 portrays the data for three JC learner groups. For each of the three variables, posttest gain, program time, and posttest gain/program time, the data are presented separately for the learners in octiles 2 through 4, octiles 2 through 7, and octiles 5 through 7.

In the top third of Figure 10.3 are the data on posttest gain scores. The top set of four bars represents one target group sought in this study, namely, those JC learners who fell in the second, third, and fourth highest octiles. These learners were comparable to those in the bottom half of the SC group so far as the range of test-measured ability was concerned. They were for the most part students who could have entered a state college but who opted for a junior college. The bottom set of four bars represents the other target group sought in this study, namely, those JC learners having scholastic abilities in octiles 5 through 7, using high school seniors as a reference group. The middle set of four bars represents the above two JC groups combined and thus includes learners from octiles 2 through 7.

For learners at any level of ability, the branching format with its small steps and thematic prompting achieved the most learning. In Figure 10.2, for the SC learners, particularly those of lower ability, overt responding (plus question reading) seemed to be the most critical principle to include in a format. Indeed, the difference between the posttest gains of the BC and OR formats was statistically significant. However, on all the JC samples, feedback seemed to be the most critical principle to include, with small steps assuming importance also for learners in octiles 5, 6, and 7.

On posttest gain, either of the groups BR or AE were significantly superior to either of the groups OR or BC. According to the formal analysis of the formats in terms of principles incorporated, the significant difference between the formats, OR and AE, supported the feedback principle. However, the support is qualified by the fact that the posttest gains on the OR format, at all ability levels of JC learners, were actually less than those on the BC format. Thus, it would be more accurate to say that responding plus feedback made a contribution to learning at all ability levels of JC learners. These results are in harmony with Evans' (1962) opinion that overt responding and immediate feedback are more critical in situations where correct responses have low probability.

In view of the relatively great number of errors made by the JC samples and in view of the similarity in the patterns of the four posttest gain bars over all ability levels, with the OR format systematically giving rise to the least posttest gain, it is dangerous to require JC learners to emit responses without giving them KCR. With KCR, the AE format gave rise to far better posttest gains even though the AE learners had almost the identical number

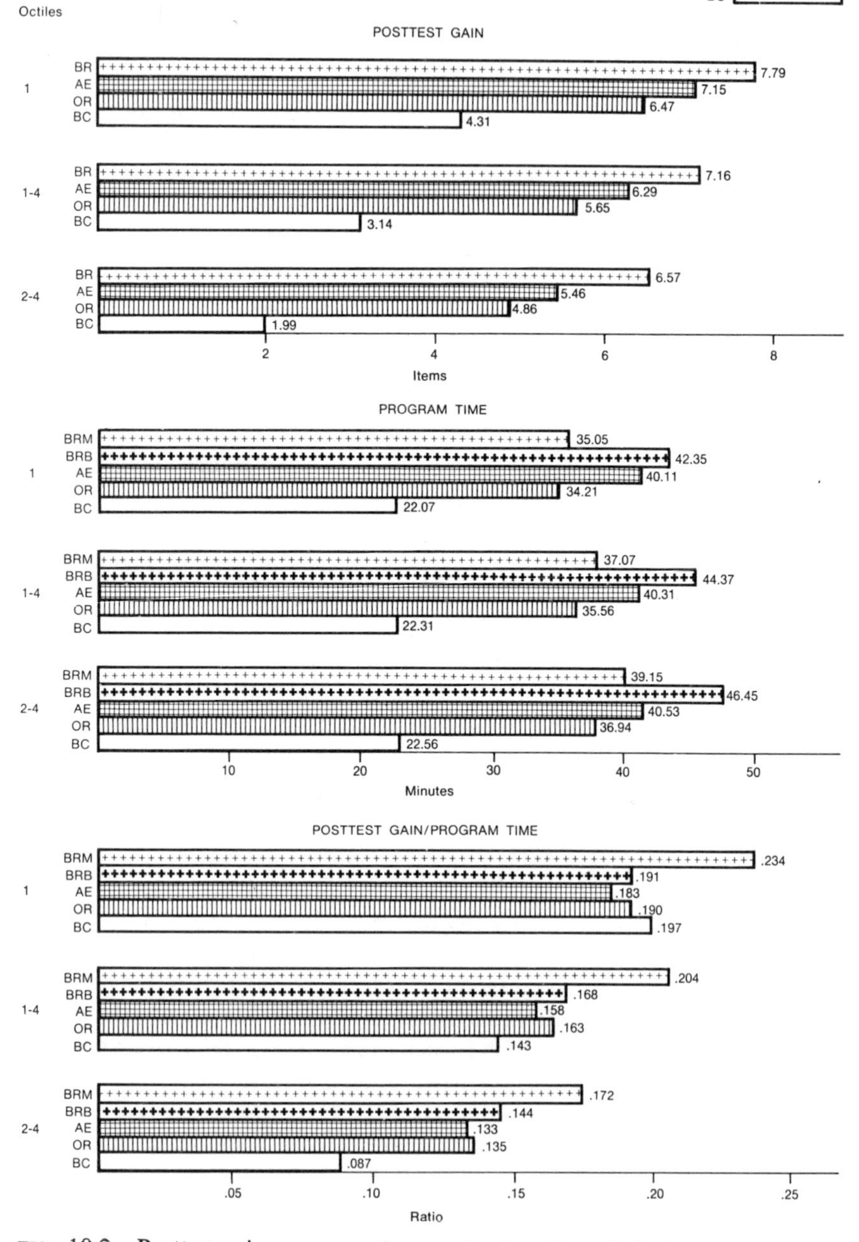

FIG. 10.2 Posttest gain, program time, and a learning efficiency index for each of four experimental formats presented to state college learners, differentiated and undifferentiated according to scholastic ability.

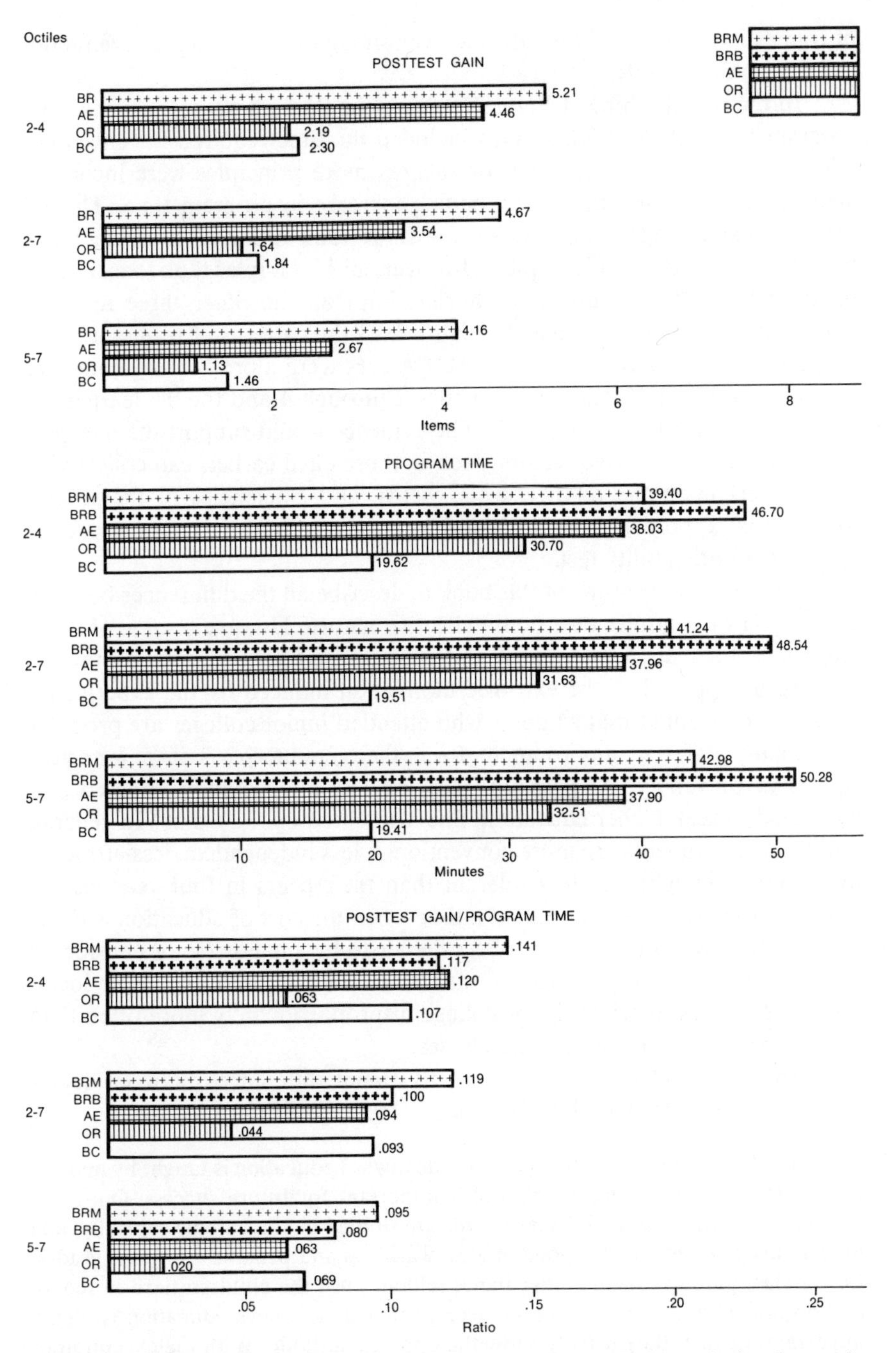

FIG. 10.3 Posttest gain, program time, and a learning efficiency index for each of four experimental formats presented to junior college learners, differentiated and undifferentiated according to scholastic ability.

of frames in error as did the OR and even though they averaged seven more errors than did the OR.

In the middle third of Figure 10.3 are the data on program times. The program times of the BRB groups included the time required for envelope-opening. For the nonbranching formats, as more principles were incorporated, there was a general corresponding increase in program time. The JC samples maintained approximately the same rank order of program times that characterized the SC samples. However, all JC samples took longer times on the BRM/BRB format and shorter times on the other three formats, particularly on the OR format. In Figure 10.3 the patterns of program times of the JC samples having different ACT scores were more similar than were the patterns of the JC learners in octiles 2 through 4 and the SC learners in octiles 2 through 4 in Figure 10.2. The evidence would support the interpretation that nonintellective factors, such as those cited earlier, can collectively have effects upon the relative costs, yields, and efficiencies of the several formats that approach those attributable to the intellective factors measured by the scholastic ability test.

It is beyond the scope of this book to describe all the differences between the JC and SC samples of a nonintellective nature. However, some of these differences bear upon the relative differences in intrinsic motivation toward learning as opposed to the extrinsic motivation induced by the experiment. Cross (1968) found that students who attended junior colleges are products of a totally different environment from their counterparts in a four-year college or university. As a group, they are less intellectually oriented and motivated to seek higher education. She also noted (p. 32) that "In general, junior college students are more conventional, less independent, less attracted to reflective thought and less tolerant than their peers in four-year institutions." Cross also reported that, at a time when the cost of education is rising steadily, the low cost of junior colleges tends to be a major factor considered by many students. The expense consideration leads those of the lower socioeconomic classes to select junior college disproportionately more often than those of middle or higher income classes.

Another good description of motivational differences between socioeconomic classes is given by Havighurst (1951, p. 21).

> The characteristic middle-class attitude toward education is taught by middle-class parents to their children. School is important for future success. One must do one's very best in school. Report cards are studied by the parents carefully, and the parents give rewards for good grades, warnings and penalties for poor grades. Lower-class parents, on the other hand, seldom push the children hard in school and do not show by example or by precept that they believe education is highly important. In fact, they usually show the opposite attitude. With the exception of a minority who urgently desire mobility for their children, lower-class parents tend to place little value on high achievement in school or on school attendance beyond minimum age.

When the middle-class child comes to a test, he has been taught to do his very best on it. Life stretches ahead of him as a long series of tests, and he must always work himself to the very limit on them. To the average lower-class child, on the other hand, a test is just another place to be punished, to have one's weaknesses shown up, to be reminded that one is at the tail end of the procession. Hence this child soon learns to accept the inevitable and to get it over with as quickly as possible. Observation of the performance of lower-class children on speed tests leads one to suspect that such children often work very rapidly through a test, making responses more or less at random. Apparently they are convinced in advance that they cannot do well on the test, and they find that by getting through the test rapidly they can shorten the period of discomfort which it produces.

The JC learners came from a lower socio-economic level, on the whole, than did the SC learners. If Havighurst is correct, it would be expected that the average JC student has a lower need for achievement and less intrinsic motivation toward study than his SC counterpart. Also, as acknowledged earlier, the lowered motivation could stem from the conditions of administration arousing less extrinsic motivation in the JC learner. At any rate, to the observer, the JC learners seemed less highly motivated, relative to the SC learners. It would be expected that their program times would be shorter, and this expectation was the outcome on three of the formats. The greatest disparity between JC and SC learners occurred on the OR and BC formats. It happens, that on these two formats, the learners encountered the least novelty among the four formats of instructional materials; they merely read text on the BC format, and they read text and took a test on the OR format. In contrast, both the AE and BRM/BRB formats had novelty.

The AE and BRM/BRB formats also provided feedback so that learners became aware immediately of their errors. Because the JC group made more errors, they had to emit more responses on the AE and BRM/BRB formats. The time it took them to emit extra responses, coupled with a slowing down effect these extra errors might have induced, would account for the smaller disparity between the program times of the JC and SC learners on the AE format. Moreover, if the greater number of errors made by the JC learners caused them to slow down, they should have slowed down most on the BRM/BRB format, where the text and test items are interspersed and where review of text is permitted prior to responding. They apparently slowed down so much that their program times were actually longer than those of the SC learners on the BRM/BRB format. Among the five JC formats, the only two program times not significantly different were the BRM and AE.

In the bottom third of Figure 10.3 are the data on the efficiency indices. At all JC ability levels, the simulated machine-presented branching format again appeared to be the most efficient. However, in contrast to the results using SC learners, the OR format appeared to be the least efficient at all JC ability levels. On the SC learners in octiles 2 through 4, overt responding seemed the most critical principle to include in a format. However, at all JC ability levels, feedback seemed to be the most critical principle to include, with small steps assuming importance also for learners in octiles 5 through 7.

For learners who will make many errors, whether due to low ability or questionable motivation, the results suggest that, if the instructional technologist is going to incur the time penalty of introducing an overt-response feature into the format of an instructional instrument, he had better also introduce feedback and, hopefully, small steps. It does not appear to be a sound practice to encourage, or even permit, learners with low-motivation levels to make mistakes, particularly if they are not immediately corrected.

The superiority in efficiency of the BRM format over the BRB was statistically significant at all ability levels of JC learners. In addition, the OR format was significantly less efficient than:

(*a*) the BRM, AE, and BRB formats on learners from octiles 2 through 4;
(*b*) the BRM and BRB formats on learners from octiles 5 through 7;
(*c*) the BRM, BRB, AE, and BC formats on learners from octiles 2 through 7.

Intercorrelations

Table 10.8 contains the intercorrelations between all variables within each of the four experimental groups. Those values differing significantly from zero parameter value are indicated by numerals, as signified in the footnote to the table, using a two-tailed test in every instance. Those within-group correlations[1] that were significantly different from each other do not share a common underline. These correlations may be compared to those obtained on the SC learners. However, in interpreting differences between Tables 8.1 and 10.8, it must be remembered that the SC and JC samples of learners differed both intellectively and nonintellectively.

As was the case with the SC learners (see Table 8.1), posttest corrects shared a great deal of variance with the scholastic ability measure. The correlation coefficients were significant within each of the four groups. However, while the correlations for the BRM and AE formats were only slightly depressed from their values for the SC learners, the values for the OR and BC formats were considerably depressed. Thus, for those two formats incorporating a lesser number of PI principles, the correlations between ability and learning were less than for those two formats incorporating a greater number of PI principles. These results conflict with the often heard opinion that programmed instruction reduces the disparity between the bright and the dull in performance on criteria of learning. Furthermore, they are the reverse of

[1] Statistical tests were actually performed upon the z-transformations of the correlations.

Table 10.8 Product-Moment Correlation Coefficients Between Variables within Four Experimental Formats, Using Learners Who Were Junior College Students

Algebraically Low → Algebraically High

Between Posttest Corrects and Scholastic Ability

OR	BC	BRM	AE
.269[1]	.291[1]	.356[3]	.375[3]

Between Posttest Corrects and Program Time

BRM	BC	AE	OR
−.047	.135	.154	.315[2]

Between Posttest Corrects and Program Items in Error

OR	AE	BRM
−.583[6]	−.383[4]	−.354[3]

Between Posttest Corrects and Program Errors

OR	AE	BRM
−.583[6]	−.388[4]	−.351[3]

Between Scholastic Ability and Program Time

BRM	OR	AE	BC
−.235[1]	−.195	−.070	.023

Between Scholastic Ability and Program Items in Error

BRM	AE	OR
−.417[5]	−.339[3]	−.313[2]

Between Scholastic Ability and Program Errors

BRM	AE	OR
−.428[5]	−.323[2]	−.313[2]

Between Program Time and Program Items in Error

OR	AE	BRM
−.229[1]	−.145	.277[1]

Between Program Time and Program Errors

OR	AE	BRM
−.229[1]	−.143	.195

Between Program Items in Error and Program Errors

AE	BRM	OR
.946[6]	.973[6]	1.000[6]

Note. Coefficients not sharing a common underline are significantly different at the .05 level. Superscripts indicate how significantly coefficients differ from zero.

[1] indicates .05 significance level
[2] indicates .01 significance level
[3] indicates .005 significance level
[4] indicates .001 significance level
[5] indicates .0005 significance level
[6] indicates .0001 significance level

the relationships for the SC learners. The apparent conflict can be accounted for, however, by the same interpretation made earlier in discussing program time. Seemingly, the JC group had less motivation toward study. Therefore, on the BC and OR formats, they did not fully mobilize their intellectual resources and the correlations between intellect and posttest performance were relatively low. However, because the AE and BRM/BRB formats contained both novelty and feedback, the intelligence of the learners was actualized and the correlations between intellect and posttest performance approached those obtained for the SC learners.

With reference to the correlations between posttest corrects and program time, the values for the JC learners, except for the BC format, seemed to trend more positively than did the values for the SC learners. There appeared to be a closer relationship between the amount of time a JC learner spent on a program and how much he learned than there was for a SC learner, particularly, on the OR format. The elevated correlation between program time and posttest corrects on the OR format supports the earlier interpretation that the JC learners on the whole were taking insufficient time. On the other hand, the times taken by even the fastest of the SC learners were apparently long enough to reduce the effects upon learning due to differences in the duration of exposure to the instructional materials.

With reference to the correlations between posttest corrects and program items in error, the values for the three formats, OR, AE, and BRM, were quite negative. The values for the BRM format differed negligibly between the JC and SC learners. In contrast, the negative correlations for the JC learners on the OR and AE formats were somewhat less in absolute magnitude than the values for the SC learners. Hence, the correlations for the OR, AE, and BRM formats did not differ significantly from each other for the JC learners. We might account for the correlation on the BRM format resembling so closely the value for the SC learners by the fact that the errors made by the JC learners on the BRM format were only slightly in excess of those made by the SC learners. This result, in turn, might be due to the BRM features of thematic prompting, small steps, and the opportunity to examine text before responding. The correlations between posttest corrects and program errors behaved similarly to the correlations between posttest corrects and program items in error and lead to identical interpretations.

The correlations between scholastic ability and program time were in the same ordinal sequence as for the SC learners, and the values were, in fact, quite similar. If we accept the proposition that those with less ability should spend more time in contact with the instructional materials by way of compensation, then the high negative correlation associated with the BRM format was a good feature, and the negligible correlation associated with the BC format was a bad feature.

The correlations between scholastic ability and program items in error all remained negative. However, the values for the OR and AE formats became less negative, and the value for the BRM format became more negative. The correlations between scholastic ability and program errors behaved similarly to the correlations between posttest corrects and program items in error.

The correlations between program time and program items in error retained the same ordinal sequence with a possible trend toward more negative relationships. There seemed to be a greater inverse relationship between the amount of time a JC learner spent on the program and how many frames he erred on than was the case for the SC learner. And since an inverse correlation indicates that those learners emitting the greater number of errors were spending the lesser amounts of time on their programs, this condition is not desirable. It is however, compatible with the observation that the JC learners were, on the whole, taking insufficient time. Also, the fact that the branching format gave rise to the most positive correlations, for both junior college and state college learners, is favorable to the branching technique. The branching features of small steps, thematic prompting, and the opportunity to review text prior to responding, apparently, led those learners making the greater number of errors to spend longer times with their instructional materials. The correlations between program time and program errors behaved similarly to the correlations between program time and program items in error and lead to the same interpretations.

Above it was noted that the correlations between posttest corrects and program time, while trending higher for the JC learners than for the SC learners, were still fairly low in an absolute sense. Figure 10.4 shows the

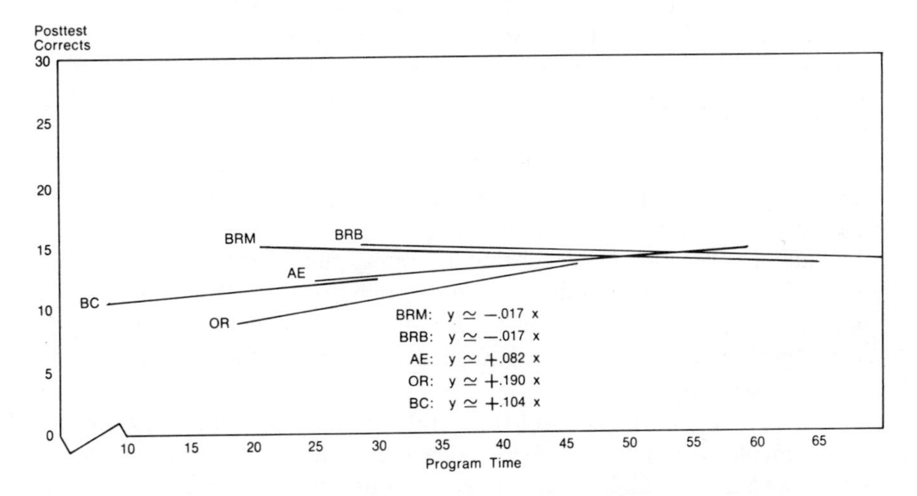

FIG. 10.4 Regression lines, posttest corrects on program time, within each experimental group of junior college students, for formats BRM, BRB, AE, OR, and BC.

regression equations and regression lines within each of the formats tested with JC learners. The regression lines for the BRM, AE, and OR formats became somewhat more positive than they were on the SC sample. With the exception of the OR format, the lines remained fairly close to horizontal. As was the case with the SC learners, the positive slopes reflected the relationship: the more time spent studying, the more learned. The negative slopes of the BRM and BRB regression lines seemed again to suggest that a format which permits the learner to inspect the text after he views a test item, and before responding, is going to have a negative correlation between program time and posttest corrects. The more difficulty the learner experiences in responding to the items, the slower he reads the text, or the more he rereads the text.

To test for significant departures from linear regression, posttest corrects on program time, an *eta* coefficient was computed within each group. Below are the values of *eta* and Pearson *r* for each group. In none of the formats were the departures from linearity significant.

	BC	OR	AE	BRM/BRB
eta	.178	.369	.337	.229
r	+.135	+.316	+.154	−.074

Summary

On program formats calling for overt responding, the error rate decreased significantly as scholastic ability increased. This generalization held true even in the presence of feedback, small steps, thematic prompting and the opportunity to reread text prior to responding. The correlations were negative for both state college and junior college learners. Furthermore, the greater error rate of junior college learners, as compared to state college learners, was due to intellective rather than nonintellective factors among the learner population.

The learning yield of every format increased as ability increased. This pattern occurred regardless of the number and configuration of PI principles and features employed. The direct relationship was true for both state college and junior college learners, showing the strong influence upon learning yield of intellective factors. On the other hand, only for the OR format did nonintellective factors prove their influence upon learning yield: if ability is held constant, junior college students learned less from the OR format than did state college students.

Program time, in contrast to error rate and learning yield, was a function of nonintellective factors to about as great an extent as it was a function of intellective factors. Significant differences in program time due to intellective factors were found only for the OR and BRM/BRB formats and only for state college learners (octile 1 *versus* octiles 2 through 4). Significant differences in program time due to the nonintellective factors separating the state college and junior college learners were found on both the BC and OR formats.

In order to consider the relative advantages of the several PI principles and features and of the different formats, for dealing with state college learners, on the one hand, and junior college learners, on the other, these two groups of learners, unmatched on ability, were compared. These comparisons thus lumped together the differences between the two learner populations whether due to intellective or nonintellective factors. For junior college learners, it appeared that feedback was the most important PI principle to include in order to obtain learning yield. For lower ability learners, small steps and thematic prompting also assumed a more important role. The increased importance of immediate feedback, small step, and thematic prompting, relative to their importance for state college learners, appears to be due to the lower probability of junior college learners emitting unprompted correct responses.

As with the state college learners, the branching format gave rise to the greatest amount of learning yield, and the other formats fell in the same rank order, except that the overt-responding format was much poorer in both relative and absolute terms. The program times of the junior college learners were approximately in the same rank order as those of the state college learners. The only discrepancy being due to the junior college learners taking longer times on the branching formats and shorter times on the other three formats. The program times were particularly short on the OR format. The pattern of program times was more similar for junior college learners of different ability than it was for learners of the same ability but differing in institutional affiliation (junior *versus* state college). Nonintellective factors seemed to influence program times as much as did intellective factors. But whether due to low motivation or to low ability, the foreshortening of time spent on a program can be counteracted to a large extent by introducing novelty and feedback into the structural characteristics of the program. Feedback brings to the attention of the learner his high-error rate and causes him to emit additional responses and probably to take more time on his initial response to each test item. Also helpful are certain features of the branching format, such as small steps and the opportunity to review text prior to responding. These features of the branching format were apparently responsible for that format being the only one upon which junior college learners had longer program times than did state college learners.

As with the state college learners, the machine-presented branching format appeared the most efficient. However in contrast to the results using state college learners, the OR format was the least efficient at all ability levels. For learners who will make many errors, whether due to low ability or questionable motivation, the results suggest that if the instructional technologist is going to incur the time penalty of introducing an overt response feature into the format of an instructional instrument, he had better also introduce feedback, and hopefully, small steps. It does not appear to be a sound practice to encourage, or even permit, learners with low motivation levels to make mistakes, particularly if they are not immediately corrected.

For junior college learners, the correlations between posttest corrects and scholastic ability were considerably depressed below the corresponding values for state college learners for the OR and BC formats. Because these two formats incorporated a lesser number of PI principles than did the BRM/BRB and AE formats, these findings conflict with the often heard opinion the programmed instruction reduces the disparity between the bright and the dull in performance on criteria of learning. This opinion was sustained by the results using state college learners. The apparent conflict can be accounted for, however, by the seemingly lower motivation level of the junior college learners. On the OR and BC formats, the junior college learners apparently did not fully mobilize their intellectual resources so that the correlations between intellect and posttest performance were relatively low. However because the BRM/BRB and AE formats contained both novelty and feedback, the intelligence of the learners apparently was actualized, and the correlations between intellect and posttest performance approached those for the state college learners.

With regard to the correlations between posttest corrects and program time, the values appeared to trend more positively for junior college than for state college learners, and this trend seemed particularly evident for the OR format. There appeared to be a closer relationship between the amount of time a JC learner spent on a program and how much he learned than there was for a state college learner. The particularly elevated correlation between program time and posttest corrects on the OR format supports the interpretation that the junior college learners on the whole were taking insufficient time. On the other hand, the times taken by even the fastest state college learners were apparently long enough to reduce the effects upon learning due to differences in the duration of exposure to the instructional materials. When the formats are compared, the negative correlation of the branching format suggests that permitting a learner to inspect the text after he views a test item and before responding is favorable. The more difficulty the learner experiences in responding to the items, the slower he reads text or the more he rereads the text.

The correlations between scholastic ability and program time were negligible in magnitude for the BC format and appreciably (although not significantly) negative for the BRM/BRB format. This finding would be favorable to the branching technique if we accept the proposition that those with less ability should spend correspondingly more time in contact with the instructional materials by way of compensation.

The correlations between program time and either of the program error variables seemed to trend toward more negative values than was true for state college learners. There seemed to be a greater inverse relationship between error behavior and program time for junior college learners as compared to state college learners. And because an inverse correlation indicates that those learners emitting the greater number of errors were spending the lesser amounts of time on their programs, this condition is not desirable, It is, however, compatible with the observation that junior college learners were, on the whole, taking insufficient time. Also, the fact that the branching format gave rise to the most positive correlations, for both junior college and state college learners, is favorable to the branching technique. The branching features of the small steps, thematic prompting, and the opportunity to review text prior to responding, apparently led those learners making the greater number of errors to spend longer times with their instructional materials.

11

Efficient for Whom? A Comparison of Formats on Naval Enlisted Men

From the foregoing studies on both state college and junior college students, it became increasingly obvious that the relative merit of a format and of the principles comprising it are very much determined by intellective and nonintellective factors. Using twelfth grade norms, the sample drawn from the state college populations occupied:

(*a*) octile 1, and
(*b*) octiles 2 through 4.

The sample drawn from the junior college population occupied:

(*a*) octiles 2 through 4, and
(*b*) octiles 5 through 7.

In addition, a sample of enlisted men drawn from the population at the Naval Training Center occupied:

(*a*) octile 1,
(*b*) octiles 2 through 4, and
(*c*) octiles 5 through 7.

Therefore, the effects of intellective factors can be investigated by comparing the naval enlisted men (NEM) in the three ability levels: octile 1; octiles 2 through 4; and octiles 5 through 7. And the effects of nonintellective factors can be investigated by comparing:

(*a*) the NEM octiles 1 through 4 to the SC octiles 1 through 4,
(*b*) the NEM octiles 2 through 7 to the JC octiles 2 through 7,
(*c*) the NEM octile 1 to the SC octile 1,
(*d*) the NEM octiles 2 through 4 to the SC and JC octiles 2 through 4,
(*e*) (and the SC octiles 2 through 4 to the JC octiles 2 through 4), and
(*f*) the NEM octiles 5 through 7 to the JC octiles 5 through 7.

Included among the nonintellective factors differentiating the NEM sample from the SC and JC samples is the fact that the NEM group was 100 percent male.

Again, in recognition of possible differences between the NEM, SC, and JC samples in terms of the input level of information concerning the subject matter of the program, the simulated pretest was readministered to a group of NEM matched in ability to those NEM receiving experimental formats. The number of items correctly responded to by the NEM, JC and SC samples were:

OCTILES		NEM	JC	SC	
1	GCT 68-74[a]	12.92		12.74	ACT 24-30
1 - 4	GCT 58-74	11.52		11.94	ACT 16-30
2 - 4	GCT 58-67	10.94	11.19	11.05	ACT 16-23
2 - 7	GCT 45-67	10.84	10.82		ACT 6-23
5 - 7	GCT 45-57	10.66	10.46		ACT 6-15

[a] T-scores on the Naval General Classification Test were converted into the stated octile classification on the basis of twelfth-grade norms computed in Project Talent by the American Institute for Research.

The six formats investigated again included the BC, OR, AE, and BRM/BRB. In addition, because this study was conducted after the completion of the SC studies which found the AE-OR format to be very efficient, it was decided to include the AE-OR format in order to test the degree to which its efficiency would generalize from one population to another. Moreover, because the studies reported in Chapter 7 suggested that a two-response version of the AE-OR might be even more efficient, such a format was constructed and empirically tested upon NEM learners. On each format, there were 26 NEM learners in octile 1, 63 in octiles 2 through 4, and 32 in octiles 5 through 7. Thus, over the six formats and the pretest group, there were 847 learners tested.

Table 11.1 shows the means and standard deviations of the several variables investigated. The variable, scholastic ability, again served the two functions it served in the studies of SC and JC learners. GCT (Naval General Classification Test) scores were used to separate learners into levels of ability, and within these levels, the GCT scores stratified the learners in order that the experimental analysis would be more sensitive to true differences between formats.

Table 11.1. Means and Standard Deviations of Variables Investigated. Using Learners Who Were Naval Enlisted Men

		Experimental Formats						
		BC	OR	AE	BRM	BRB	AE-OR	AE-OR_2
Posttest corrects	M:	13.37	15.41	15.84	16.55	16.55	15.71	15.68
	SD:	3.88	4.15	5.11	4.68	4.68	4.26	4.53
Scholastic ability	M:	61.76	61.76	61.76	61.76	61.76	61.76	61.76
	SD:	6.22	6.22	6.22	6.22	6.22	6.22	6.22
Program time	M:	21.45	38.97	40.22	36.77	44.07	29.56	28.07
	SD:	4.70	8.06	8.67	8.09	8.09	5.73	5.24
Program items in error	M:	na [a]	12.30	12.20	3.98	3.98	na	na
	SD:	na	4.93	4.81	2.65	2.65	na	na
Program errors	M:	na	na	16.69	4.53	4.53	na	na
	SD:	na	na	7.26	3.25	3.25	na	na

[a] na indicates variable is not applicable for that experimental group.

Chapter 10 showed that the relative efficiencies of the experimental formats changed depending upon the scholastic ability of the JC learner group. Chapter 6 showed this same phenomenon for SC learners. Clearly, the efficiency of a format must be empirically tested upon the target population of learners. Figure 11.1 summarizes the results on the BRM/BRB, AE, OR, and BC formats for three NEM learner groups comparable in ability to the SC learners. Figure 11.2 summarizes the results for three NEM learner groups comparable in ability to the JC learners. For each of the three variables, posttest gain, program time, and posttest gain/program time, the data are presented separately for the learners in octile 1, octiles 1 through 4, octiles 2 through 4, octiles 2 through 7, and octiles 5 through 7. Figure 11.3 summarizes the results of the AE-OR_2, AE-OR, and AE formats for NEM learners in the various octile groups.

In the top third of both Figures 11.1 and 11.2 are the data on posttest gain scores. In Figure 11.1, the top set of four bars represents one target group sought in this study, namely, those NEM learners who fell in octile 1. These learners were comparable to the SC learners in octile 1, so far as test-measured ability was concerned. The bottom set of four bars represents those NEM learners who fell in octiles 2 through 4. These learners were comparable to the SC learners in octiles 2 through 4. The middle set of four bars represents the above two NEM groups combined and thus includes learners

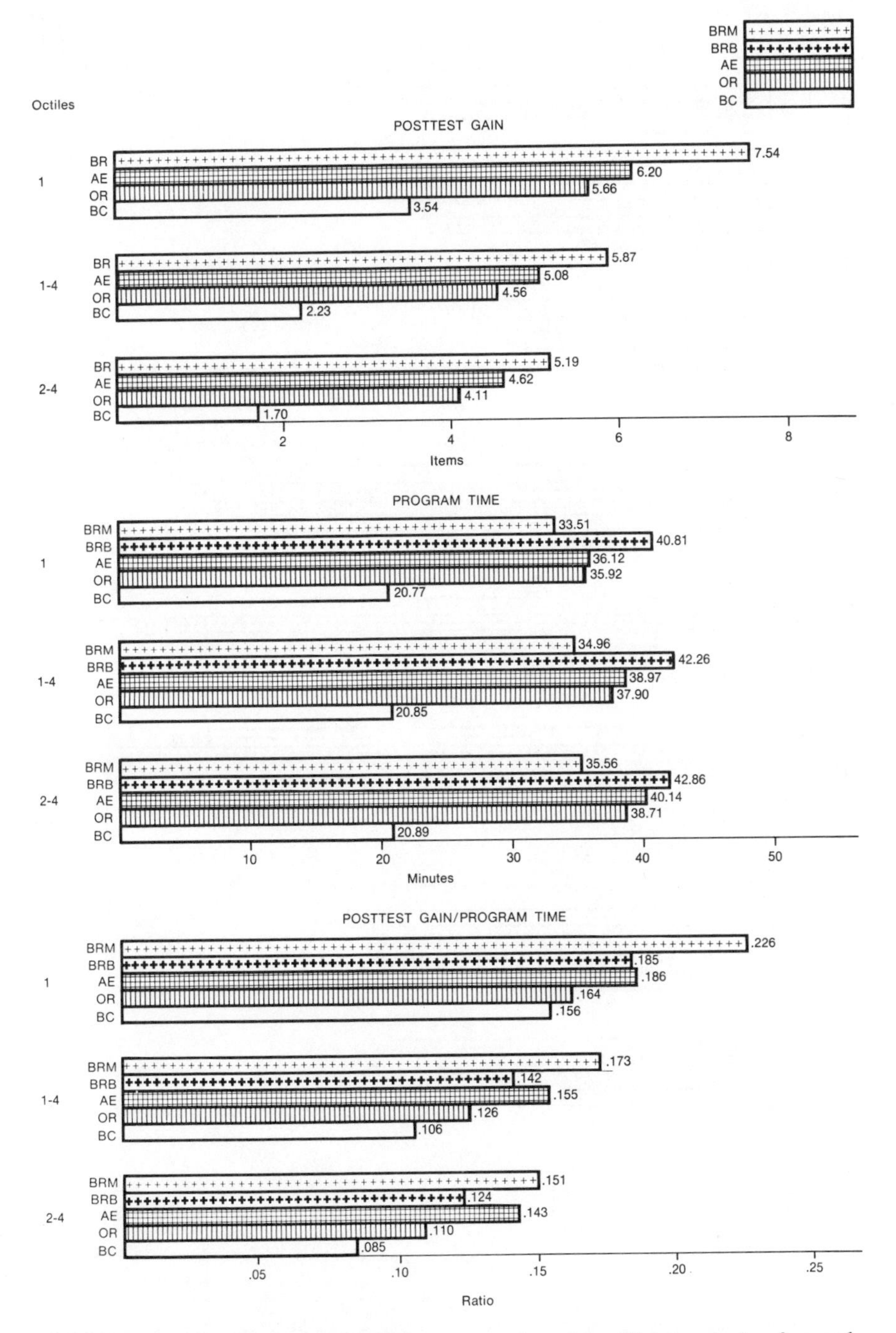

FIG. 11.1 Posttest gain, program time, and a learning efficiency index for each of four experimental formats (BRM/BRB, AE, OR, and BC) presented to naval enlisted men, differentiated and undifferentiated according to scholastic ability, for comparison to state college students.

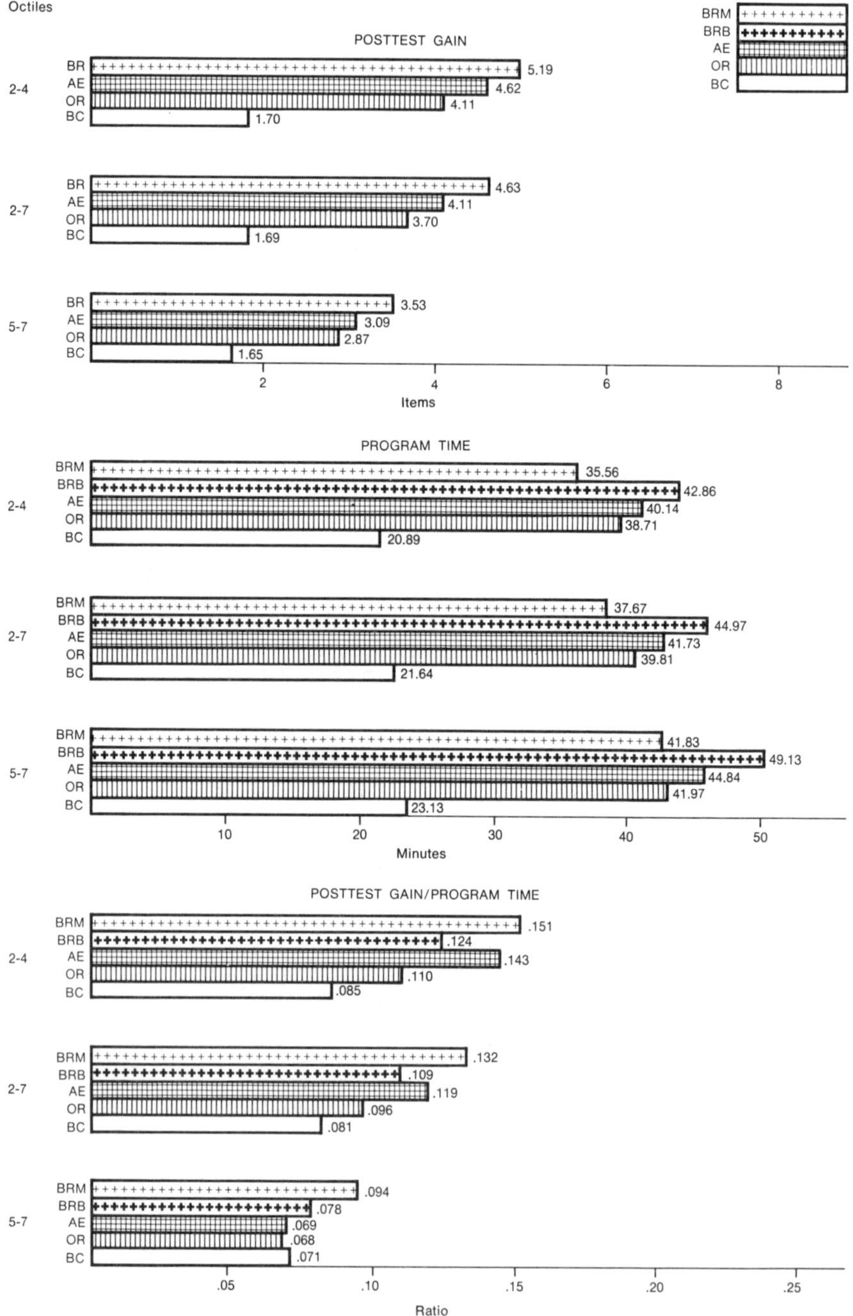

FIG. 11.2 Posttest gain, program time, and a learning efficiency index for each of four experimental formats (BRM/BRB, AE, OR, and BC) presented to naval enlisted men, differentiated and undifferentiated according to scholastic ability, for comparison to junior college students.

from octiles 1 through 4. These learners were comparable to the entire SC sample. In Figure 11.2, the top set of four bars represents those NEM learners who fell in octiles 2 through 4. These learners are comparable in ability to the SC and JC learners in octiles 2 through 4. The bottom set of four bars represents those NEM learners who fell in octiles 5 through 7. These learners were comparable in ability to the JC learners in octiles 5 through 7. The middle set of four bars represents the above two NEM groups combined and thus includes learners from octiles 2 through 7. These learners were comparable to the entire JC sample.

For NEM learners at any level of ability, the branching format with its small steps and thematic prompting achieved the most learning. Figure 10.2, shows that for the SC learners, particularly those of lower ability, overt responding (including question reading) seemed to be the most critical principle to include in a format. Indeed, the difference between the posttest gains of the BC and OR formats was statistically significant. Referring back to Figure 10.3, we note that on the JC learners, feedback seemed to be the most critical principle to include, with small steps assuming importance also for learners in octiles 5 through 7. Now in Figures 11.1 and 11.2, the NEM learners seem to resemble the SC learners more than the JC, because for the NEM learners, overt responding seemed to be the most critical principle to include in a format.

Figure 11.3 indicates that the AE format, incorporating the overt-responding principle and the confirmation feature, fails to show any systematic advantage in posttest gain over the AE-OR and AE-OR_2 formats, that do not incorporate the overt-responding principle and exchange confirmation for formal prompting.

On posttest gain, the significant differences were as follows:

(*a*) for octile 1 learners, – between BC and OR, BRM/BRB, AE-OR, and AE-OR_2
(*b*) for octile 1-4 learners, – between BC and OR, AE, BRM/BRB, AE-OR, and AE-OR_2
– between OR and BRM/BRB
(*c*) for octile 2-4 learners, – between BC and OR, AE, BRM/BRB, AE-OR, and AE-OR_2.
(*d*) for octile 2-7 learners, – between BC and OR, AE, BRM/BRB, AE-OR, and AE-OR_2
(*e*) for octile 5-7 learners, – between BC and BRM/BRB.

According to the formal analysis of the formats in terms of principles incorporated, the posttest corrects of the NEM learners may be summarized as supporting overt responding (including question reading) unless formal prompting is present or unless the learners are below average in ability. In that event, it would seem wise to incorporate both the immediate-feedback and small-step principles. On the other hand, let us consider the JC learners, who tended to have more program test items in error and had significantly

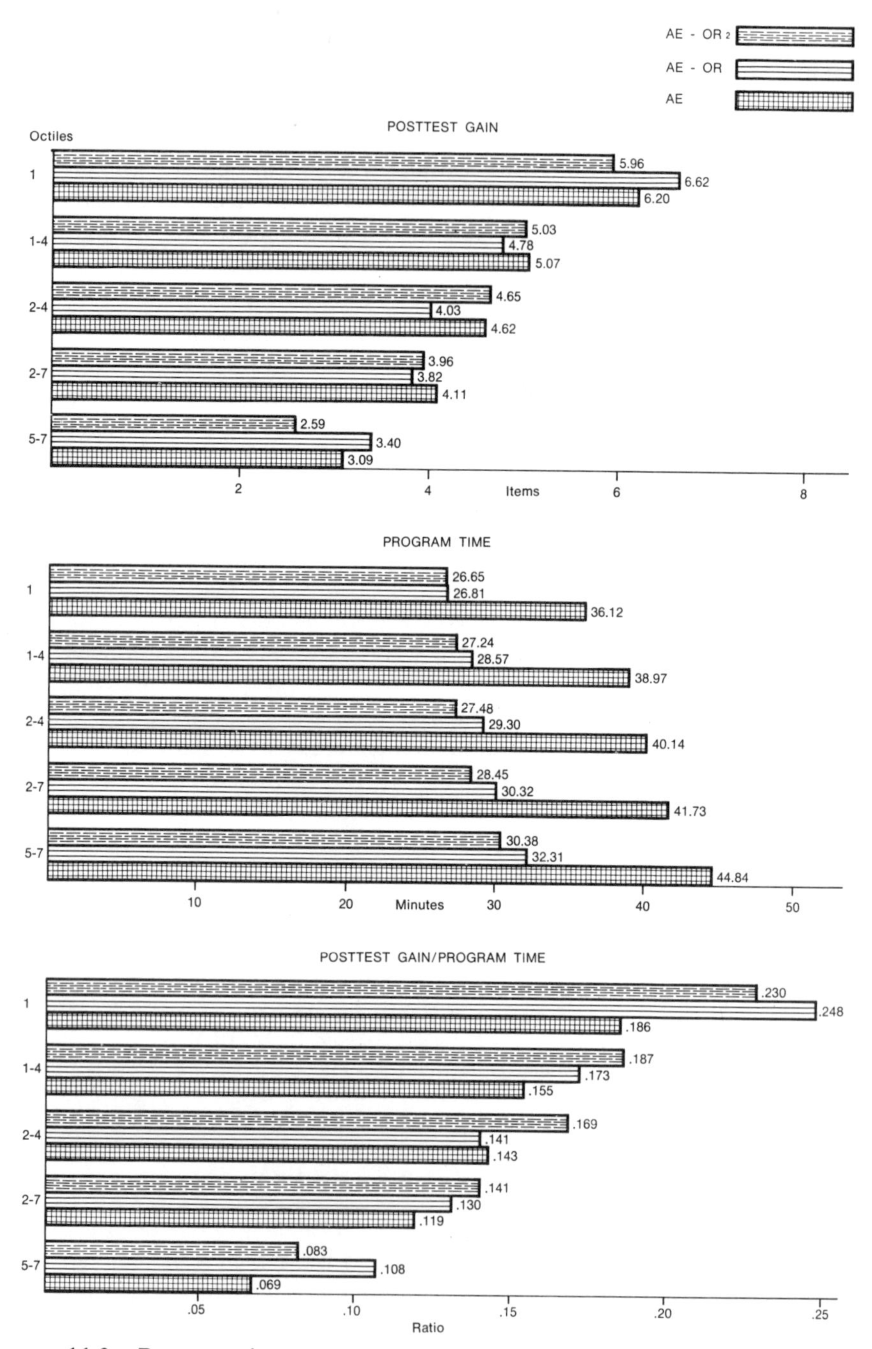

FIG. 11.3 Posttest gain, program time, and a learning efficiency index for each of three experimental formats (AE-OR$_2$, AE-OR, and AE) presented to naval enlisted men, differentiated and undifferentiated according to scholastic ability, for comparison to state college students.

more total errors on their programs than did their NEM counterparts. Even if the JC learners were not below average in ability, it would be prudent to incorporate immediate feedback and small steps into any format calling for overt responses.

In the middle third of Figures 11.1 and 11.2 are the data on program times. The program times of the BRB groups included the time required for envelope-opening. For the nonbranching formats, as more principles were incorporated, there was a general corresponding increase in program time ranging from BC through OR to AE. In Figure 11.3, at every ability level, the AE format required far more program time than either of the AE-OR formats.

On program time, all formats differed significantly from each other except for the following:

(*a*) for octile 1 learners, – between OR and AE, BRM
between AE and BRM
between AE-OR and $AE\text{-}OR_2$
(*b*) for octile 1-4 learners, – between OR and AE
between AE-OR and $AE\text{-}OR_2$
(*c*) for octile 2-4 learners, – between OR and AE
between AE-OR and $AE\text{-}OR_2$
(*d*) for octile 2-7 learners, – between OR and AE, BRM
(*e*) for octile 5-7 learners, – between OR and AE, BRM
between AE and BRB, BRM
between AE-OR and $AE\text{-}OR_2$

In the bottom third of Figures 11.1 and 11.2 are the data on the efficiency indices. At all NEM ability levels, the simulated machine-presented branching format again appeared to be more efficient than the BC, OR, AE, and BRB. Figure 11.3 casts considerable doubt upon the efficiency of the AE technique *versus* the prompted AE-OR formats. The differences that were statistically significant are indicated in Appendix G.

On the whole, the more efficient formats were the two- and three-response versions of the AE-OR format, and the machine-presented branching format. The less efficient were the BC, the OR, and for the lower ability learners to some extent, the book-presented branching format. This hierarchy of efficiencies was similar to that obtained on SC learners. In many ways, the NEM and SC learners seemed to have more in common with each other than either group had in common with the JC learners. The example of this trend was for the OR format to be very inefficient for JC learners but to be only moderately inefficient for SC and NEM learners. Because the JC learners appeared to be more poorly motivated than the SC and NEM learners and overt responding without feedback, prompting, or small steps is predisposed to a high-error rate for poorly motivated learners, the inefficiency of the OR format by JC learners is intuitively understandable. Also understandable is the fact that the AE format, with its confirmation feature, required much more program time than did the AE-OR formats, in both the two- and three-response versions, with their formal prompting feature. And because the AE format showed no better learning yield than did either of the AE-OR formats, the latter appeared somewhat more efficient, particularly at the upper ability levels. Regarding the relative efficiencies of the various formats, the NEM learners differed in one striking way from the SC learners in that the BC format was not efficient at any level of ability, even the top octile. It did not seem efficient to have naval enlisted men learn from mere plain text.

The NEM learners, like both the SC and JC learners, had significantly less items in error on the small-step format (BRM/BRB) than on either of the large-step formats (OR and AE). Similarly, the NEM learners, like the SC and JC learners, had significantly less total program errors on the BRM/BRB format than on the AE. These differences are attributable to the fact that the small-step permits examination of text after a test item is read, whereas a large-step format does not.

Comparison of the Navy and College Samples

In Table 11.2 are the data in Table 11.1 less the data for the NEM learners in octiles 5 through 7. Table 11.2 enables the NEM results to be

Table 11.2 Means and Standard Deviations of Variables Investigated, Using Learners Who Were Naval Enlisted Men in Octiles 1 through 4

		Experimental Formats						
		BC	OR	AE	BRM	BRB	AE-OR	AE-OR$_2$
Posttest corrects	M:	13.75	16.08	16.60	17.39	17.39	16.30	16.55
	SD:	3.85	4.05	5.43	4.77	4.77	4.37	4.67
Scholastic ability	M:	64.54	64.54	64.54	64.54	64.54	64.54	64.54
	SD:	4.61	4.61	4.61	4.61	4.61	4.61	4.61
Program time	M:	20.85	37.90	38.97	34.96	42.26	28.57	27.24
	SD:	4.67	7.60	7.62	6.80	6.80	5.69	5.04
Program items in error	M:	na[a]	11.61	11.45	3.33	3.33	na	na
	SD:	na	4.99	4.89	2.19	2.19	na	na
Program errors	M:	na	na	15.63	3.73	3.73	na	na
	SD:	na	na	5.32	2.68	2.68	na	na

a na indicates variable is not applicable for that experimental group.

Table 11.3 Means and Standard Deviations of Variables Investigated, Using Learners Who Were Naval Enlisted Men in Octiles 2 through 7

		Experimental Formats						
		BC	OR	AE	BRM	BRB	AE-OR	$AE\text{-}OR_2$
Posttest corrects	M:	12.53	14.54	14.95	15.47	15.47	14.66	14.80
	SD:	3.41	3.76	4.87	4.18	4.18	3.53	4.28
Scholastic ability	M:	59.36	59.36	59.36	59.36	59.36	59.36	59.36
	SD:	4.67	4.67	4.67	4.67	4.67	4.67	4.67
Program time	M:	21.64	39.81	41.73	37.67	44.97	30.32	28.45
	SD:	4.22	8.29	7.29	8.51	8.51	5.81	5.37
Program items in error	M:	na[a]	13.66	13.26	4.51	4.51	na	na
	SD:	na	4.36	4.34	2.67	2.67	na	na
Program errors	M:	na	na	18.25	5.16	5.16	na	na
	SD:	na	na	6.74	3.31	3.31	na	na

a na indicates variable is not applicable for that experimental group.

compared to the SC results in Table 5.1. In Table 11.3 are the data in Table 11.1 less the data for the NEM learners in octile 1. Table 11.3 enables the NEM results to be compared to the JC results in Table 10.1. While the data in Tables 5.1 and 11.2 represent the results of learners comparable in ability, as is also true of the data in Tables 10.1 and 11.3, the ability values in Tables 5.1 and 10.1 are ACT scores, and the values in Tables 11.2 and 11.3 are GCT scores. The equating of a given NEM octile to a given SC or JC octile rests upon the assumption that both tests are comparable and that the norm samples are as similar as they are described in the literature.

Tables 11.1 through 11.3 are organized to compare differences between experimental formats and, thus, hold constant the institutional affiliations and ability levels. Because the comparison of formats within one institutional setting was a prime goal of all the studies, the NEM learners, like the SC and JC learners, were matched perfectly on ability test scores from one experimental format to another.

Tables 11.4 through 11.9 are organized differently. The organization of Tables 11.4, 11.6, and 11.8 holds constant the institutional affiliation and experimental format and compares the results between ability levels. The organization of Tables 11.5, 11.7, and 11.9 holds constant the ability level

Table 11.4 Program Items in Error and Program Errors Made by Learners in State College, Junior College, and Navy Samples: Comparison of Effects of Intellective Factors

	SC Octiles		JC Octiles		NEM Octiles		
	1	2-4	2-4	5-7	1	2-4	5-7
			BRM/BRB				
Program items in error	2.68	3.84	4.76	7.00	2.04	3.86	5.78
			AE				
	8.30	12.84	14.54	16.41	8.31	12.75	14.28
			OR				
	9.05	11.94	14.68	16.33	7.31	13.38	14.22
			BRM/BRB				
Program errors	2.84	4.49	5.43	8.56	2.23	4.35	6.75
			AE				
	10.61	16.64	20.57	23.56	11.00	17.54	19.66

Note. Means not sharing a common underline are significantly different at the .05 level.

and experimental format and compares the results between institutional affiliation. It was a simple matter to match learners on the variables institutional affiliation and experimental format. It was not so simple to match learners on such a finely calibrated scales as test scores. The matching that was accomplished on ability level within an institution, such as state college system, junior college system, or Naval Training Center, did not generalize across institutions. In order to match learners on ability level across institutions, some learners from each of the three institutions had to be discarded. For this reason, the mean values listed in Tables 11.5, 11.7, and 11.9 are not identical to those in Tables 11.4, 11.6, and 11.8. The number of cases in each shrunken sample are indicated in Tables 11.5, 11.7, and 11.9.

Program Errors

Tables 11.4 and 11.5 contain the means for both error variables. The values in Table 11.4 were grouped first by institution and then by octiles in order to compare the effects of intellective factors upon error behavior. The values in Table 11.5 were grouped first by octiles and then by institution in order to compare the effects of nonintellective factors upon error behavior.

Table 11.4 shows that intellective factors do affect error behavior. Except for those few octile groupings sharing a common underline all other

Table 11.5 Program Items in Error and Program Errors Made by Learners in State College, Junior College, and Navy Samples: Comparison of Effects of Nonintellective Factors

Octiles:		1-4		2-7		1		2-4						5-7	
Institution:		SC	NEM	NEM	JC	SC	NEM	SC	NEM	SC	JC	NEM	JC	NEM	JC
N:		79	76	77	56	46	26	33	50	23	23	56	31	21	25
Program items in error	BRM/BRB	3.18	3.21	4.47	5.46	2.57	2.04	4.03	3.82	4.39	4.35	3.95	4.77	5.86	6.32
	AE	10.42	10.99	13.66	14.77	7.96	8.31	13.85	12.38	13.83	14.39	12.95	14.61	15.57	14.96
	OR	10.46	11.01	14.00	14.96	8.76	7.31	12.82	12.94	13.35	14.17	13.70	14.36	14.81	15.72
Program errors	BRM/BRB	3.61	3.57	5.14	6.50	2.74	2.23	4.82	4.26	5.30	5.13	4.50	5.52	6.86	7.72
	AE	13.28	15.01	18.83	20.93	10.09	11.00	17.73	17.10	17.87	20.22	17.80	20.84	21.57	21.04

Note. Means not sharing a common underline are significantly different at the .05 level.

differences between mean values within an institutional grouping were statistically significant at the .05 level. On all formats calling for overt responding, the error rate decreased significantly as scholastic ability increased. This pattern occurred even in the presence of feedback, small steps, thematic prompting and the opportunity to reread text prior to responding. The inverse relationship was true for SC, JC, and NEM learners, and was particularly true at the upper levels of learner ability and where the formats incorporated the greater number of PI features. Table 11.5 shows that nonintellective factors exert a weaker effect upon error behavior. Those few institutional groupings not showing a common underline are the only differences between mean values within an octile grouping which were statistically significant. The sample sizes underlying the two comparisons on the extreme left of Table 11.5 were sufficiently great so that even with the shrinkage, they each retained a considerable number of cases. For this reason, they are of greater interest. Whether for program items in error or program errors, when ability level was held constant, there was a trend for SC learners to make the least errors, NEM the next least, and JC learners the most.

Table 11.6 Program Times for the State College, Junior College, and Navy Samples: Comparison of Effects of Intellective Factors

	SC Octiles		JC Octiles		NEM Octiles		
	1	2-4	2-4	5-7	1	2-4	5-7
$AE\text{-}OR_2$					26.65	27.48	30.38
AE-OR	26.21	29.11			26.81	29.30	32.31
BRM	35.05	39.16	39.40	42.98	33.51	34.56	41.82
BRB	42.35	46.46	46.70	50.28	40.81	42.86	49.12
AE	40.11	40.53	38.03	37.90	36.12	40.14	44.84
OR	34.21	36.96	30.70	32.51	35.92	38.71	41.97
BC	22.07	22.56	19.62	19.41	20.77	20.89	23.12

Note. Means not sharing a common underline are significantly different at the .05 level.

Table 11.7 Program Times for the State College, Junior College, and Navy Samples: Comparison of Effects of Nonintellective Factors

Octiles:	1-4		2-7		1		2-4						5-7	
Institution:	SC	NEM	NEM	JC	SC	NEM	SC	NEM	SC	JC	NEM	JC	NEM	JC
N:	79	76	77	56	46	26	33	50	23	23	56	31	21	25
AE-OR	27.96	28.07			26.54	26.81	29.94	28.72						
BRM	37.14	34.15	37.31	40.86	35.05	33.51	40.06	34.48	39.53	40.74	35.75	39.80	41.46	42.18
BRB	44.44	41.45	44.61	48.16	42.35	40.81	47.36	41.78	46.83	48.04	43.05	47.10	48.76	49.48
AE	39.82	38.82	41.22	37.80	39.41	36.12	40.39	40.22	40.30	39.43	40.07	37.94	44.29	37.64
OR	35.47	37.42	39.78	31.11	34.48	35.92	36.85	38.20	37.87	30.78	39.34	30.52	40.95	31.84
BC	22.00	21.22	21.58	19.68	21.41	20.77	22.82	21.46	23.22	18.91	20.95	19.77	23.29	19.56

Note. Means not sharing a common underline are significantly different at the .05 level.

In both Tables 11.4 and 11.5, the means of the variable, total program errors, tended to differ from each other more than did the means of the variable, program items in error. The differences between the means tended to be greater on the BRM/BRB and AE format than they did on the OR format.

Program Times

Tables 11.6 and 11.7 contain the mean program times. The values in Table 11.6 were grouped first by institution and then by octile in order to compare the effects of intellective factors upon program time. The values in Table 11.7 were grouped first by octile and then by institution in order to compare the effects of nonintellective factors upon program time. Table 11.6 shows that intellective factors do affect program time. Except for the JC students and the SC students given the BC and AE formats, learners with less ability appeared to take more time on the program. Table 11.7 shows that nonintellective factors also exerted an effect upon program time, but the direction of the influence was less systematic. SC learners typically took more time than did NEM learners on the BRM/BRB format. Differences between the SC and NEM learners on the other formats are less pronounced. JC learners

Table 11.8 Posttest Corrects for the State College, Junior College, and Navy Samples: Comparison of Effects of Intellective Factors

	SC Octiles		JC Octiles		NEM Octiles		
	1	2-4	2-4	5-7	1	2-4	5-7
$AE\text{-}OR_2$					18.88	15.59	13.25
AE-OR	20.32	18.27			19.54	14.97	14.06
BRM/BRB	20.53	17.62	16.40	14.62	20.46	16.13	14.19
AE	19.90	16.54	15.65	13.13	19.12	15.56	13.75
OR	19.21	15.91	13.38	11.59	18.58	15.05	13.53
BC	17.05	13.04	13.49	11.92	16.46	12.64	12.31

Note. Means not sharing a common underline are significantly different at the .05 level.

Table 11.9 Posttest Corrects for the State College, Junior College, and Navy Samples: Comparison of Effects of Nonintellective Factors

Octiles:	1-4		2-7		1		2-4						5-7	
Institution:	SC	NEM	NEM	JC	SC	NEM	SC	JC	SC	NEM	NEM	JC	NEM	JC
N:	79	76	77	56	46	26	23	23	33	50	56	31	21	25
AE-OR	19.60	16.76			20.83	19.54			17.88	15.32				
BRM/BRB	19.42	17.71	15.78	15.80	20.87	20.46	17.17	16.48	17.39	16.28	16.38	16.16	14.19	15.36
AE	18.54	16.88	14.73	14.75	20.30	19.12	15.48	14.87	16.09	15.72	15.14	15.68	13.62	13.60
OR	17.89	16.38	14.34	12.29	19.67	18.58	15.44	13.22	15.39	15.24	14.77	13.36	13.19	10.96
BC	15.33	14.22	12.49	12.94	17.02	16.46	12.78	13.44	12.97	13.06	12.59	13.58	12.24	12.20

Note. Means not sharing a common underline are significantly different at the .05 level.

typically took more time than did NEM learners on the BRM/BRB format and less time on the AE, OR, and BC formats. Although the evidence is weaker, it also appears that JC learners typically took more time than did SC learners on the BRM/BRB format and less time on the AE, OR, and BC formats.

Posttest Corrects

Table 11.8 and 11.9 contain the mean posttest corrects. The values in Table 11.8 were grouped first by institution and then by octile in order to compare the effects of intellective factors upon posttest performance. The values in Table 11.9 were grouped first by octile and then by institution in order to compare the effects of nonintellective factors upon posttest performance. Table 11.8 shows that intellective factors highly affected posttest performance: all the differences were in favor of the higher ability learners, and almost all the differences were statistically significant. This trend occurred regardless of the number and configuration of PI features employed. The direct relationship was true for SC, JC, and NEM learners, and was particularly true at the upper levels of learner ability and where the formats incorporated the greater number of PI features, such as immediate feedback, small steps, thematic prompting, and the opportunity to reread text prior to responding. Table 11.9 shows that nonintellective factors exerted a weaker effect upon posttest performance. Nonintellective factors appeared to have the greatest influence in differentiating SC learners from both the JC and NEM. Except for the BC format, the SC learners typically posttested higher than did the NEM learners. The SC and NEM learners typically posttested higher than did the JC learners only on the OR format.

Recapitulation

Collectively, nonintellective factors did not seem to have as pronounced effects upon the relative amounts of error behavior and learning yield associated with each of the several formats as did the intellective factors measured by the ability tests. Nevertheless, nonintellective factors did seem to play an important role in determining the relative merit of the formats for the learners from the three separate institutions. The influence of nonintellective factors was primarily upon program time. To the observers, it appeared that the JC sample were the least motivated of all the learners. A possible reason for the apparently higher motivation of the NEM sample was that they were all recent graduates of recruit training. Their motivation might have been therefore largely induced by military discipline and therefore extrinsic in nature.

The principle, overt responding, in the absence of immediate feedback and small steps, seemed to be contra-indicated for the JC learners, whether in octiles 2 through 4 or in octiles 5 through 7. On the other hand, the SC learners in octiles 2 through 4 seemed to profit from overt responding (plus question reading), as did the NEM learners in octiles 2 through 4. The NEM learners in octiles 5 through 7 profited from overt responding (plus question reading) in terms of posttest gain, but the cost in program time resulted in the OR format not being any more efficient than the BC. It does appear, therefore, that overt responding should not be used in the absence of immediate feedback and small steps for low-ability learners, particularly when the motivation level is questionable. Where motivation is known to be low, the use of an overt-response feature without immediate feedback in the format of an instructional instrument is contra-indicated. If an instructional technologist does incur the time penalty of overt responding, he had better also introduce feedback, and hopefully, small steps. It would not be a sound practice to encourage or permit learners with low-ability and low-motivation levels to make mistakes because through the use of small steps, mistakes can be efficiently reduced to one quarter or one third. If for some reason large-step size must be used, immediate feedback should be present so that the mistakes can be promptly corrected.

Intercorrelations

Table 11.10 contains the intercorrelations between all variables within each of the six experimental groups. Those values differing significantly from zero parameter value are indicated by numerals, as signified in the footnote to the table, using a two-tailed test in every instance. Those within-group correlations[1] that were significantly different from each other do not share a common underline.

In order to make comparisons between the correlations computed upon the NEM learners and the SC learners, Table 11.11 contains correlations computed upon those NEM learners in octiles 1 through 4 only. In order to make the comparisons between the correlations computed upon the NEM learners and the JC learners, Table 11.2 contains correlations computed upon those NEM learners in octiles 2 through 7 only. Thus, the values in Tables 8.1 and 11.11 are based on learners comparable on intellective factors but differing on nonintellective factors. The same holds for the values in Tables 10.3 and 11.12. In contrast, the values in Tables 11.10, 11.11, and 11.12 are based on learners comparable on nonintellective factors but differing on intellective factors.

As was the case with the SC and JC learners (see Tables 8.1 and 10.3), posttest corrects shared a great deal of variance with the scholastic ability measure for the NEM learners. The correlation coefficients were significant for each of the six formats, except in Table 11.12, lacking octile 1 learners. The systematically greater values in Table 11.11 than in Table 11.12, with the BC format differing significantly, suggests that the influence of ability

[1] Statistical tests were actually performed upon the z-transformations of the correlations.

Table 11.10 Product-Moment Correlation Coefficients between Variables within Six Experimental Formats, Using Learners Who Were Naval Enlisted Men

Algebraically Low → Algebraically High

Between Posttest Corrects and Scholastic Ability

BC	BRM	AE	AE-OR$_2$	OR	AE-OR
$.356^{6}$	$.430^{6}$	$.461^{6}$	$.463^{6}$	$.470^{6}$	$.490^{6}$

Between Posttest Corrects and Program Time

BRM	AE	AE-OR	OR	BC	AE-OR$_2$
−.157	−.097	−.068	−.012	.007	.063

Between Posttest Corrects and Program Items in Error

AE	OR	BRM
$-.689^{6}$	$-.652^{6}$	$-.339^{5}$

Between Posttest Corrects and Program Errors

AE	OR	BRM
$-.687^{6}$	$-.652^{6}$	$-.310^{4}$

Between Scholastic Ability and Program Time

BRM	AE-OR	AE	OR	AE-OR$_2$	BC
$-.392^{6}$	$-.331^{5}$	$-.329^{5}$	$-.293^{3}$	$-.284^{3}$	$-.185^{1}$

Between Scholastic Ability and Program Items in Error

BRM	OR	AE
$-.530^{6}$	$-.526^{6}$	$-.555^{6}$

Between Scholastic Ability and Program Errors

BRM	OR	AE
$-.542^{6}$	$-.526^{6}$	$-.495^{6}$

Between Program Time and Program Items in Error

OR	AE	BRM
.012	.056	$.236^{2}$

Between Program Time and Program Errors

AE	OR	BRM
.008	.012	$.272^{3}$

Between Program Items in Error and Program Errors

AE	BRM	OR
$.963^{6}$	$.973^{6}$	1.000^{6}

Note. Coefficients not sharing a common underline are significantly different at the .05 level. Superscripts indicate how significantly coefficients differ from zero.

^{1} indicates .05 significance level
^{2} indicates .01 significance level
^{3} indicates .005 significance level
^{4} indicates .001 significance level
^{5} indicates .0005 significance level
^{6} indicates .0001 significance level

Table 11.11 Product-Moment Correlation Coefficients between Variables within Six Experimental Formats, Using Learners Who Were Naval Enlisted Men in Octiles 1 through 4

Algebraically Low → Algebraically High

Between Posttest Corrects and Scholastic Ability

BRM	AE-OR$_2$	AE	OR	BC	AE-OR
.373[5]	.388[5]	.439[6]	.462[6]	.482[6]	.509[6]

Between Posttest Corrects and Program Time

OR	AE	AE-OR	BRM	AE-OR$_2$	BC
−.260	−.038	.012	.013	.123	.202

Between Posttest Corrects and Program Items in Error

AE	OR	BRM
−.728[6]	−.642[6]	−.242[1]

Between Posttest Corrects and Program Errors

AE	OR	BRM
−.737[6]	−.642[6]	−.288[2]

Between Scholastic Ability and Program Time

OR	BRM	AE-OR	AE	AE-OR$_2$	BC
−.285[2]	−.256[1]	−.196	−.179	−.142	−.009

Between Scholastic Ability and Program Items in Error

OR	AE	BRM
−.611[6]	−.533[6]	−.479[6]

Between Scholastic Ability and Program Errors

OR	AE	BRM
−.611[6]	−.509[6]	−.489[6]

Between Program Time and Program Items in Error

AE	BRM	OR
.009	.013	.038

Between Program Time and Program Errors

AE	OR	BRM
−.028	.038	.044

Between Program Items in Error and Program Errors

BRM	AE	OR
.966[6]	.967[6]	1.000[6]

Note. Coefficients not sharing a common underline are significantly different at the .05 level. Superscripts indicate how significantly coefficients differ from zero.

[1] indicates .05 significance level
[2] indicates .01 significance level
[3] indicates .005 significance level
[4] indicates .001 significance level
[5] indicates .0005 significance level
[6] indicates .0001 significance level

Table 11.12 Product-Moment Correlation Coefficients between Variables within Six Experimental Formats, Using Learners Who Were Naval Enlisted Men in Octiles 2 through 7

Between Posttest Corrects and Scholastic Ability

Algebraically Low					Algebraically High
BC	BRM	AE-OR	OR	AE-OR$_2$	AE
.091	.183	.253[1]	.317[3]	.342[4]	.343[4]

Between Posttest Corrects and Program Time

BRM	BC	AE-OR	AE	OR	AE-OR$_2$
−.124	.023	.027	.067	.101	.136

Between Posttest Corrects and Program Items in Error

AE	OR	BRM
−.627[6]	−.579[6]	−.202[1]

Between Posttest Corrects and Program Errors

AE	OR	BRM
−.620[6]	−.579[6]	−.179

Between Scholastic Ability and Program Time

BRM	AE-OR$_2$	AE-OR	OR	BC	AE
−.376[5]	−.298[3]	−.261[1]	−.230[1]	−.227[1]	−.207[1]

Between Scholastic Ability and Program Items in Error

BRM	AE	OR
−.414[6]	−.339[4]	−.249[1]

Between Scholastic Ability and Program Errors

BRM	AE	OR
−.438[6]	−.315[3]	−.249[1]

Between Program Time and Program Items in Error

AE	OR	BRM
−.211[1]	−.121	.188

Between Program Time and Program Errors

AE	OR	BRM
−.261	−.121	.229

Between Program Items in Error and Program Errors

AE	BRM	OR
.950[6]	.969[6]	1.000[6]

Note. Coefficients not sharing a common underline are significantly different at the .05 level. Superscripts indicate how significantly coefficients differ from zero.

[1] indicates .05 significance level
[2] indicates .01 significance level
[3] indicates .005 significance level
[4] indicates .001 significance level
[5] indicates .0005 significance level
[6] indicates .0001 significance level

upon learning drops off as the ability level drops off. (It should be pointed out that the octiles 1 through 4 learners have a range of test scores nearly as great as the octiles 2 through 7 learners, and any differences between the values in Tables 11.11 and 11.12 need not be adjusted for the restriction in range phenomenon.) The correlations for the BC, OR, AE, and BRM formats in Table 11.11 were comparable to the values for the SC learners and the correlation for the AE-OR format was somewhat greater than the value for the SC learners. The correlations for the OR and AE formats in Table 11.12 were comparable to the values for the JC learners. The correlations for the the BC and BRM formats were somewhat lower than the values for the JC learners.

With regard to the correlations between posttest corrects and program time, the values in Table 11.0 are not statistically significant and do not differ significantly from each other. The values in Table 11.11 are similar to the values for the SC learners in that both sets of values are small in absolute magnitude. The values in Table 11.12 are similar to the values for the JC learners except that as noted in Chapter 10, the value for the OR format was elevated for the JC learners. There seemed to be a closer relationship between the amount of time a JC learner spent on a program and how much he learned than there was for either the SC or the NEM learners. This relationship seemed to be particularly true on the OR format. The earlier interpretation that the JC learners on the whole were taking insufficient time is further supported by comparing the JC correlations between program time and posttest corrects to the corresponding NEM correlations as well as to the corresponding SC correlations. The times taken by even the fastest of the SC and NEM learners were apparently long enough to wipe out most of the effects upon learning due to differences in the duration of exposure to the instructional materials.

With reference to the correlations between posttest corrects and program items in error, the values for all three formats, OR, AE, and BRM, were negative and statistically significant, as was true of both the SC and JC learners. The values for the OR and AE formats were significantly more negative than the value for the BRM format, as was true of the SC learners. In contrast, the negative correlations for the JC learners on the OR and AE formats were somewhat less in absolute magnitude than the values for the SC and NEM learners, and hence, the correlations for the OR, AE, and BRM formats did not differ significantly from each other for JC learners. The correlations between posttest corrects and program errors behaved similarly to the correlations between posttest corrects and program items in error and lead to identical interpretations.

The correlations between scholastic ability and program time were all negative and statistically significant for the entire sample of NEM learners represented in Table 11.10. None of the format values differed significantly from any other. As with the SC and JC data, if one accepts the proposition that those with less ability should spend more time in contact with the instructional materials by way of compensation, then the high negative correlations associated with the formats on the left side of Table 11.10 was a good feature, and the low negative correlations associated with the formats on the right side of Table 11.10 was a bad feature.

The correlations between scholastic ability and program items in error were all negative and statistically significant for NEM learners. None of the format values differed significantly from any other. However, in the comparison of the NEM learners in octiles 1 through 4 (Table 11.11) to the SC learners (Table 8.1), the correlations for the OR and BRM formats were considerably more negative for the NEM learners. It appears that ability is more strongly related (in an inverse direction) to errors among the NEM learners than among the SC. Motivation can act as a moderator variable between ability and performance variables: when motivation is relatively high, the correlation between ability and performance is relatively high: when motivation is relatively low, the correlations between ability and performance is relatively low. The present results suggest that motivation was higher among the NEM learners than among the SC. The correlations between scholastic ability and program errors behaved similarly to the correlations between scholastic ability and program items in error.

The correlations between program time and program items in error were most positive for the BRM format except in Table 11.11, lacking NEM learners in octiles 5 through 7. For the upper four octiles of NEM learners, errors and program time were largely independent. The correlations shown

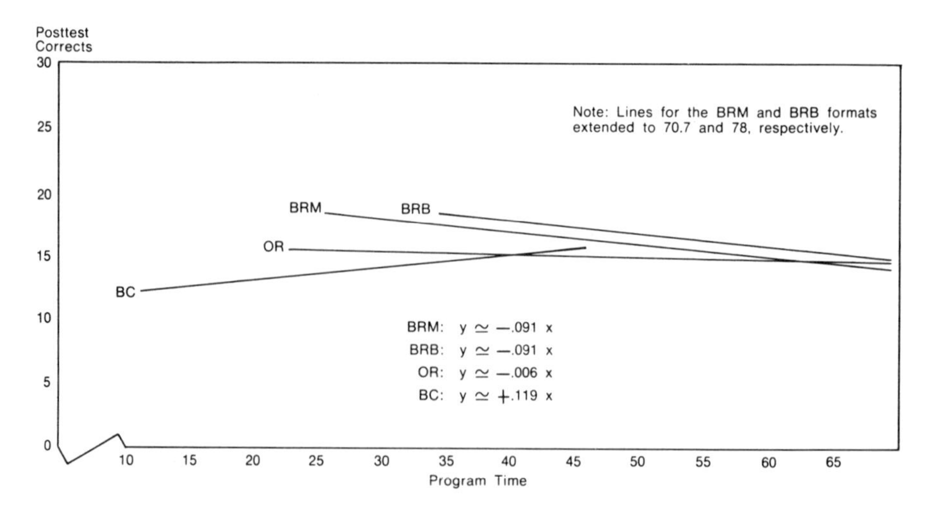

FIG. 11.4 Regression lines, posttest corrects on program time, within each experimental group of naval enlisted men, for formats BRM, BRB, OR, and BC.

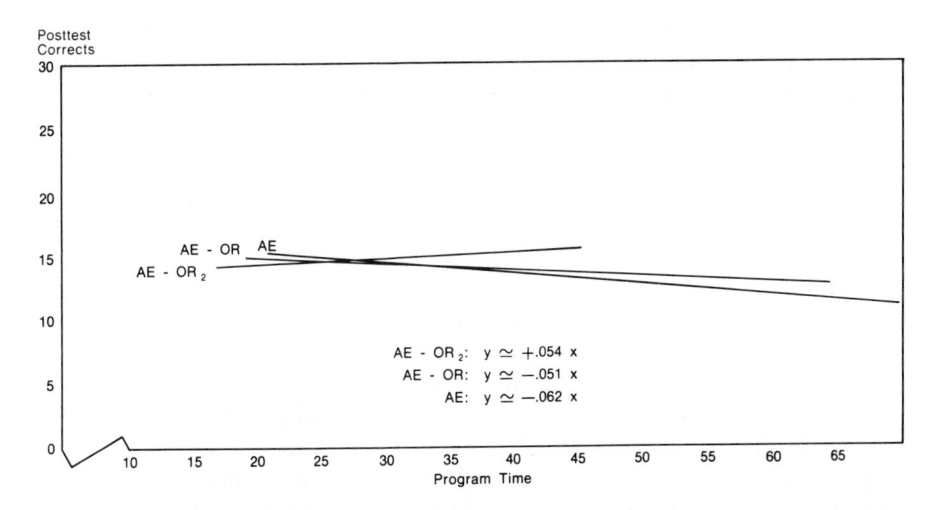

FIG. 11.5 Regression lines, posttest corrects on program time, within each experimental group of naval enlisted men, for formats AE-OR_2, AE-OR, and AE.

in Tables 11.10 and 11.12 are more similar to those for JC and SC learners in that the value for the BRM format was considerably more positive than those for the OR and AE formats. The correlations between program time and program errors behaved similarly to the correlations between program time and program items in error.

Above it was noted that the correlations between posttest corrects and program time, like those for the JC and SC learners, were fairly low in an absolute sense. Figures 11.4 and 11.5 show the regression equations and regression lines within each of the formats tested with NEM learners. Again, all the regression lines were fairly close to horizontal. The slopes were somewhat less positive than they were for the JC sample. These results are in keeping with the observations of the proctors that the NEM learners appeared more highly motivated, intent, and serious than did the JC learners. It follows that if the JC learners were less highly motivated, their learning would be more purely a function of time spent on a program; that is, the effects of program time would be greater under low levels of motivation than under high levels. As was the case with the SC learners, the positive slopes reflected the relationship: the more time spent studying, the more learned. The most negative slopes were associated with the BRM and BRB regression lines and again suggested that a format which permits the learner to inspect the text after he views a test item, and before responding, is going to have a negative correlation between program time and posttest corrects. The more difficulty the learner experiences in responding to the items, the slower he reads the text or the more he rereads the text.

To test for significant departures from linear regression, posttest corrects on program time, an *eta* coefficient was computed within each group. Below are the values of *eta* and Pearson *r* for each group. In none of the formats were the departures from linearity significant.

	BC	OR	AE	BRM/BRB	AE-OR	$AE\text{-}OR_2$
eta	.124	.045	.187	.259	.071	.161
r	+.007	−.012	−.097	−.157	−.068	+.063

Summary

Of the formats tested upon the NEM learners, the more efficient ones were the two- and three-response versions of the AE-OR format, and the machine-presented branching format. The less efficient were the BC, OR, and book-presented branching formats. This hierarchy of efficiencies was similar to that obtained on SC learners. In many ways, the NEM and SC learners seemed to have more in common with each other than either group had in common with the JC learners. The example of this trend was for the OR format to be very inefficient for JC learners but to be only moderately inefficient for SC and NEM learners. Because the JC learners appeared to be more poorly motivated than the SC and NEM learners, and overt responding without feedback, prompting, or small steps is predisposed to a high-error rate for poorly motivated learners, the inefficiency of the OR format by JC learners is intuitively understandable. Also understandable is the fact that the AE format, with its confirmation feature required much more program time than did the AE-OR formats, in both the two- and three-response versions, with their formal prompting feature. And because the AE format showed no better learning yield than did either of the AE-OR formats, the latter appeared somewhat more efficient, particularly at the upper ability levels. Regarding the relative efficiencies of the various formats, tht NEM learners differed in one striking way from SC learners in that the BC format was not efficient at any ability level, even the top octile. It did not seem efficient to have naval enlisted men learn from mere plain text.

It appears that overt responding should not be used in the absence of immediate feedback and small steps for low-ability learners, particularly when the motivation level is questionable. Where motivation is known to be low, the use of an overt-response feature without immediate feedback in the format of an instructional instrument is contra-indicated. If an instructional technologist does incur the time penalty of overt responding, he had better also introduce feedback, and hopefully, small steps. It would not be a sound practice to encourage or permit learners with low-ability and low-motivation levels to make mistakes since through the use of small steps, mistakes can be efficiently reduced to one quarter or one third. If for some reason large step-size must be used, immediate feedback should be present so that the mistakes can be promptly corrected.

Naval enlisted men were found to make significantly less errors on the small-step format (BRM/BRB) than on either of the large-step formats (OR and AE). The advantage of the small-step format may, of course, be due in part to the thematic prompting and the opportunity to reread text prior to responding. On all formats calling for overt responding, the error rate decreased significantly as scholastic ability increased. This occurred even in the presence of feedback, small steps, thematic prompting and the opportunity to reread text prior to responding. The inverse relationship was true for SC, JC, and NEM learners, and was particularly true at the upper levels of learner ability and where the formats incorporated the greater number of PI features. When ability level was held constant, there was a trend for SC learners to make the least errors, NEM the next least, and JC learners the most. Thus, nonintellective factors influence error behavior but, overall, were a weaker influence than were the intellective factors.

The learning yield of every format increased as ability increased. This pattern occurred regardless of the number and configuration of PI features employed. The direct relationship was true for SC, JC, and NEM learners, and was particularly true at the upper levels of learners ability and where the formats incorporated the greater number of PI features, such as immediate feedback, small steps, thematic prompting, and the opportunity to reread text prior to responding. When ability level was held constant, there was a trend for SC learners to acquire more learning yield than did the NEM learners, except on the BC format. Little difference was evident between the JC and NEM learners except that the NEM learners acquired more yield on the OR format. Thus, nonintellective factors influence learning yield, but overall, were a weaker influence than were the intellective factors.

Program time, in contrast to error rate and learning yield, was a function of nonintellective factors to as great an extent as it was a function of intellective factors. While there was a strong trend for program time to decrease as ability increased, the direction of influence of nonintellective factors upon program time was less systematic.

For learners who are naval enlisted men, the correlations between posttest corrects and scholastic ability decline in positive value at the lower ability levels. It appears, therefore, that the influence of ability upon learning drops off at the lower ability levels, and this relationship holds particularly true where learning is from reading plain text.

For learners who are naval enlisted men, the correlations between posttest corrects and program time were generally small in absolute magnitude. In comparing values across institutions, the most impressive finding is the previously noted elevated correlation on the OR format and the more positive values generally for JC learners. There seemed to be a closer relationship between the amount of time a JC learner spent on a program and how much he learned than there was for either the SC or the NEM learners. This trend held particularly true on the OR format. The earlier interpretation that the JC learners on the whole were taking insufficient time is further supported by comparing the JC correlations between program time and posttest corrects to the corresponding NEM correlations as well as to the corresponding SC correlations. The times taken by even the fastest of the SC and NEM learners were apparently long enough to eliminate most of the effects upon learning due to differences in the duration of exposure to the instructional materials.

12

Trends in Programmed Instruction

Contemporary PI techniques constitute only a few of the possible combinations of the PI principles and features. Some of these newer possible combinations can yield PI techniques which for some purposes are superior to those few techniques in vogue today. For example, a very efficient technique, in terms of posttest gain per unit time, was to have the learner simply read text and, then, read a series of test questions over that text, with the correct answers conspicuously indicated. This technique was far more efficient than its near relative, the auto-elucidative program, even though the auto-elucidative program is the only one of the two to incorporate the PI principle of overt responding.

Features of Contemporary Programmed Instruction Predicted to Trend Upward

Evolution of Programmed Instruction into a Technology

The field of PI will become a technology. For this development to occur, we must be able to draw upon research results which enable us to prescribe techniques for achieving specific instructional objectives with specific target populations. The research reported in this book was largely directed at discovering the optimal mix of PI principles for particular levels of learner ability. Efficiency indices were computed for these various configurations, some of which constituted conventional PI techniques. These indices help us approach the stage where we can make informed, albeit tentative, recommendations about how to teach "brights, normals, and dulls", at least in the area of associative learning.

More Empirical Testing

In the future, there will be more empirical testing of alternative instructional formats on a sample of learners from the target population before deciding on a particular format. In the present investigation, for state college learners in the top octile of ability, a conventional textbook was a fairly efficient teaching vehicle; whereas for learners in the next three octiles, it was very inefficient. The lower ability learners not only learned more but learned more per unit time from a text plus workbook, where they had an opportunity to respond overtly. However, for junior college learners comparable to the lower ability state college learners, overt responding was counter-productive and could only be recommended when coupled with immediate feedback and small-step size.

Eventual Popularization of Behavioral Analysis

While not a subject of study in the current investigation, behavioral analysis as described so ably by Mechner (1967), will gain increasing recognition. Not only will behavior be analyzed into "discriminations, generalizations, and chains", but the process will come to be accepted as a PI principle. In fact, it may supercede and incorporate the present-day principle of objective specification. Behavioral analysis will come to mean:

(*a*) specification of the behavioral objectives,
(*b*) analysis of the behavior in terms of its component discriminations, generalizations, and chains, and
(*c*) sequencing of these components for effective learning.

Behavioral analysis would therefore assume the status of a mandatory principle. However, not all of Mechner's recommendations are universally applicable. Hartley and Woods (1968), for example, failed to find support for Mechner's recommended "backward chaining" procedure for sequential learning. Learning a poem, last part first, did not prove superior to learning it first part first. Nevertheless, Mechner's formulations exemplify the kind of instructional tactics that are needed by programmers to guide their creative efforts, once the instructional objectives have been specified. Also helpful, but more at the strategic than at the tactical level, is Bruner's (1966) analysis of instructional technology. Every instructor should read his recommendations regarding how instruction should be sequenced and his discussion of activation, maintenance, and direction as essential parts of the instructional process.

Increasing Numbers of Success Experiences in Applying PI

Programs will continue to show that they can teach learners heretofore considered not to be at the age of "readiness". On the other hand, it will be a great many years before another claim of PI enthusiasts is realized. The claim is that the differences in posttest performances between the bright and dull learners will be converted mainly into differences in program time.

Persistence of Cultism in Programmed Instruction

These results will not deter programmers from prematurely "hardening" the formats into which they cast instructional material. However, these results will introduce a few more formats as candidates for the hardening process.

Features of Contemporary Programmed Instruction Predicted to Trend Downward

Less Uncritical Use of Remediation

Apart from the formulated principles of programmed instruction, there are a number of characteristic features possessed by some PI techniques but not by others. For example, consider the remediation used on branching programs. There is no compelling reason why branching programs should restate the question and the emitted response before telling the learner whether he was correct or incorrect. But branching programs tend to have this feature. They also typically supply the learner with remedial text on an error frame before returning him to the correct answer sequence. The present investigation found that branching programs without remediation teach about as much content per unit time as do those with remediation. Admittedly, there are occasions where remedial instruction is indicated. It is probable though that a good deal of the verbiage contained on the remedial frames of present-day scrambled textbooks is there to reduce conspicuous expanses of white space. Hopefully, this problem will be solved as book-presented branching programs give way to machine-presented branching programs.

Less Distractors in Test Items Used for Instructional Purposes

Today, there are certain arbitrary customs that characterize the existing PI techniques which actually hamper learning. Both the auto-elucidative and branching techniques make use of multiple-choice test items. Because multiple-choice items were originally designed for measurement purposes, there were functional reasons for having several distractors. However, for many learning applications, the less distractors, the better. Admittedly, there may be some classes of instructional objectives, such as the terminal stages of discrimination-making, for which several distractors would be desirable. However, it appears that the structural characteristics of test items in the branching and auto-elucidative techniques were adopted without sufficient empirical check by proponents of those techniques. The number of distractors will become less as their harmful effects become more widely appreciated.

Implications of the Present Investigation for the Linear Technique

While the linear technique was not investigated *per se* in these studies, the results have many implications, mostly favorable, for the linear technique *vis-à-vis* the branching and auto-elucidative. Like the branching technique, the linear incorporates all six of the mandatory and optional PI principles. Although the underlying rationales of the two techniques differ considerably, the main pragmatic differences are that the linear uses a linear frame sequence, a somewhat smaller step size, a lower error rate, a constructed response, and no remediation.

The present results support the linear technique with regard to small-step size. In fact, the linear technique is the prototype of a small-step format. The merit of the small-step principle was directly supported in the present studies in that, for all ability levels, those formats using small steps were among the highest in posttest gain and efficiency. The reason for the superiority of small steps may have been that among the PI formats of this investigation, small-step size, unlike large-step size, was associated with thematic prompting and the opportunity to reread text after viewing a test item. However, because this same confoundment exists among the PI techniques, the linear and branching techniques incorporating both thematic prompting and small- to medium-step size, the auto-elucidative technique incorporating both confirmation and large-step size, the present results are indirectly supportive of the linear technique with regard to step size.

The present results support the linear technique with regard to low-error rate. In comparing the state college and junior college learners, prompted and unprompted formats, and again in comparing two-response and three-response multiple-choice test items, the advocates of low-error rate were found to be correct in their insistence on keeping error to a minimum. Because the linear technique maintains the lowest error rate, it was supported by these results.

The present results do not support the linear technique with regard to constructed responses. Skinner (1958, p. 970) argues for the constructed response for two reasons:

(a) "we want the learner to recall rather than to recognize, – to make a response as well as see that it is right."
(b) "effective multiple-choice material must contain plausible wrong responses, which are out of place in the delicate process of 'shaping' behavior because they strengthen unwanted forms."

The present study is in agreement with Skinner's argument *(b),* at least for the introductory stages of instruction. His argument *(a),* although intuitively appealing, is too all-sweeping. If the various responses are already in the behavioral repertoire of the learner, selecting right answers from multiple-choice items has proven to be a useful procedure, at least for initial training. Moreover, Evans (1961) has successfully taught young children to "draw" the 10 digits by means of multiple-choice discrimination training, a procedure which prevented the children from practicing. Evans concluded that after learning to discriminate between correct and incorrect examples of numerals, the child is enabled to monitor the adequacy of his own productions. Ironically, Skinner (1961, p. 95), in arguing for the essentiality of constructed *versus* multiple-choice responses, states, "Our ability to remember wrong facts because we recall having read them somewhere is notorious." As detected by Klaus (1965), Skinner here confesses that facts can be remembered without necessarily having been overtly practiced.

The present study supports the linear technique in its avoidance of remediation. The experimental format, BRM-R, that lacked remediation, was a departure from a simulated branching technique in the direction of linear. The BRM-R compared favorably in efficiency to the BRB, indicating that among software formats, the omission of remediation makes for greater efficiency.

The present results also support the linear technique in confirming the degrading effects of program noise and miselicitation and nonelicitation of relevant responses. Proponents of the linear technique are the most scrupulous in editing out irrelevancies from the text and eliciting relevant responses.

Although the present investigation lends net support to the linear technique, it is still an open question as to whether the linear technique is the most efficient for all classes of learners and all classes of learning tasks. And the foregoing is not meant to imply that all of the Skinnerian arguments underlying the linear technique were also supported by the data. The central role of the hypothetical construct, reinforcement, was not proven, nor was there even evidence that the operant conditioning paradigm is the most fitting to account for what transpires in learning by means of programmed instruction. The key word is instruction. Instruction is guided direction by the teacher/program of the mentation and behavior of the student. The guidance should come first, certainly before an overt response. As Crowder points out, the emphasis should be on adequate communication that will enable the learner to emit the appropriate response when it is requested. In noninstructional settings, it may be that behavior is more randomly generated. If so, reinforcement would play a more important role in adaptive learning in the natural state of many organisms. However, it would be absurdly inefficient for an instructor not to guide the learner's behavior prior to elicitation. Only if the instructor is unable to evoke the appropriate response need he fall back upon shaping the behavior through selective reinforcement.

Skinnerian programmers are quite concerned with differentiation of responses, with linking responses to stimuli, and with discriminations between stimuli. These concerns lead them to concentrate initially upon eliciting existing responses from the learner's repertoire providing abundant stimulus support. Then, they gradually withdraw all of the parts of the stimulus configuration except the part that they wish ultimately to control the response. This focusing on the response has led too many Skinnerian novices to accept freely and to overemploy the formal prompt. Thus, a hasty indoctrination in Skinnerian "theory" frequently leads to programs only appropriate for teaching the types of learning low on Gagné's hierarchy. However, some Skinnerian programmers follow Skinner's programming practice rather than make their own free translations of Skinner's theory. These programmers use thematic prompting and create programs appropriate for teaching the higher-order learnings. Ironically, a literal translation of Skinner's theory, such as his shaping procedure, would be excellent for differentiating old responses or for teaching new responses. But linear programs are rarely directed at these particular instructional objectives, although there are many motor, language and social skills that require instructional programs.

Implications of the Present Investigation for Branching Technique

The branching technique rests, according to Crowder (1960), on a communications model. The function of the text is to teach, and the function of the test item is to find out if the learner has grasped an essential point in the text. Crowder declares (p. 288) that "the test result is used to control the behavior of the teaching machine and need not necessarily be furnished to the student at all. The student may immediately learn whether a given answer was 'right' or not, and presumably this is usually desirable, but the furnishing of this 'knowledge of result' to the student is not the primary purpose of the testing. The primary purpose is to determine whether the communication was successful, in order that correction steps may be taken by the machine if the communication process has failed."

Crowder's rationale for the text is correct. His rationale for the test item is incomplete. The test item helps:

(*a*) to focus attention upon vital points,
(*b*) to inform the learner that he has (almost always) learned correctly, and,
(*c*) (through causing the learner to emit a response) to strengthen the associative bonds.

The test item also enables the programmer to test the program empirically and revise it. It is too bad that some branching proponents either fail to test their material empirically or direct their secondary efforts at writing remedial material rather than improving the original text. In practice, many branching programmers unfortunately *dry-lab* the responses to the multiple-choice items; that is, they conjure up what they believe are logical errors for the learner to make. Whether one is constructing survey interview questionnaires, test items, or programmed instruction materials, it is very important to discover empirically what responses people actually make. In developing survey interview questionnaires, if one wants to end up with "poll-type" (multiple-choice) questions, it is still established procedure to commence with "open-ended" questions, in order to ascertain what the most typical responses will be. In developing tests if one wants to end up with multiple-choice questions, it is still established procedure to commence with completion-type questions in order to generate some realistic and appealing distractors. Pressey, in developing the multiple-choice test items for his auto-elucidative technique, specifies that essay questions should be used to detect the actual misconceptions that learners acquire from reading he expository text. The responses made to these questions by a pilot group of learners are used as distractors on the multiple-choice test items in the auto-elucidative technique.

Branching programs, if they truly underwent the empirical testing typical of linear programs, would perhaps grow to resemble linear programs more closely. Let us anticipate that someday a branching programmer will empirically test the text of each branching frame coupled with a completion-type test question. From the responses of a pilot sample of learners, he finds that the frame lends itself to one or two misinterpretations. What is now his most sensible action in order to conserve his own time and effort and that of the learner? Should he write remedial frames for each misconceptualization, or rewrite the original frame so that it is more lucid? When is the best time for a program "to adapt to the learner"; before it is published or after?

The preceding does not rule out the branching tactic altogether in programmed instruction. Branching can be used on certain critical frames to track learners onto sequences lean or fat in redundancy. It can be used in the terminal stages of the training of trouble shooters or internes. It can be used to grant the learner an option with regard to aspects of a topic in which he is interested. Form should follow function, and in each of the above examples, there is a definite need for the branching function. However, many existing programs in branching format are directed at teaching rudimentary skills, and these programs branch on every paragraph or two. Such usage would seem to be a misapplication of a programming tool.

Implications of the Present Investigation for the Auto-Elucidative Technique

Pressey (1926) declares that "other things being equal, the response which has been made most often, and most recently, is most likely to be made again." Thus, it could be argued that the auto-elucidative technique has some theoretical basis in the law of frequency and the law of postremity (referred to by Pressey as the law of recency.). The law of postremity could be invoked even in today's "trainer-tester response cards" because the correct response is the last one made. It could also be argued that the auto-elucidative technique has a theoretical basis in the law of effect since indicating to a learner that his response is correct is satisfying to him. However, Pressey's descriptions of his technique are usually based not on theory, but on straightforward evidence that his original hardware device and its contemporary software manifestations do teach.

Many, including Gilbert (1960), have argued that the form and structure of a program be tailored to the instructional objectives and not be constrained by the nature of available gadgets. The wisdom of this advice is borne out by:

(a) the fact that Pressey's (1950) original device was designed in part to perform an automatic testing function, and
(b) by the relatively poor showing of the experimental format (AE) simulating the auto-elucidative technique.

The auto-elucidative technique as it stands today is the heir of an unwise decision to test and teach simultaneously. Unfortunately, this decision compelled the technique to forego prompting for confirmation. It also resulted in small-step units of text reading not being interspersed with the test items and in error rate not being small.

In the future, it would appear that users of the auto-elucidative technique would be limited to those persons having a considerable investment in existing instructional materials in conventional format. If the number of trainees were too small to warrant the expense of redoing the material in a format incorporating objective specification, empirical testing, and small-step size, the trainer, at the end of conventional instruction, could simply give the trainees some critical test questions over the material and have them respond on the trainer-tester response cards. Of course, under these same circumstances, the trainer might more profitably administer the test questions formally prompted according to the AE-OR format style. Not only would the prompted questions be less expensive, they would probably teach more effectively and in less time.

Implications of the Present Investigation for Computer-assisted-instruction

Computer-assisted-instruction (CAI) ranges in nature from nothing more than expensive page-turners for branching programs to sophisticated systems following strategies having little in common with mainstream PI. Where the programs are simply branching they serve an another exemplification of the gadget-centeredness of which Gilbert warned us. Just because the branching program is presented by a computer does not negate its shortcomings. As with any program:

(a) prior to publication, the text plus completion type test items should be tested empirically,
(b) improvements should be primarily in the form of revisions, not in the form of remedial material,

(c) when multiple-choice items have to be used, the response options should be based on earlier responses actually emitted by pilot study learners, and,
(d) distractors should be minimized.

At least one CAI researcher, Coulson (1961), has already ceased using the same test items for both teaching and diagnosis.

If these few guidelines were followed, then perhaps a greater proportion of effort would be directed at exploring new ways for a computer to assist instruction. Some interesting developments are reported by Licklider (1961). He has used a computer to control conditional progression from one section of a course to another and also has faded in prompts as a function of response latency. This latter development is one example of how the technological capabilities of the computer may eventually displace such a PI principle as self-pacing. In addition, Licklider is examining the potential of a computer for student-controlled exploration and investigation and for teaching the relations between the algebraic and graphical representations of mathematical functions.

The researchers in CAI might take a hint from Skinner (1968, p. 218). He suggests that the correct response could be revealed in stages so that the learner, after emitting an erroneous constructed response, could:

(a) discover that his emitted response was incorrect, and then,
(b) receive some additional (formal) prompting which would permit him to emit the correct response and secure reinforcement.

Without necessarily adopting Skinner's reinforcement rationale, we could agree that the prompted correct response thus elicited would be preferable to the mere copying response performed on linear programs following an erroneous response. The prompted response is more likely to be associated with the controlling relations of the stimulus configuration. We could, also, for the same reason, agree with Skinner's further recommendation that the prompting be thematic. It would be a simple matter for a computer to supply the learner some essential feature possessed by the correct response but not by the incorrect response emitted by the learner. While such prompting might resemble present-day remediational frames, the prompts would be shorter, more trenchant and more helpful.

CAI has the potential for enhancing student motivation above present levels by permitting a student to select, to a large extent, the sequence with which groupings of substantive material are presented. Furthermore, in the terminal stages of training in professional and technical skills CAI could assume much of the training presently accomplished through internships or practicums. Let us consider for example, the residency period in medical training. Many of the objectives of this training period could be accomplished by CAI. Various syndromes could be stored in the memory of a computer. A pattern of presenting symptoms could be supplied by the computer to the student-doctor. He then could attempt a differential diagnosis by sequentially requesting various tests. The computer, by requiring him to state his tentative diagnostic impressions as he proceeded, could not only rectify gross errors of judgment but could finely tune his diagnostic skills by pointing out how certain critical tests should have occurred earlier in a sequence or that the sequence of tests was not parsimonious in time and effort, and hence suboptimal. One of the deficiencies in having a fledging doctor spend a short period on a certain ward of a general hospital is that he may never encounter many of the rarer diseases which are nevertheless important to detect. A computer can remedy this shortcoming by insuring that all such disease conditions are presented for detection despite their rarity. Moreover, CAI could be used for refresher training or for up-grading of doctors in private practice or in remote localities. Even doctors in group practice close to research centers require continual training to keep abreast of the state of the art. An additional by-product of such training would be that it might encourage the next generation of doctors to utilize computers as ancillary aids.

The Future of the Techniques

To the degree that a true technology of instruction develops, the cultish aspects of the present-day PI schools will recede. Auto-elucidation will drop out as a viable technique since the unhappy combination of large-steps and confirmation cannot be rescued and should be scrapped outright. Some training directors and educators have been attracted to the auto-elucidation technique because it seemed to make possible the salvaging of existing instructional materials in conventional format at small expense. These parties might consider the formally prompted AE-OR techniques.

There will be a melding of the linear and branching techniques. Linear programmers do some right things (use prompting, small steps, and low-error rate) for an oversimplified reason (to achieve reinforcement of an emitted response). Branching programmers do some wrong things (which were itemized earlier) for the right reasons (to try to enable the learner to emit a correct response).

Let us anticipate the form and structure that programs will assume a few years hence. For Simplicity, we will restrict our concern to programs directed at teaching content to learners of intermediate ability. A greater proportion of the programs will be presented by computer than at present. The sequence will be primarily linear, but there will be branching at frequent critical test frames. All the text will have been empirically pretested on pilot study learners emitting constructed responses. Revisions will have been primarily in the text although remedial sequences will have been written for each "wrong" response to occasional "critical" or "test" frames.

There will be more text per frame than in present-day linear programs, but thematic prompting will be used heavily to keep error rate low enough to please Skinnerians. The pacing on the CAI programs will be modified self-pacing. The computer will measure the individual learner's preferred rate and accelerate it moderately. This development will be accomplished by formal prompting (fading in cues) and additional thematic prompting (asking leading questions or presenting analogies).

The computer will adapt the program according to the learner's attributes, his age, ability, etc. Adaptation will not be limited to just adding or deleting redundant text. The computer will also alter the form and structure of the frames. The older learners will be treated as more task-oriented and given terse KCR. The younger will be treated as more ego-involved and given encouragement.

Validity data will be gathered automatically and standards of quality will be accepted and enforced. The present day emphasis on techniques will give way to an emphasis on the optimum combination of PI features to accomplish specific objectives with specific target groups of learners.

Appendix A

The Frames of the BRM (&BRB) Format

Instructions

This is a programmed textbook about the structure and function of the human eye. The text material is presented paragraph by paragraph in small steps. At the end of each paragraph you will find a multiple-choice question about the information contained in the paragraph. The paragraph of text plus the test question is referred to as a frame.

The answers to the questions are contained in the envelopes on the page to the right of the frame. In working through the book you will take the following steps:

(1) read the paragraph of text material;
(2) read the question and alternate answers of the test item;
(3) choose the answer you believe to be correct and open the envelope marked with the same letter as the answer you believe to be correct;
(4) follow the instructions contained in the envelope.

There is only **one** correct answer for each question; you must keep choosing answers until the correct one is located. You may re-examine a text paragraph as much as you like before answering the question.

In the response receptacle with which you have been provided there are two compartments. One compartment is for the opened envelopes and the other is for the answer sheets contained in the envelopes. Keep them separate.

During your reading you will be referred to another booklet labeled "Figures." These figures are drawings or illustrations which are useful in understanding the text. You may refer to these figures as often as you wish, but do not advance to a new figure until told to do so by the text.

The first frame is a sample to help you become familiar with the format of the book. Work through it. If you do not understand how to work through the program, raise your hand and ask the proctor to help you.

When you have completed the entire book, so signify to the proctor.

YOU MAY TURN THE PAGE AND BEGIN

Sample Frame

This is a sample frame. The remainder of this book is identical in format to this frame. When you finish reading this paragraph you may answer the question below. Choose the answer which you find most correct. Note that the envelopes on the right page correspond to the answers given below, i.e. (a), (b), and (c). After you have chosen an answer open the corresponding envelope and follow the instructions it contains. On any given frame you may choose one, two, or all three of the answers before you choose the correct one. KEEP CHOOSING until you do find the ONE right answer for that frame.

Regarding this sample frame which of the following is a true statement?
(a) I do not understand how to work this textbook
(b) I understand completely how to work this textbook
(c) I am lost!

Frame 1

The front or foremost covering of the eyeball is a transparent membrane known as the cornea. To the rear, behind the cornea are two cavities, connecting with one another, which are called, going from the outside inward, the anterior and posterior chambers. In the normal eye these two chambers are filled with a clear fluid known as the aqueous humour. (See Fig. 1)

Regarding the eyeball structures, which of the following is true?
(a) The **anterior** chamber contains **vitreous** humour.
(b) The **anterior** chamber contains **aqueous** humour.
(c) The **posterior** chamber contains **vitreous** humour.

REMEDIATION FOR FRAME 1

Frame 1 Answer a

You responded that the anterior chamber contains vitreous humour.
WRONG
Note again Fig. 1. See that the anterior chamber is in front of the lens, and that the vitreous humour is located behind the lens.
Deposit answer and envelope in their receptacles.
Return to frame 1 and select another answer.

Frame 1 Answer b

You responded that the anterior chamber contains aqueous humour.
CORRECT
Deposit answer and envelope in their receptacles.
Advance to the next frame of the text.

Frame 1 Answer c

You responded that the posterior chamber contains vitreous humour.

WRONG

Note again Fig. 1. See that the posterior chamber is in front of the lens and that the vitreous humour is behind the lens.

Deposit answer and envelope in their receptacles.

Return to frame 1 and select another answer.

Frame 2

The anterior and posterior chambers are separated by a pigmented structure, known as the iris, which gives the eye its color. The iris forms an adjustable diaphragm in front of the lens; the aperture of this diaphragm is called the pupil. (See Fig. 1)

Regarding eyeball structure, which of the following is true?

(a) The pupil surrounds the iris.
(b) The lens forms an adjustable diaphragm around an aperture.
(c) The iris surrounds the pupil.

Frame 3

Located directly behind the iris is the lens of the eye. During the visual processes the lens, because of its elastic structure, is contracted and expanded by its two supporting structures (one on either side) which are called the suspensory ligaments. (See Fig. 1)

Regarding eyeball structures, which of the following is true? The function of the suspensory ligaments is to contract and expand the

(a) lens
(b) pupil
(c) iris

Frame 4

To the rear of the lens is located the largest chamber of the eye. This chamber extends from the back of the lens to the rear wall of the eyeball. The chamber is filled with a clear fluid, mostly water, called the vitreous humour. (See Fig. 1)

Regarding the eyeball structures, which of the following is true?

The vitreous humour is located

(a) between the iris and the lens
(b) between the lens and the rear wall of the eye
(c) between the cornea and the lens

Frame 5

The human eye is covered by three tissue coats. The outer-most of these coats is called the sclerotic coat, and helps to form the characteristic shape of the eyeball. The sclerotic coat also provides an attachment for the extrinsic movement muscles of the eye. The second or middle tissue coat contains pigment and is known as the choroid coat.

Regarding eyeball structures, which of the following is true?
(a) The innermost coat is the sclerotic.
(b) The innermost coat is the choroid.
(c) The outermost coat is the sclerotic.

Frame 6

The third and innermost tissue coat of the eye is the retina. The retina contains a specialized visual area, known as the fovea, which occupies an indented region located in the center of the rear wall of the eye. The retina is composed of neural tissue, and is the only part of the central nervous system which can be observed without the use of surgical techniques.

Regarding eyeball structure, which of the following is true?
(a) The fovea is the tissue coat in front of the retina.
(b) The retina is the tissue coat which contains the fovea.
(c) The fovea is the tissue coat which contains the retina.

Frame 7

The retina contains three layers of cells. The innermost layer, which lies against the vitreous humour, is called the ganglion layer. The middle layer is called the bipolar layer, and the outermost layer is called the rod and cone layer. Each of these three layers is named after the type of cells from which it is constructed. (See Fig. 2)

Incoming light waves strike which layer of the retina first?
(a) Ganglion
(b) Bipolar
(c) Rod and cone

Frame 8

At a point slightly to the nasal side of the fovea, the optic nerve pierces the rear wall of the eye at an area called the optic disc. The optic nerve is made-up of nerve fibers coming from the ganglion layer of the retina. (See Figs. 1 and 2)

Regarding eyeball structures, which of the following is true?
The optic nerve is made-up of nerve fibers coming from the
(a) outermost, or bipolar layer of the retina.
(b) middlemost, or ganglion layer of the retina.
(c) innermost, or ganglion layer of the retina.

Frame 9

Each optic nerve exchanges neural fibers with its counterpart at a point, known as the optic chiasma, which is located internally mid-way between the eyes. From the optic chiasma the neural pathways (right and left) which contain fibers from each optic nerve, continue inward to their termination in the primary visual center of the occipital lobe located on their respective side of the brain.

In the brain, the primary visual center is located in the
(a) optic chiasma
(b) occipital lobe
(c) parietal lobe

Frame 10

The stimuli to which the human eye is sensitive are radiations from the electromagnetic spectrum. The electromagnetic spectrum is composed of waves of energy varying in length from very short gamma waves to the extremely long radio waves. The eye can see (sense) only those electromagnetic waves which lie in the visual area located between the shorter ultraviolet waves and the longer infrared waves. Thus, the visual area is confined to energy waves having an approximate length of about 400 to 700 millimicrons. (See Fig. 3)

The stimuli from the electromagnetic spectrum which the retina is ordinarily sensitive to are
(a) longer than the ultraviolet waves.
(b) shorter than the gamma waves.
(c) longer than the infrared waves.

Frame 11

The phenomenon we perceive as color is influenced by three **physical** attributes of the electromagnetic waves. These three variables are the wavelength, the intensity, and the relative purity of a particular wavelength. However, the colors which a person perceives can also be described in terms of psychological dimensions which correspond approximately to the above physical ones. The **psychological** dimensions of color are:
hue, which corresponds to physical wavelength;
brightness, which corresponds to physical intensity;
saturation, which corresponds to the physical purity of the electromagnetic wave.

The perception of color is influenced by which of the following physical properties of electromagnetic stimulation?
(a) Brightness, wavelength, purity
(b) Wavelength, intensity, saturation
(c) Intensity, purity, wavelength

Frame 12

The eye perceives four primary colors from the electromagnetic spectrum. These four primary colors are: blue (450 millimicrons); green (550 millimicrons); yellow (590 millimicrons); red (700 millimicrons). (See Fig. 3) Combinations of the primary colors can be perceived as intermediate colors. White (or gray) is perceived by combining all of the primary colors, and black is the total absence of color stimulation. Certain colors are said to be complementary to one another; that is, if they are mixed together the resulting combination will appear as gray. Three complementary pairs of color stimuli are: red-green, blue-yellow, and black-white.

In the visual portion of the electromagnetic spectrum the four primary colors (from longest to shortest wavelength) are:
(a) red, yellow, green, violet
(b) blue, green, yellow, red
(c) red, yellow, green, blue

Frame 13

Waves of light entering the eye are refracted by the eye's internal structures, but most importantly by the lens. The phenomenon of refraction occurs whenever there are changes in the density of the media through which light passes. As light rays pass through a surface from a less dense to a more dense medium – as is the case when light passes from the aqueous humour to the lens – the rays, in effect, bend or refract toward a line perpendicular to the surface at the point of crossing. The degree of refraction phenomenon depends upon the angle at which light enters the lens which, in turn, depends upon the degree of curvature of the front lens surface. (See Fig. 4)

When a light ray passes from the aqueous humour to the lens it will refract
(a) toward a line perpendicular to the surface at the point of crossing.
(b) toward a line tangent to the surface at the point of crossing.
(c) away from a line perpendicular to the surface at the point of crossing.

Frame 14

As light rays pass through a surface from a more dense to a less dense medium – as is the case when light rays pass from the lens to the vitreous humour – the light rays, in effect, bend or refract away from a line perpendicular to the surface at the point of crossing. The degree of bending depends upon the angle at which the light leaves the lens which, in turn, depends upon the degree of curvature of the rear lens surface. (See Fig. 4)

When a light ray passes from the lens to the vitreous humour it will refract
(a) away from a line tangent to the surface at the point of crossing.
(b) away from a line perpendicular to the surface at the point of crossing.
(c) toward a line perpendicular to the surface at the point of crossing.

Frame 15

The lens of the eye is geometrically biconvex in form, that is, both the front and rear surfaces are convex in shape. The cumulative effect of both refractions (at the front and rear surfaces of the lens) is to cause the light waves to converge and thus focus on a point rearward of the lens . . . and then to diverge and project an image on the retina which is both inverted (upside-down) and virtual (reversed). The inverted and virtual image is perceived as upright and normal by the viewer, a phenomenon which is learned by the organism. The inverted and virtual image is clearest on a certain plane. Optimally this plane of clear image will fall on the visual receptors of the retina. Whether or not the plane of clear image falls on the retina is controlled by the degree of convexity or bulging of the lens, that is, the lens bulges as the eye fixates near objects, and flattens as the eye fixates far objects. This variable focusing movement is called accommodation, and is made necessary by the change in the angle of entering light rays due to change in distance. (See Fig. 4)

To change focus from a distant to a near object the lens would
(a) flatten
(b) bulge
(c) become more dense

Frame 16

In some eyes, either the eyeball is abnormally long, or the lens is unable to flatten enough to allow the plane of clear image for far objects to fall on the retina. When one of these defects occurs, the resulting abnormal condition is known as myopia or nearsightedness. (See Fig. 5)

If an eyeball were abnormally long, which condition would most likely result?
(a) Farsightedness
(b) Under-refraction
(c) Nearsightedness

Frame 17

In some eyes the eyeball is abnormally short or the lens is unable to bulge enough to allow the plane of clear image for near objects to fall on the retina. When defects of this type occur, the resulting abnormal condition is known as hypermetropia or farsightedness.
If the lens is unable to bulge enough to project the plane of clear image on the retina the condition most likely to result is
(a) farsightedness
(b) nearsightedness
(c) over-refraction

Frame 18

As a person grows older the lens of the eye tends to lose some of its characteristic elasticity. Because of this phenomenon the lens is no longer able to accommodate to a degree adequate for normal vision, and, thus, the viewed image is often blurred and out of focus. This condition is known as presbyopia, and is often accompanied by the formation of opaque areas in the lens . . . called cataracts. The formation of cataracts prevents the incoming light rays from reaching the receptors in the retina, and, so, a portion of the perceived image will be totally absent. As cataracts become larger and increase in number the person will eventually become blind.

Which of the following would most likely be a causative factor in the development of presbyopia?
(a) Advancing age
(b) Large cataracts
(c) Opaque blindness

Frame 19

The human visual system is binocular in structure, that is, it contains two eyes and their accessory structures. During the evolutionary process both eyes have moved to the front of the head; because of this arrangement man is able to focus both eyes simultaneously on the same object. This type of visual system is called stereoscopic. Stereoscopic vision provides man with many of the cues which are necessary for the perception of depth.

In regard to man's stereoscopic visual system, which of the following is true?
(a) It allows binocular vision to develop.
(b) It provides cues for depth perception.
(c) It allows each eye to focus independently on different objects.

Frame 20

Fusion is a neurological phenomenon which is partially responsible for the perception of depth. In the process of fusion the separate images from each eye are seen as one by the observer. Fusion takes place primarily where the fibers from the separate optic nerves exchange at the optic chiasma before continuing inward to the visual centers of the brain.

Regarding fusion, which of the following is true?
(a) It allows the observer to see a separate object with each eye.
(b) It takes place primarily at the optic chiasma.
(c) It is caused, in part, by the perception of depth.

Frame 21

In order for fusion to occur the viewed image must fall on approximately the same retinal area of each eye simultaneously; thus, both eyeballs must adjust themselves to view an object at about the same angle relative to the plane of the central axis of each eye. This lining up action of the eyeballs is called convergence, and it is accomplished by the extrinsic muscles of each eye. (See Fig. 6)

In regard to convergence, which of the following is a true statement?
(a) It allows simultaneous stimulation of the same retinal area.
(b) It is caused by movements of the intrinsic eye muscles.
(c) It occurs as a result of fusion.

Frame 22

Sensory excitation in the eye takes place in the outermost of the three neural layers of the retina. This outer layer, in contact with the choroid coat, contains the eye's two types of stimuli receptors . . . the rods and cones. (See Fig. 2).

The rods and cones are located in the
(a) innermost layer of the retina.
(b) next to the retina.
(c) outermost layer of the retina.

Frame 23

The rods are the eye's receptors for dim light vision. The rods are totally color blind, and see all visual stimuli as varying shades of gray. The dim light and color blind reception by the rods is known as scotopic vision. The rods are twice as numerous as the cones (the retina's second type of receptor), and are located in the peripheral areas of the retina. Two areas of the retina contain no rods; the first is the fovea, and the second is the optic disc which is often called the 'blind spot' because it contains no receptors of any kind.

Which of the following statements is true?
(a) There are no cones in the fovea.
(b) There are approximately twice as many rods as cones in the optic disc.
(c) There are no rods in the fovea.

Frame 24

The rods adapt to dimmer light conditions by means of a visual pigment they contain . . . called rhodopsin. Rhodopsin is often called visual purple because of its characteristic dark blue color. The raw material from which rhodopsin is made is vitamin A, and, thus, a deficiency of vitamin A will result in poor dim-light vision.

Which of the following statements regarding rhodopsin is true?
(a) It contains a pigment called visual purple.
(b) It becomes deficient in the presence of vitamin A.
(c) It is dark blue in color.

Frame 25

Receptors of a second type in the retina are the flask-shaped cones. These structures are responsible for the visual perception of bright light and color. This type of color and high intensity reception by the cones is known as photopic vision. There are approximately one-half the number of cones as there are rods in the retina.

Which of the following statements is true?
(a) The dimmer the light the more responsible for vision are the cones.
(b) The dimmer the light the more responsible for vision are the rods.
(c) The rods enable the visual perception of color.

Frame 26

Like the rods, the cones are scattered randomly throughout the periphery of the retina, but, unlike the rods, the majority of them are packed into the indented region of the fovea. Because of the concentration of receptors in its relatively small area, the fovea possesses the most acute bright light and color vision of any portion of the retina.

Which of the following is true?
(a) The periphery of the retina contains no cones.
(b) The periphery of the retina contains no rods.
(c) Most bright light receptors are in the fovea.

Frame 27

Visual acuity is the ability to distinguish detail in images projected on the retina. Visual acuity is better for close objects than for far objects, because at close range the eye is able to perceive much more accurately the spatial pattern of a viewed object. Visual acuity increases in direct relation to the number of receptors which are stimulated, and, thus, the fovea is the area of maximum acuity for bright light and color vision. For dim light vision, acuity is best in the peripheral areas of the retina where the greatest concentration of rods are located; however, visual acuity under dim light conditions is never as good as it is under bright light conditions.

Regarding visual acuity, which of the following is true?
(a) It is greatest in the fovea.
(b) It is greatest in the periphery of the retina.
(c) It is greatest under dim light conditions.

Frame 28

Color blindness is a sex-linked characteristic which occurs more often in males than in females. The most common type of color blindness is called dichromatism. A person afflicted with dichromatism is unable to perceive or define either of the two primary colors . . . red and green.

Which of the following would be the most probable if you knew only that a person was color blind?
(a) The color blindness is for reds, yellows, greens and blues.
(b) The color blindness is for reds and greens only.
(c) The color blindness is for blues and yellows only.

Frame 29

Occasionally, a person is born totally color blind; this condition is called achromatism, and is one in which the eye perceives all visual stimuli as varying shades of gray. In achromatism the fovea is totally blind and all visual perception is accomplished by the rods. An achromatic person is unable to see in very bright light.

Which of the following is true of a person having achromatism?
(a) He sees only the primary colors.
(b) He has no rod vision.
(c) He has no cone vision.

Frame 30

Color vision is not universal throughout the animal kingdom. Fish, bees and birds have color vision, but most mammals do not. An exception to this rule are the primates, the order to which man belongs. Monkeys and the great apes possess various degrees of color vision, and the chimpanzee has a structural and perceptual visual system which is almost identical to that of man.

Regarding color vision, which of the following is true?
(a) Most mammals see at least the primary colors.
(b) Primates have some color perception.
(c) Birds and bees are typically color blind.

YOU ARE NOW FINISHED.
MAKE SURE THAT YOUR NAME IS CLEARLY **PRINTED**, LAST NAME FIRST, WHERE IT IS SUPPOSED TO BE.
RAISE YOUR HAND TO SIGNAL THE ROOM PROCTOR.
AFTER YOUR MATERIALS ARE CHECKED BY THE PROCTOR YOU ARE FREE TO LEAVE.

REMEMBER TO RETURN IN ONE WEEK TO COMPLETE THE SECOND PART OF THIS STUDY.

Appendix B

The Instruction Sheets of the Other Experimental Formats

BC

Instructions

This is a programmed textbook about the structure and function of the human eye.

During your reading you will be referred to another booklet labeled "Figures." These figures are drawings or illustrations which are useful in understanding the text. You may refer to these figures as often as you wish, but do not advance to a new figure until told to do so by the text.

If you do not understand how to work through the program, raise your hand and ask the proctor to help you.

When you have completed the entire book, so signify to the proctor.

YOU MAY TURN THE PAGE AND BEGIN

CR

Instructions

This is a programmed textbook about the structure and function of the human eye. The book is divided into two sections. At the end of each section are 15 study questions which refer to the text material just read.

For each study question three possible answers are shown. One of the three answers will be the **correct** answer. You may study the question and three answers as much as you wish. However, you are not being asked to identify the correct answer, and hence you will have no need of pencil or paper. In working through the book you will take the following steps:

(1) read the first half of the text material;
(2) read each of the 15 study questions. In each case, examine the three possible answers noting the one which is correct and the two which are not correct. There is only **one** correct answer to each question.
(3) read the second half of the text;
(4) read each of the 15 study questions following the second half of the text.

You may **not** re-examine the preceding text as you examine the study questions.

During your reading you will be referred to another booklet labeled "Figures." These figures are drawings or illustrations which are useful in understanding the text. You may refer to these figures as often as you wish, but do not advance to a new figure until told to do so by the text. **When studying the questions, however, keep the booklet of figures closed.**

If you do not understand how to work through the program, raise your hand and ask the proctor to help you.

When you have completed the entire book, so signify to the proctor.

YOU MAY TURN THE PAGE AND BEGIN

OR

Instructions

This is a programmed textbook about the structure and function of the human eye. The book is divided into two sections. At the end of each section are 15 multiple choice questions which refer to the text material just read.

Each question will have three possible answers identified as (a), (b), or (c). On the answer sheet provided notice that there are 30 lines, numbered 1 through 30. Each line contains three circles also identified as (a), (b), or (c). To respond to a question, locate on the answer sheet the line of circles whose number corresponds to the number on the question. Then choose the answer, (a), (b), or (c), which you believe to be correct. Blacken in the circle in the proper column on the answer sheet. There is only **one** correct answer for each question.

When you have finished a section of text do **not** refer back to it when answering the questions.

During your reading you will be referred to another booklet labeled "Figures." These figures are drawings or illustrations which are useful in understanding the text. You may refer to these figures as often as you wish, but do not advance to a new figure until told to do so by the text. **When answering the questions, however, keep the booklet of figures closed.**

If you do not understand how to work through the program, raise your hand and ask the proctor to help you.

When you have completed the entire book, so signify to the proctor.

YOU MAY TURN THE PAGE AND BEGIN

AE

Instructions

This is a programmed textbook about the structure and function of the human eye. The book is divided into two sections. At the end of each section are 15 multiple choice questions which refer to the text material just read.

Each question will have three possible answers identified as (a), (b), or (c). On the answer card provided notice that there are 30 lines, numbered 1 through 30. Each line contains three dots also identified as (a), (b), or (c). To respond to a question, locate on the card the line of dots whose number corresponds to the number on the question. Then choose the answer, (a), (b), or (c), which you believe to be correct. Erase the black dot in the proper column on the answer card. If your response is correct you will find the letter **R** under the dot, and you may then proceed to the next question. However, if your response is incorrect, you will find the letter **X** under the dot, and you must then make another choice for that question. On each question, keep choosing answers, and erasing dots, until you locate the correct answer indicated by **R**. There is only **one** correct answer for each question.

When you have finished a section of text do **not** refer back to it when answering the questions.

During your reading you will be referred to another booklet labeled "Figures." These figures are drawings or illustrations which are useful in understanding the text. You may refer to these figures as often as you wish, but do not advance to a new figure until told to do so by the text. **When answering the questions, however, keep the booklet of figures closed.**

If you do not understand how to work through the program, or how to use the answer card, raise your hand and ask the proctor to help you.

When you have completed the entire book, so signify to the proctor.

YOU MAY TURN THE PAGE AND BEGIN

BRM-R

Instructions

This is a programmed textbook about the structure and function of the human eye. The text material is presented paragraph by paragraph in small steps. At the end of each paragraph you will find a multiple choice question about the information contained in the paragraph. The paragraph of text plus the test question is referred to as a frame.

Each question will have three possible answers identified as (a), (b), or (c). On the answer card provided you notice that there are 30 lines, numbered 1 through 30. Each line contains three dots also identified as (a), (b), or (c). To respond to the question on a frame, locate on the card the line of dots whose number corresponds to the number on the frame containing the question. Then choose the answer, (a), (b), or (c), which you believe to be correct. Erase the black dot in the proper column on the answer card. If your response is correct you will find the letter **R** under the dot, and you may then proceed to the next frame of material. However, if your response is incorrect, you will find the letter **X** under the dot, and you must then make another choice for that question. On each question keep choosing answers, and erasing dots, until you locate the correct answer indicated by **R**. There is only **one** correct answer for each question.

You may re-examine a text paragraph as much as you like before answering the question.

During your reading you will be referred to another booklet labeled "Figures." These figures are drawings or illustrations which are useful in understanding the text. You may refer to these figures as often as you wish, but do not advance to a new figure until told to do so by the text.

If you do not understand how to work through the program, or how to use the answer card, raise your hand and ask the proctor to help you.

When you have completed the entire book, so signify to the proctor.

YOU MAY TURN THE PAGE AND BEGIN

BRM-F

Instructions

This is a programmed textbook about the structure and function of the human eye. The text material is presented paragraph by paragraph in small steps. At the end of each paragraph you will find a multiple-choice question about the information contained in the paragraph. The paragraph of text plus the test question is referred to as a frame.

Each question will have three possible answers identified as (a), (b), or (c). On the answer sheet provided you notice that there are 30 lines, numbered 1 through 30. Each line contains three circles also identified as (a), (b), or (c). To respond to the question on a frame, locate on the answer sheet the line of circles whose number corresponds to the number on the frame containing the question. Then choose the answer, (a), (b), or (c), which you believe to be correct. Blacken in the circle in the proper column on the answer sheet. In working through the book you will take the following steps:

(1) read the paragraph of text material;
(2) read the question and the alternate answers of the test item;
(3) choose the answer you believe to be correct and blacken in the circle marked with the same letter as the answer you believe to be correct.
There is only **one** correct answer for each question.

You may re-examine a text paragraph as much as you like before answering the question.

During your reading you will be referred to another booklet labeled "Figures." These figures are drawings or illustrations which are useful in understanding the text. You may refer to these figures as often as you wish, but do not advance to a new figure until told to do so by the text.

If you do not understand how to work through the program, raise your hand and ask the proctor to help you.

When you have completed the entire book, so signify to the proctor.

YOU MAY TURN THE PAGE AND BEGIN

BRM-OR

Instructions

This is a programmed textbook about the structure and function of the human eye. The text material is presented paragraph by paragraph in small steps. At the end of each paragraph you will find a study question about the information contained in the paragraph. The paragraph of text plus the study question is referred to as a frame.

For each study question three possible answers are shown. The **correct** answer is indicated by an asterisk (*) in front of it. In working through the book you will take the following steps:

(1) read the paragraph of text material;
(2) read the study question;
(3) examine the three possible answers noting the one which is correct and the two which are not correct. There is only **one** correct answer for each question.

You may re-examine a text paragraph as much as you like as you examine the study question.

During your reading you will be referred to another booklet labeled "Figures." These figures are drawings or illustrations which are useful in understanding the text. You may refer to these figures as often as you wish, but do not advance to a new figure until told to do so by the text.

If you do not understand how to work through the program, raise your hand and ask the proctor to help you.

When you have completed the entire book, so signify to the proctor.

YOU MAY TURN THE PAGE AND BEGIN

AE-OR

Instructions

This is a programmed textbook about the structure and function of the human eye. The book is divided into two sections. At the end of each section are 15 study questions which refer to the text material just read.

For each study question three possible answers are shown. The **correct** answer is indicated by an asterisk (*) in front of it. In working through the book you will take the following steps:

(1) read the first half of the text material;
(2) read each of the 15 study questions. In each case, examine the three possible answers noting the one which is correct and the two which are not correct. There is only **one** correct answer to each question.
(3) read the second half of the text;
(4) read each of the 15 study questions following the second half of the text.

You may **not** re-examine the preceding text as you examine the study questions.

During your reading you will be referred to another booklet labeled "Figures." These figures are drawings or illustrations which are useful in understanding the text. You may refer to these figures as often as you wish, but do not advance to a new figure until told to do so by the text. **When studying the questions, however, keep the booklet of figures closed.**

If you do not understand how to work through the program, raise your hand and ask the proctor to help you.

When you have completed the entire book, so signify to the proctor.

YOU MAY TURN THE PAGE AND BEGIN

Appendix C

The Six Illustrations

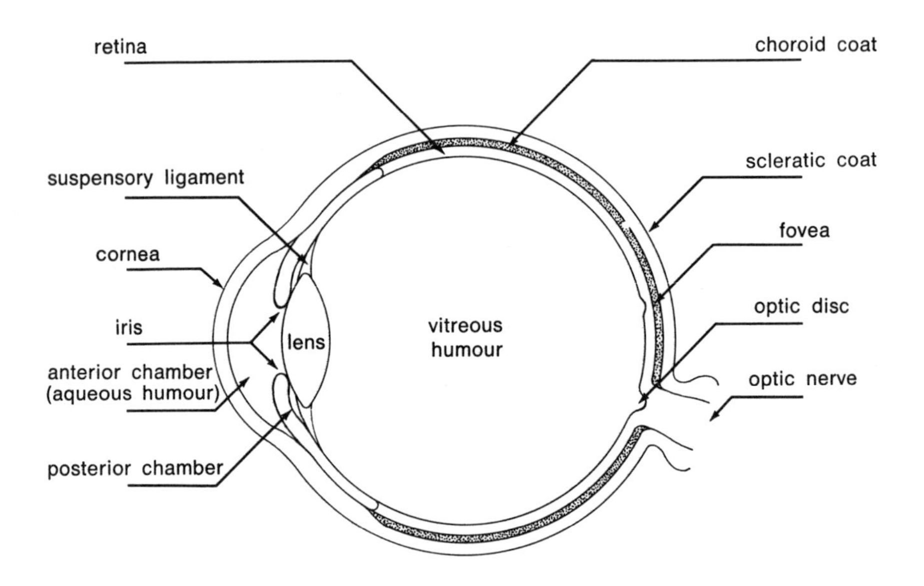

FIG. C.1 Anatomy of the human eye.

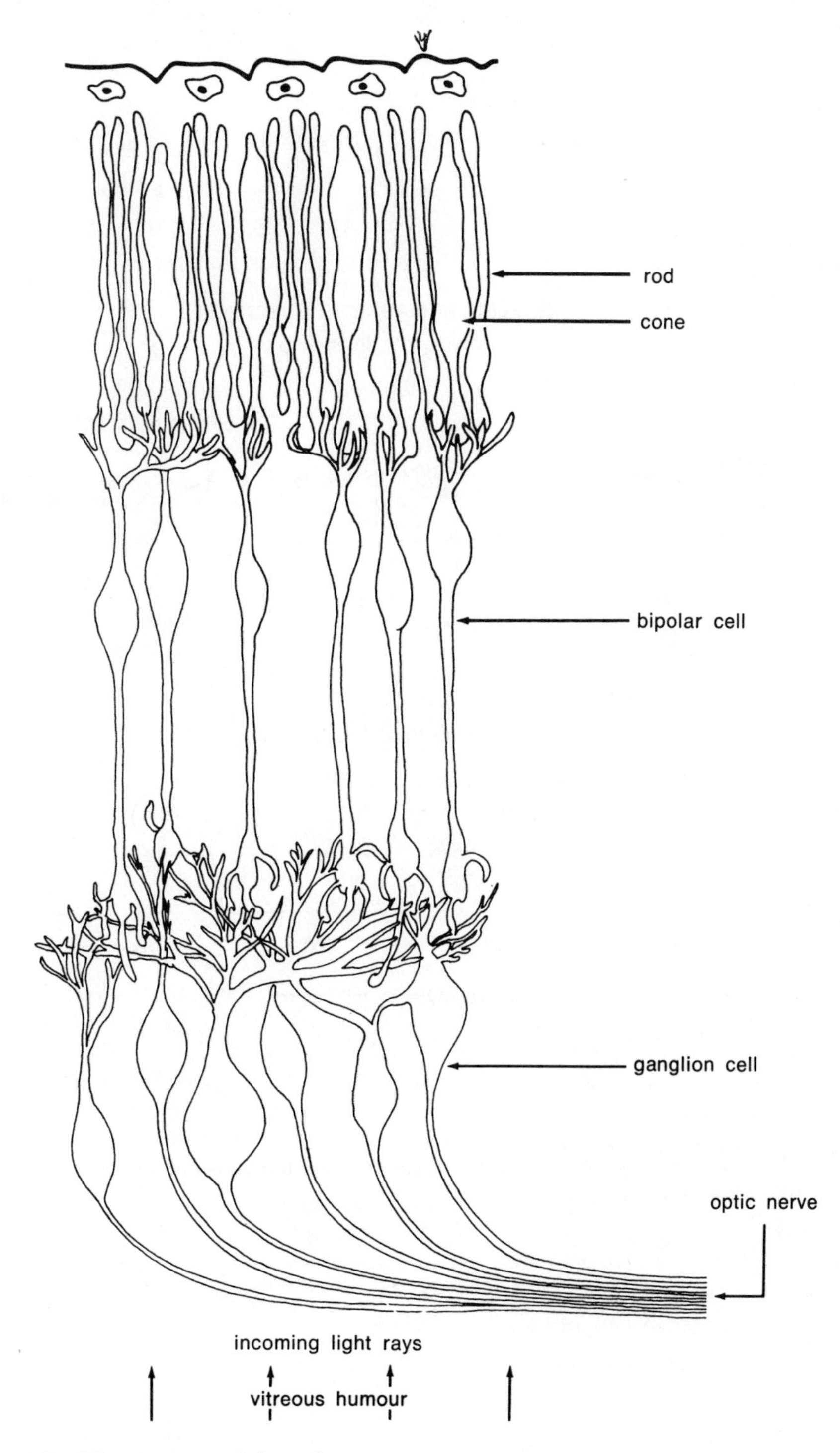

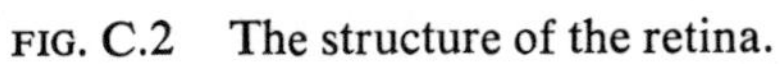
FIG. C.2 The structure of the retina.

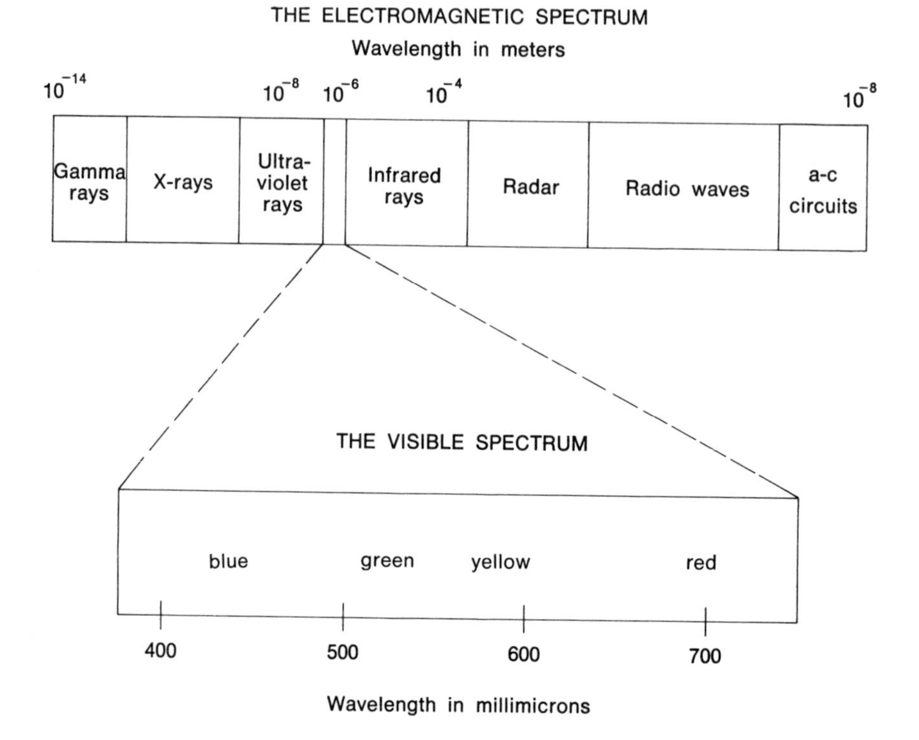

FIG. C.3 Diagram of the electromagnetic spectrum showing the relative size of the visible spectrum.

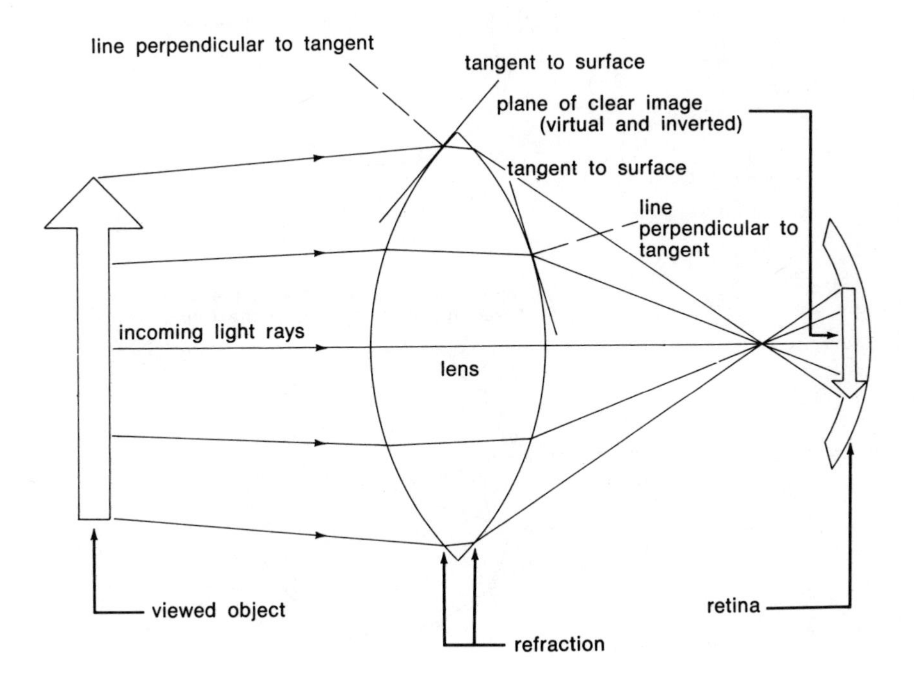

FIG. C.4 Effects of refraction in the eye.

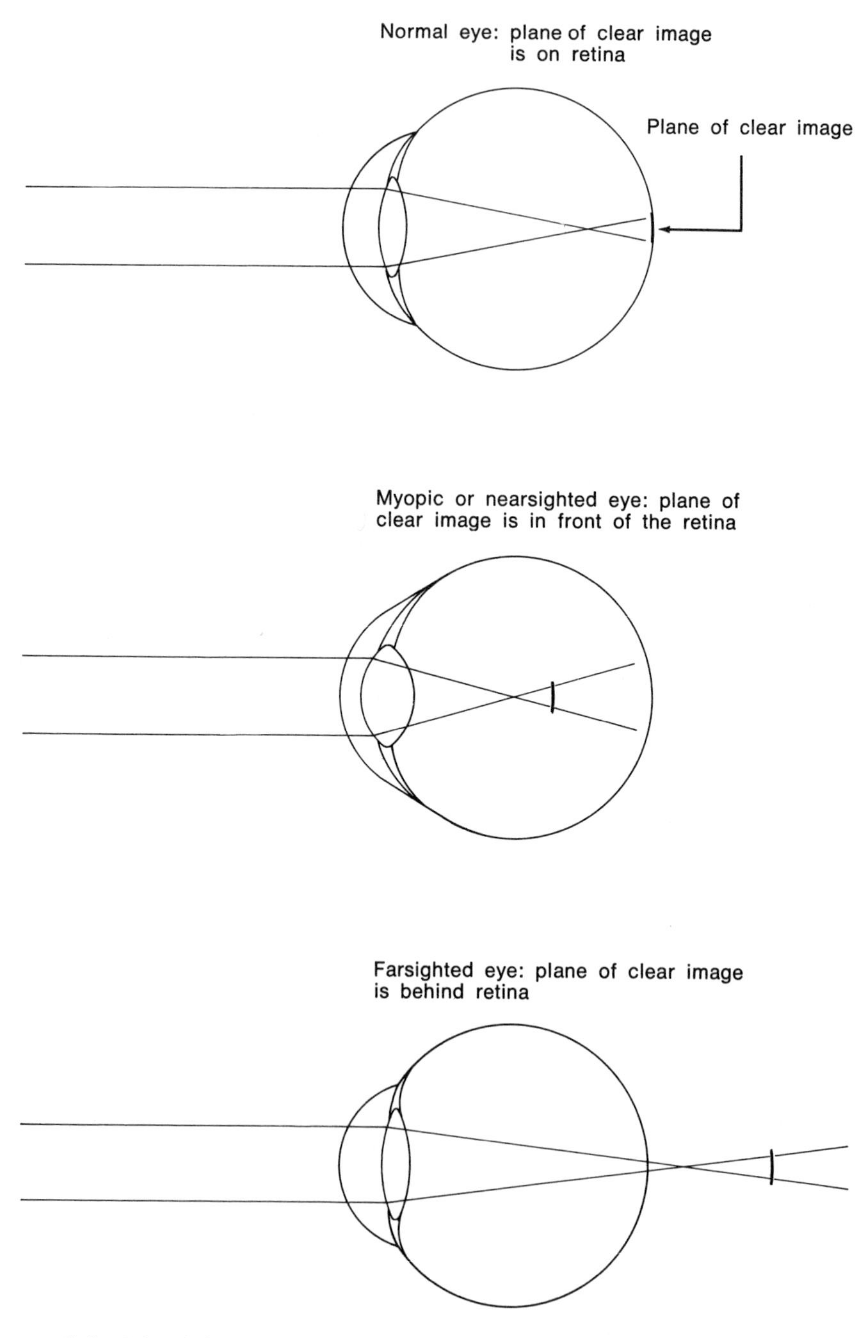

FIG. C.5 Visual defects.

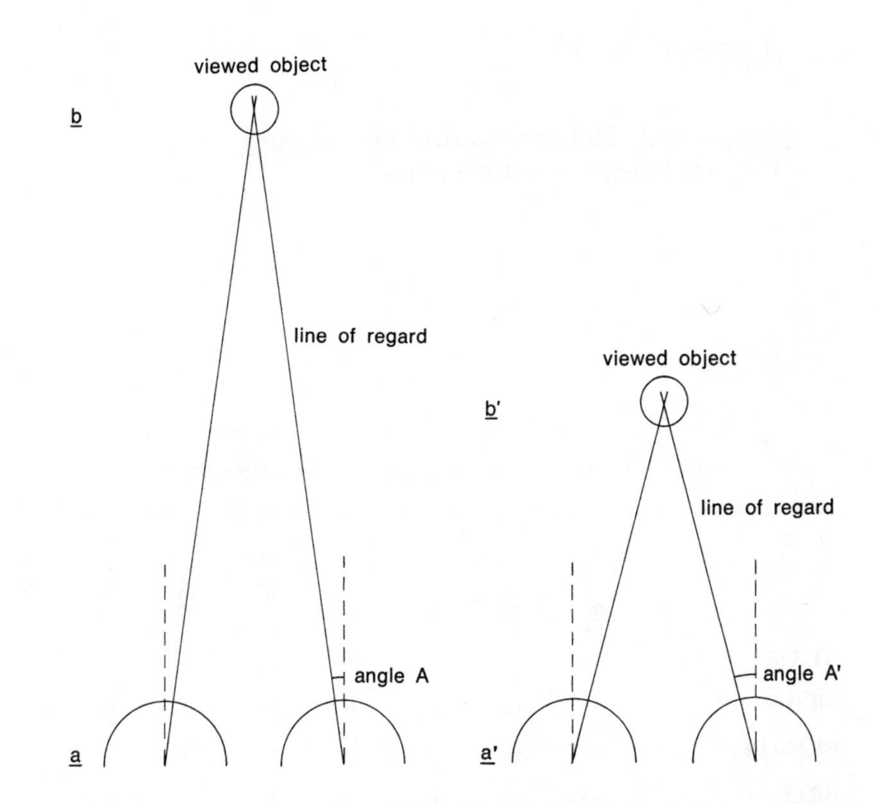

FIG. C.6 Convergence: as a viewed object draws nearer the eyeballs turn toward one another to allow convergence of their separate visual fields.

Appendix D

Significantly Different Indices of Efficiency For All Experimental Formats

D. 1 Learners in the First Octile of Scholastic Ability

	AE	OR	BRB	CR	BC	BRM-R	BRM	BRM-OR	BRM-F
AE-OR	←	←	←	←	←	←	←	←	0
BRM-F	←	←	←	←	0	0	0	0	
BRM-OR	←	←	←	0	0	0	0		
BRM	←	←	←	0	0	0			
BRM-R	←	0	0	0	0				
BC	0	0	0	0					
CR	0	0	0						
BRB	0	0							
OR	0								

← indicates direction of a significantly greater mean

0 indicates no significant difference in means

D. 2 Learners in Second, Third, and Fourth Octiles of Scholastic Ability

	BC	AE	OR	CR	BRB	BRM	BRM-R	BRM-F	BRM-OR
AE-OR	←	←	←	←	←	←	←	←	←
BRM-OR	←	←	←	←	←	0	0	0	
BRM-F	←	←	←	←	←	0	0		
BRM-R	←	0	0	0	0	0			
BRM	←	←	←	0	←				
BRB	←	0	0	0					
CR	0	0	0						
OR	0	0							
AE	0								

← indicates direction of a significantly greater mean
0 indicates no significant difference in means

D. 3 Learners in the First Four Octiles of Scholastic Ability

	BC	AE	OR	CR	BRB	BRM	BRM-R	BRM-OR	BRM-F
AE-OR	←	←	←	←	←	←	←	←	←
BRM-F	←	←	←	←	←	0	0	0	
BRM-OR	←	←	←	←	←	0	0		
BRM-R	←	←	←	←	←	0			
BRM	←	←	←	←	←				
BRB	0	0	0	0					
CR	0	0	0						
OR	0	0							
AE	0								

← indicates direction of a significantly greater mean
0 indicates no significant difference in means

BRM-OR_2

Instructions

This is a programmed textbook about the structure and function of the human eye. The text material is presented paragraph by paragraph in small steps. At the end of each paragraph you will find a study question about the information contained in the paragraph. The paragraph of text plus the study question is referred to as a frame.

For each study question two possible answers are shown. The **correct** answer is indicated by an asterisk (*) in front of it. In working through the book you will take the following steps:

(1) read the paragraph of text material;
(2) read the study question;
(3) examine the two possible answers noting the one which is correct and the one which is not correct. There is only **one** correct answer for each question.

You may re-examine a text paragraph as much as you like as you examine the study question.

During your reading you will be referred to another booklet labeled "Figures." These figures are drawings or illustrations which are useful in understanding the text. You may refer to these figures as often as you wish, but do not advance to a new figure until told to do so by the text.

If you do not understand how to work through the program, raise your hand and ask the proctor to help you.

When you have completed the entire book, so signify to the proctor.

YOU MAY TURN THE PAGE AND BEGIN

AE-OR_2

Instructions

This is a programmed textbook about the structure and function of the human eye. The book is divided into two sections. At the end of each section are 15 study questions which refer to the text material just read.

For each study question two possible answers are shown. The **correct** answer is indicated by an asterisk (*) in front of it. In working through the book you will take the following steps:

(1) read the first half of the text material;
(2) read each of the 15 study questions. In each case, examine the two possible answers noting the one which is correct and the one which is not correct. There is only **one** correct answer to each question.
(3) read the second half of the text;
(4) read each of the 15 study questions following the second half of the text.

You may **not** re-examine the preceding text as you examine the study questions.

During your reading you will be referred to another booklet labeled "Figures." These figures are drawings or illustrations which are useful in understanding the text. You may refer to these figures as often as you wish, but do not advance to a new figure until told to do so by the text. **When studying the questions, however, keep the booklet of figures closed.**

If you do not understand how to work through the program, raise your hand and ask the proctor to help you.

When you have completed the entire book, so signify to the proctor.

YOU MAY TURN THE PAGE AND BEGIN

Appendix F

Significantly Different Indices of Efficiency For All Experimental Formats (Including Those with the Two-Response Options)

F. 1 Learners in the First Octile of Scholastic Ability

	AE	OR	BRB	CR	BC	BRB_2	BRM-R	BRM	BRM-OR	$BRM-F_2$	$BRM-OR_2$	BRM-F	AE-OR
BRM_2	←	←	←	←	←	←	←	←	0	0	0	0	0
AE-OR	←	←	←	←	←	←	←	←	←	←	0	0	
BRM-F	←	←	←	←	0	0	0	0	0	0	0		
$BRM-OR_2$	←	←	←	←	0	0	0	0	0	0			
$BRM-F_2$	←	←	←	←	0	0	0	0	0				
BRM-OR	←	←	←	0	0	0	0	0					
BRM	←	←	←	0	0	0	0						
BRM-R	←	0	0	0	0	0							
BRB_2	←	0	←	0	0								
BC	0	0	0	0									
CR	0	0	0										
BRB	0	0											
OR	0												

← indicates direction of a significantly greater mean
0 indicates no significant difference in means

F. 2 Learners in Second, Third, and Fourth Octiles of Scholastic Ability

	BC	AE	OR	CR	BRB	BRM	BRM-R	BRM-F	BRM-OR	BRB$_2$	BRM-F$_2$	BRM-OR$_2$	AE-OR
BRM$_2$	←	←	←	←	←	←	←	←	←	←	0	0	0
AE-OR	←	←	←	←	←	←	←	←	←	0	0	0	
BRM-OR$_2$	←	←	←	←	←	←	←	0	←	0	0		
BRM-F$_2$	←	←	←	←	←	←	←	0	0	0			
BRB$_2$	←	←	←	←	←	0	0	0	0				
BRM-OR	←	←	←	←	←	0	0	0					
BRM-F	←	←	←	←	←	0	0						
BRM-R	←	0	0	0	0	0							
BRM	←	←	←	0	←								
BRB	←	0	0	0									
CR	0	0	0										
OR	0	0											
AE	0												

← indicates direction of a significantly greater mean

0 indicates no significant difference in means

F. 3. Learners in the First Four Octiles of Scholastic Ability

	BC	AE	OR	CR	BRB	BRM	BRM-R	BRB_2	BRM-OR	BRM-F	$BRM\text{-}F_2$	$BRM\text{-}OR_2$	AE-OR
BRM_2	←	←	←	←	←	←	←	←	←	←	←	0	0
AE-OR	←	←	←	←	←	←	←	←	←	←	←	0	
$BRM\text{-}OR_2$	←	←	←	←	←	←	←	0	0	0	0		
$BRM\text{-}F_2$	←	←	←	←	←	←	←	0	0	0			
BRM-F	←	←	←	←	←	0	0	0	0				
BRM-OR	←	←	←	←	←	0	0	0					
BRB_2	←	←	←	←	←	0	0						
BRM-R	←	←	←	←	←	0							
BRM	←	←	←	←	←								
BRB	0	0	0	0									
CR	0	0	0										
OR	0	0											
AE	0												

← indicates direction of a significantly greater mean
0 indicates no significant difference in means

Appendix G

Significantly Different Indices of Efficiency For Experimental Formats Given to Learners, Who Were Naval Enlisted Men

G.1 Learners in the First Octile of Scholastic Ability

	BC	OR	BRB	AE	BRM	$AE\text{-}OR_2$
AE-OR	0	←	0	0	0	0
$AE\text{-}OR_2$	0	0	0	0	0	
BRM	0	0	←	0		
AE	0	0	0			
BRB	0	0				
OR	0					

← indicates direction of a significantly greater mean
0 indicates no significant difference in means

G.2 Learners in the Second, Third, and Fourth Octiles of Scholastic Ability

	BC	OR	BRB	AE-OR	AE	BRM
$AE\text{-}OR_2$	←	←	0	0	0	0
BRM	←	0	←	0	0	
AE	0	0	0	0		
AE-OR	←	←	0			
BRB	←	0				
OR	0					

← indicates direction of a significantly greater mean
0 indicates no significant difference in means

G.3 Learners in the Fifth, Sixth, and Seventh Octiles of Scholastic Ability

	OR	AE	BC	BRB	$AE\text{-}OR_2$	BRM
AE-OR	0	0	←	0	0	0
BRM	0	0	0	←	0	
$AE\text{-}OR_2$	0	0	0	0		
BRB	0	0	0			
BC	0	0				
AE	0					

← indicates direction of a significantly greater mean
0 indicates no significant difference in means

G. 4 Learners in the First Four Octiles of Scholastic Ability

	BC	OR	BRB	AE	BRM	AE-OR
$AE\text{-}OR_2$	←	←	←	0	0	0
AE-OR	←	←	0	0	0	
BRM	←	←	←	0		
AE	0	0	0			
BRB	←	0				
OR	0					

← indicates direction of a significantly greater mean
0 indicates no significant difference in means

G. 5 Learners in the Second Through Seventh Octiles of Scholastic Ability

	BC	OR	BRB	AE	AE-OR	BRM
$AE\text{-}OR_2$	←	←	0	0	0	0
BRM	←	←	←	0	0	
AE-OR	←	←	0	0		
AE	0	0	0			
BRB	←	0				
OR	0					

← indicates direction of a significantly greater mean
0 indicates no significant difference in means

G. 6 Learners in the First Through Seventh Octiles of Scholastic Ability

	BC	OR	BRB	AE	BRM	AE-OR
AE-OR$_2$	←	←	←	0	0	0
AE-OR	←	←	←	0	0	
BRM	←	←	←	0		
AE	0	0	0			
BRB	←	0				
OR	0					

← indicates direction of a significantly greater mean
0 indicates no significant difference in means

Glossary

Program: whatever information and instructions are presented to the learner and which lead to his acquisition of certain specified behavioral objectives.

Frame: the fundamental unit of programs using small- or medium-step size. On programs using overt responding, at least one overt response per frame will be required of the learner. On programs using immediate feedback, the learner will be informed of the correctness of his emitted responses.

Reinforcement: a technical psychological term to denote a hypothetical process whereby the probability that a certain response will occur in the future is elevated, due to the response having been followed in the past by some stimulus having reward value. In programmed instruction, this stimulus is the display of the correct response by the program following the emission of the correct response by the learner.

Shaping: the building of a desired behavior in a learner through reinforcing selectively forms of the behavior which are progressively more adequate. Common behavior is variable. When the learner, in the ordinary course of events, emits a response which resembles in some respect the behavior desired by the trainer, the trainer rewards the behavior by providing some form of positive reinforcement. Gradually, the criteria for reinforcement are shifted in the direction of the desired behavior and through successive approximations the desired behavior eventually occurs and is reinforced. This training technique was popularized by Skinner as a means of training learners to emit unusual responses to any chosen stimulus. Shaping is rarely used in programmed instruction because it is usually far easier to evoke a response through prompts. However, shaping can be helpful whenever a response is difficult to evoke for the first time, that is when the response is not already in the learner's repertoire of behaviors, or when for some other reason, the response cannot be called forth verbally. Therefore, shaping is a useful tool for training in certain families of skills, such as motor skills, language skills, or social skills. For example, a trainer might use shaping to teach an English-speaking learner to speak the German equivalent of the English word, overestimate, but not to teach him to speak the English equivalent of the German word **ueberschaetzen.**

Principles of programmed instruction: those characteristics that either define instructional material as programmed or that tend to occur in programmed instruction under certain conditions. Three of the principles are considered to be mandatory in that they must be present if instruction is to be considered programmed. The mandatory principles are objective specification (or behavior analysis), empirical testing, and self-pacing. Three of the principles are considered to be optional in that one or two of them may or may not be incorporated into an instructional format depending upon the theoretical position of the programmer or upon the pragmatic efficiency of a certain configuration of principles for a certain learning task by a certain target population of learners. The optional principles are overt responding, immediate feedback, and small-step size.

Objective specification: the terminal behaviors sought in the learners when they complete the program, are stated in observable form. The programmer describes intended outcomes rather than substantive content. He also indicates the conditions under which the terminal behaviors are to be manifested, and states explicitly any restrictions to be imposed, or resources to be provided. He specifies a standard for judging if, upon completion of the program, the learner's performance is acceptable. Objective specification typically results in the creation of a posttest. The principle of objective specification is evolving into a more broadly-conceived principle embracing not only the specification of objectives but the specification of the tactics to be used in the creative effort of generating programmed materials that will attain these objectives. Thus, behavior will be analyzed in terms of its component discriminations, generalizations, and chains. Those components will then be sequenced most effectively for learning.

Empirical testing: the performance of tryout groups of learners from the target population is used as a basis for program development and validation. The data from responses to both the program and the posttest are examined. In the program development phase these responses identify shortcomings of each successive draft of the program and provide clues as to how it can be improved. A frame may simply be unclear, or a prior sequence may have insufficient redundancy, or prerequisite information assumed by the program may not be present among the learners, or prompts may have been faded too soon. After all these defects are remedied, empirical testing is used again in the program validation phase. When the program is believed ready for publication, it is administered to yet another sample of learners from the target population. The posttest scores obtained on this last administration must, in fact, attain the predetermined criterion level. This level may take a form, such as, some minimum specified percentage of the learners must score correctly on some minimum percentage of posttest items.

Self-pacing: each learner sets the rate at which new information is introduced to him or the rate at which new behaviors are called for by the program. The rate of progress is determined by the individual learner, not by an entire class.

Overt responding: the learners are asked to respond to explicit or implicit questions as they progress through the program. These responses may take many forms, such as: supplying a word left blank in a sentence, providing a numerical answer to a mathematical problem, choosing from several statements the one which best describes a concept, or identifying a particular element on a chart. Overt responses may take the form either of constructed responses or multiple-choice responses. A response is considered OVERT when upon request the learner performs some physical, as opposed to strictly mental, act. Otherwise, responding is considered to be COVERT. The overt response insures that the learner will become and remain attentive to the instructional material and more highly motivated. Moreover, emitting a correct overt response is considered by many to facilitate learning, particularly if the response is reinforced by some form of reward, such as, being informed that the response was correct. The overt response is also believed to be more resistant to extinction than a covert response. Apart from the instructional merits of overt responding to completed programs, overt responding by pilot samples of learners during program development are essential so that the programmer can study the response records for clues regarding how the program should be improved.

(Immediate) feedback: the information is communicated to the learner regarding which of two or more alternate answers to an implicit or explicit test question is the correct answer. Ordinarily, this information will be communicated to the learner immediately after he has emitted a response to the question, in the confirmation feedback mode. If his original response was incorrect, he must emit the correct response before proceeding to new text. In the prompting feedback mode, the cues may occasionally be so heavy as to effectively supply the learner in advance with the information as to what response is correct. This latter instructional tactic is employed by programmers sympathetic with Guthrie's theoretical position because in their view the important thing is to get a correct response emitted. Emitted responses are learned. Linear programmers, sympathetic with Skinner's theoretical position, use the prompting tactic also but for a different reason. In their view, the important thing is to get the response reinforced. But getting the response reinforced also requires getting the response emitted. Pure-confirmation tends to be employed only by auto-elucidative programmers. Branching programmers employ some thematic prompting and some confirmation, but they do so, not by intent, but as a by-product of the structure of the branching program. The branching program is based upon the rationale that the text, not the test item, instructs. The test item merely supplies feedback. But branching programmers are sympathetic to communications theory that uses feedback to mean information supplied from the learner to the program. Of course, information is also supplied from the branching program to the learner. And therefore, in fact, branching programs supply feedback as the term is ordinarily used in programmed instruction.

KCR: a commonly used abbreviation for knowledge of correct response. KCR is the irreducible minimum form that feedback can take. As operationalized in a program, KCR may simply be the correct response printed out in a designated location for inspection by the learner. In programmed formats using the procedure of confirmation of overt responses, KCR would be provided only after the emission of responses. In such formats, KCR may also be operationalized as an indication of correct/incorrect.

Remediation: additional feedback over and above KCR. Remediation occurs most often in branching programs and then takes the form of:

(a) the question and emitted response are restated before the indication of correctness or incorrectness is given, and
(b) additional remedial text is provided to the emitter of an incorrect response before returning him to the test item.

(Small-) step size: the amount of new information introduced per frame is kept small. Step size is sometimes used also to refer to the number of sequential inferences the learner may have to make in order to arrive at the correct response. But the most satisfactory definition of small-step size is the improbability of the learner emitting the correct response. Therefore, step size is defined empirically to be sufficiently small if the error rate is kept below a predetermined value, such as 10 percent.

Constructed response: a response that is supplied by the learner. The constructed response is analogous to the response emitted to a completion or short-answer type of test item. The response may be to supply the numerical solution to an algebraic problem, the missing word in a sentence, the answer to a question, or the identity of an element upon a chart. The linear technique relies heavily upon constructed responses because the underlying theory has it that learning occurs when responses are emitted and reinforced.

Multiple-choice response: a response that is selected by the learner from two or more alternatives presented by the program. The multiple-choice response is analogous to the response emitted to a multiple-choice type of test item. The multiple-choice response is particularly appropriate for those instructional objectives requiring discriminations between alternatives. The branching technique relies heavily upon multiple-choice responses because:

(a) the technique only requires an indication that the learner understood the text properly or which of several common misunderstandings occurred.
(b) the branching machine or "scrambled book" can, in practice only branch in a very few ways on each frame, and erroneous constructed responses may vary in many ways.

The auto-elucidative technique relies exclusively upon multiple-choice responses because:

(*a*) the technique is based upon the assumption that learning occurs either in text-reading or from the KCR supplied by the special-purpose response cards.
(*b*) the special-purpose response cards can only be used with multiple-choice items, because the original concept of the technique was that objective testing and learning were to occur simultaneously.

Multiple-choice test items frequently are answered on the basis of recognition while completion-type test items are frequently answered on the basis of recall. Thus, completion-type test items are typically more difficult, as a group, than are multiple-choice test items. However, in programmed instruction, responding to constructed response frames is typically less difficult than responding to multiple-choice response frames. The discrepancy is due to the fact that frames using constructed responses tend to be more heavily prompted than are frames using multiple-choice responses.

Confirmation: a feedback mode whereby the learner emits a response, then receives immediate feedback including at least KCR.

Prompting (or Cueing): a feedback mode whereby the learner is supplied so much "stimulus support" by the program that the correct response is evoked with a high degree of probability. The prompts may be in the form of additional text, or accompanying illustrations, etc. The frame stimulus consists of two portions:

(*a*) that portion which will eventually elicit the proper response, and,
(*b*) the prompt(s).

The establishment or strengthening of the bond between portion (a) of the stimulus and the proper response is an instructional objective. A prompt is simply an instrumentality for accomplishing that objective.

Formal prompt: a prompt that suggests the form of the response. Examples of formal prompts are such cues as indicating by dashes the number of letters in the proper verbal response or supplying some of the significant digits in the numerical solution to a quantitative problem.

Thematic prompt: a prompt that has meaningful implications regarding the response. Examples of thematic prompts are such cues as analogies or the restatement of a rule or principle that governs the solution of a particular class of quantitative problems.

Fading (or Vanishing): on successive frames, the gradual reduction of prompts for evoking a proper response. The rate of reduction is empirically determined so as to avoid a too rapid rate, that would result in an incorrect response, or a too slow rate, that would result in program inefficiency and boredom to the learner. As the learner proceeds through a sequence of frames, the amount of stimulus support is reduced to a bare minimum on a final frame in the sequence. This final frame is referred to as a test, critical or criterion frame, and may differ negligibly from a posttest item.

Error rate: the percentage of learners within a specified population who respond erroneously on a frame. Sometimes by extension, error rate also means the average error rate over all the frames in a program. This index is computed after every revision and tryout of a linear program, prior to its eventual validation and publication. Linear programmers do not permit error rates in excess of 10 percent. By this criterion level, a "low" error rate is considered by linear programmers to be a necessary but not sufficient condition for a program to undergo its final validation stage. In pursuit of a low-error rate, the programmer must not rely too heavily upon "copying" frames or other formal prompting devices. The low-error rate should be maintained as well upon test frames and delayed posttest items.

Redundancy: the degree to which a program will restate in a seemingly non-repetitious way, essentially the same information, or the degree to which a particular response class will be repeatedly elicited by a particular stimulus configuration. The degree of redundancy is determined by empirical test upon a sample of learners from the target population. Redundancy is a means of insuring the overlearning of material so that it will be consolidated before the introduction of new material. Redundancy is particularly important in the learning of introductory material upon which subsequent higher-order material depends.

Lean programming: the deliberate act of including insufficient redundancy into the early drafts of a program. Based upon instructional objectives, the programmer commences by writing only the "critical frames" which are frames having to do with the essential concepts logically sequenced. To the critical frames, he may add some "redundancy frames" where it is evident that the learner will require some repeated instruction in order to acquire the terminal behaviors. The rationale for programming lean is that it is quite feasible to compute error rates from the responses of tryout learners to the first draft of a program to find out where additional redundancy is needed and how much. On the other hand, if the programmer were to build into the first draft more than enough redundancy, this unwanted outcome would not be so easy to detect. Error rates, particularly in linear programs, are kept low anyway, and it would be difficult for the programmer to detect a superabundance of redundancy.

Overlearning: the learning that occurs due to the learner continuing to practice beyond the point at which the criterion level of learning has been reached. If the criterion were for a learner to identify each and every letter of the alphabet from hearing that letter in Morse code, overlearning would occur during all practice periods following the first perfect recital by the learner. Because memory ordinarily drops off precipitously immediately after learning, immediate recall is not a very good indication of whether material will be remembered to the criterion level. Overlearning slows the rate of forgetting and raises the probability that delayed recall will not slip below the criterion level.

Linear technique: the most common technique of programmed instruction. The technique is also referred to as "Skinnerian" after its founder, or as constructed response after the response mode employed. The linear technique presents information in a fixed sequence and maintains a very low-error rate on each frame. Thus, individual differences between learners are accommodated by the rates of progress through the program. The low-error rate makes branching sequences unnecessary. The linear technique utilizes all six principles of programmed instruction and has the smallest step size of any technique. Overt responding is deemed essential by linear proponents, who typically feel that responses must be emitted and reinforced, in order for learning to occur effectively. For the same rationale, constructed responses are much preferred over multiple-choice responses. Prompting, both thematic and formal, is used in order to make correct responses highly probable.

Branching technique: the second most common technique of programmed instruction. A branching frame presents text, examines the learner over the text by means of a multiple-choice test item, and if his response is correct, advances him to new text. If the response is incorrect, the learner will be given remediation (corrective instruction) and then may be directed back to the original test item or to a specially designed remedial sequence of frames, or "washed-back" to some prior frame to commence anew a sequence he has already travelled. Occasionally, test frames may be presented in a branching program so that brighter learners may be "looped-forward" around redundancy or review frames. The branching technique utilizes all six principles of programmed instruction although, compared to the linear technique, the step size is not so small, and the error rate is not so low. Like the linear technique, the branching technique requires the learner to respond overtly, but only to a multiple-choice test item. Constructed responses are unnecessary, in the view of branching proponents, because the function of the test item is not to teach, but merely to diagnose whether the text has been understood properly. Thus, the branching technique rests upon a communications model rather than the reinforcement model underlying the linear technique. Though not spelled out in the rationale of the branching technique, effectively the technique uses thematic prompting. Formal prompting is never used.

Scrambled book: a term used to describe a book-presented branching program. A scrambled book is the software equivalent of the more typical machine-presented branching program. The term scrambled book refers to the fact that the pages of the book are not read consecutively. Depending upon which answer the learner chooses for the multiple-choice item on a given page, he may be sent either forward or backward for his next frame, and on any particular response, the number of pages he must turn can be several. For this reason, there is a time penalty associated with book presentations of branching programs *versus* machine presentations. This situation is reversed with linear programs where the time penalty is associated with machine presentations *versus* book presentation. Apart from the differences in time costs, the software and hardware versions of either branching or linear programs appear to give comparable learning yields.

Wash-back: a form of branching whereby the learner is returned to a frame earlier in the instructional sequence than the one upon which he emitted an incorrect response.

Loop-forward: a form of branching whereby the learner is advanced from a correct response upon a critical frame to the next successive critical frame, thereby by-passing a sequence of frames containing either rudimentary or review material.

Auto-elucidative technique: the third most common technique of programmed instruction. The auto-elucidative technique is simply the conventional (large-step) text followed by multiple-choice test items to which the learner responds on a custom-designed response card that supplies immediate feedback by telling him if his answers are correct. He continues responding to each item until he responds correctly. The auto-elucidative technique differs from both the linear and branching technique in that it foregoes the small-step principle and also relies upon pure confirmation. It does not use prompting, nor does it permit the learner to review text prior to responding. Like the linear technique, the auto-elucidative limits its feedback to KCR. Like the branching technique, the auto-elucidative rests upon a communications model, although proponents do feel that a significant amount of learning occurs in the test-taking situation. The auto-elucidative technique is based mainly upon empirical evidence although some claims are made upon the laws of frequency, postremity, and effect. These laws hold that, of several responses emitted by a learner, the probability of any given response being learned depends upon whether it was emitted often, whether it was emitted last, or whether it was followed by satisfying or nonsatisfying consequences.

Computer-assisted-instruction (CAI): a type of programmed instruction which uses a computer to determine the identity and sequence of instructional material that the learner receives. CAI ranges from straightforward branching programs using a computer as a page turner to sophisticated systems following strategies having little in common with mainstream programmed instruction. Some CAI is more akin to information retrieval in that the learner controls the direction of instruction to a large extent. Computers are also being used to accelerate moderately the pace of self-instruction. Sometimes, this acceleration is accomplished by supplying prompts if no response has occurred within a specified latency interval.

References and Author Index[1]

American College Testing Program (1967). *Using ACT on the campus.* Iowa City: American College Testing Program. *23*

Anderson, R. C. (1967) Educational psychology. *Annual Review of Psychology, 18,* 129–164. *54*

Angell, G. W. (1949) The effect of immediate knowledge of quiz results and final examination scores in freshman chemistry. *Journal of Educational Research, 42,* 391–394. *52*

Bower, G. H., *See* Hilgard and Bower (1966).

Braden, W. *See* Buss, Braden, Orgel, and Buss (1956).

Briggs, L. J., Goldbeck, R. A., Campbell, V.N., and Nichols, D. G. (1961) Experimental results regarding form of response, size of step, and individual differences in automated programs. In J. E. Coulson (Editor), *Programmed learning and computer-based instruction.* New York: John Wiley and Sons, 86–98. *55, 83*

Bruner, J. S. (1966) *Toward a theory of instruction.* New York: Norton and Company. *144*

Buss, A. H., Braden, W., Orgel, A., and Buss, E. H. (1956) Acquisition and extinction with different verbal reinforcement combinations. *Journal of Experimental Psychology, 52,* 288–295. *55*

Buss, E. H., *See* Buss, Braden, Orgel, and Buss (1956).

Campbell, V. N. *See* Briggs, Goldbeck, Campbell, and Nichols (1961).

Carr, W. J. (1962) A review of the literature on certain aspects of automated instruction. In W. I. Smith and J. W. Moore (Editors), *Programmed learning.* New Jersey: D. Van Nostrand, 57–80. *97*

Cohen, I. R. (1962) Programmed learning and the Socratic dialogue. *American Psychologist, 17,* 772–775. *2*

Cook, J. O. (1963) "Superstition" in the Skinnerian. *American Psychologist, 18,* 516–518. *6*

Coulson, J. E. (1961) A computer-based laboratory for research and development in education. In J. E. Coulson (Editor), *Programmed learning and*

[1] The numbers in italics following each reference give the text pages on which the paper is cited. Citations in the text ar made by author and date of publication.

computer-based instruction. New York: John Wiley and Sons, 191–204. *151*

Coulson, J. E. (Editor) (1961) *Programmed learning and computer-based instruction.* New York: John Wiley and Sons, 13–24, 86–98, 191–204, 217–239. *55, 56, 83, 151*

Cross, P. (1968) *The junior college student: a research description.* Princeton: Educational Testing Service. *106*

Crowder, N. A. (1960) Automatic tutoring by intrinsic programming. In A. A. Lumsdaine and R. E. Glaser (Editors), *Teaching machines and programmed learning.* Washington, D.C.: National Education Association of the United States, 286–298. *7, 148*

Crowder, N. A. (1962) The rationale of intrinsic programming. *Programmed Instruction, 1,* No. 5 April, 3–6 *9*

DeCecco, J. P. (Editor) (1964) *Educational technology.* New York: Holt, Rinehart and Winston. *54*

Eells, K. (Editor) (1951) *Intelligence and cultural differences.* Chicago: University of Chicago. *106*

Eigen, L. D., and Margulies, S. (1963) Response characteristics as a function of information level. *Journal of Programmed Instruction, (2)1,* 45–54. *56*

Evans, J. L. (1961) Multiple choice discrimination programming. Paper read at the American Psychological Association Convention, New York, September. *147*

Evans, J. L., Glaser, R., and Homme, L. E. (1962) An investigation of 'teaching machine' variables using learning programs in symbolic logic. *Journal of Educational Research, 55,* 433–452. *103*

Gagné, R. M. (1965) *The conditions of learning.* New York: Holt, Rinehart and Winston. *13*

Gates, A. I. (1917) Recitation as a factor in memorizing. *Archives of Psychology, 7.* *50*

Gilbert, T. F. (1960) On the relevance of laboratory investigation of learning to self-instructional programming. In A. A. Lumsdaine and R. E. Glaser (Editors) *Teaching Machines and Programmed Learning.* Washington, D.C.: National Education Association of the United States, 475–485. *150*

Glaser, R. *See* Evans, Glaser, and Homme (1962).

Glaser, R. E. (Editor) (1965) *Teaching machines and programming learning, II, data and direction.* Washington, D.C.: National Education Association of the United States, 66–161. *6, 8, 147*

Glaser, R. E., and Lumsdaine, A. A. (Editors) (1960) *Teaching machines and programmed learning.* Washington, D.C.: National Education Association of the United States, 286–298, 475–485. *7, 148, 150*

Goldbeck, R. A. *See* Briggs, Goldbeck, Campbell, and Nichols (1961).

Guthrie, E. R. (1938) *The psychology of human conflict.* Boston: Beacon Press. *65*

Hartley, J., and Woods, P. M. (1968) Learning poetry backwards. *NSPI Journal, VII,* 9–13. *144*

Havinghurst, H. J. (1951) What are the cultural differences which may affect performance on intelligence tests. In K. Eells (Editor), *Intelligence and cultural differences.* Chicago: University of Chicago Press. *106*

Hilgard, E. R. (Editor) (1964) *Theories of learning and instruction: Sixty-Third Yearbook, National Society for the Study of Education.* Chicago: University of Chicago Press, 371–401. *8*

Hilgard, E. R., and Bower, G. H. (1966) *Theories of learning.* New York: Appleton-Century-Crofts. *13*

Hirsch, R. S. (1952) The effects of knowledge of test results on learning of meaningful material. Pennsylvania State Univ. Instruct. Film Res. Program, U.S. Naval Train. Device Cent., ONR. Tech Report No. SDC 269-7-30. Port Washington, N.Y. *52*

Holland, J. G. (1965) Research on programming variables. In R. E. Glaser (Editor) *Teaching machines and programming learning, II, data and direction.* Washington, D.C.: National Education Association of the United States, 66–117. *6, 8*

Homme, L. E. *See* Evans, Glaser, and Homme (1962).

Hovland, C. I., Lumsdaine, A. A., and Sheffield, F. D. (1949) *Experiments on mass communication: Studies in social psychology in World War II, Vol. II.* Princeton: Princeton Univ. Press. *55*

Jones, I. E. *See* Morse and Jones (1961).

Kaess, W., and Zeaman, D. (1960) Positive and negative knowledge of results on a Pressey-type punchboard. *Journal of Experimental Psychology, 60,* 12–17. *52, 65*

Kaufman, R. A. (1963) Experimental evaluation of the role of remedial feedback in an intrinsic program. *Journal of Programmed Instruction, 2*(4), 21–30. *52*

Kinzer, J. R. *See* Pressey and Kinzer (1964).

Klaus, D. D. (1965) An analysis of programming techniques. In R. E. Glaser Editor) *Teaching machines and programming learning, II, data and directions.* Washington, D.C.: National Education Association of the United States, 118–161. *147*

Krumboltz, J. D., and Weisman, R. G. (1962) The effect of overt *versus* covert responding to programmed instruction on immediate and delayed retention. *Journal of Educational Psychology, 53,* 89–92. *50*

Lange, P. C. (Editor) (1967) *Programmed instruction. The Sixty-Sixth Yearbook of National Society for the Study of Education. Part II.* Chicago: University of Chicago Press, 81–103. *144*

Licklider, J. C. R. (1961) Preliminary experiments in computer-aided teaching. In J. E. Coulson (Editor), *Programmed learning and computer-based instruction.* New York: John Wiley and Sons, 217–239. *151*

Lippert, H. T. *See* Stolurow and Lippert (1964).

Lumsdaine, A. A. *See* May and Lumsdaine (1958).

Lumsdaine, A. A., and Glaser, R. E. (Editors) (1960) *Teaching machines and programmed learning.* Washington, D.C.: National Education Association of the United States, 286–298, 475–485. *7, 148, 150*

Lumsdaine, A. A. (1964) Educational technology, programmed learning, and instructional science. In E. R. Hilgard (Editor) *Theories of learning and instruction: Sixty-Third Yearbook, National Society for the Study of Education.* Chicago: Univ. of Chicago Press, 371–401. *8*

Lumsdaine, A. A. *See* Hovland, Lumsdaine, and Sheffield (1949).

Mager, R. F. (1962) *Preparing objectives for programmed instruction.* San Francisco: Fearon Publishers. *2*

Margulies, S., *See* Eigen and Margulies (1963).

May, M. A., and Lumsdaine, A. A. (1958) *Learning from films.* New Haven, Conn.: Yale University Press. *26*

Mechner, F. (1967) Behavioral analysis and instructional sequencing. In P. C. Lange (Editor) *Programmed instruction. The Sixty-Sixth Yearbook of the National Society for the Study of Education. Part II.* Chicago: University of Chicago Press, 81–103. *144*

Merrill, M. D. (1965) Correction and review on successive parts in learning a hierarchial task. *Journal of Educational Psychology, 56,* 225–234. *22*

Moore, J. W., and Smith, W. I. (Editors) (1962) *Programmed learning.* Princeton: D. Van Nostrand, 57–80. *97*

Morse, R. J., and Jones, I. E. (1961) *Programmed teaching in an industrial setting.* Santa Monica: General Telephone Co. of California. *17*

Nichols, D. G. *See* Briggs, Goldbeck, Campbell, and Nichols (1961).

O'Day, E. F. (1968) *Programmed instruction and how to use it in educational applications.* Englewood Cliffs: Prentice-Hall. *2*

Orgel, A. *See* Buss, Braden, Orgel, and Buss (1956).

Pressey, S. L. (1926) A simple apparatus which gives tests and scores-and-teaches. *School and Society, 23,* 373–376. *149*

Pressey, S. L. (1950) Development and appraisal of devices providing immediate automatic scoring of objective tests and concomitant self-instruction. *The Journal of Psychology, 29,* 417–447. *150*

Pressey, S. L. and Kinzer, J. R. (1964) Auto-elucidation without programming. *Psychology in the Schools, 1,* 359–365. *8, 11*

Rothkopf, E. Z. (1966) Learning from written instructive material: I. An exploration of the control of inspection behavior by testline events. *American Education Research Journal, 3,* 241–249. *49*

Schramm, W. (1964) *Programmed instruction.* New York: Fund for the Advancement of Education. *8*

Sheffield, F. D. *See* Hovland, Lumsdaine, and Sheffield.

Silberman, H. F. (1961) Characteristics of some recent studies of instructional methods. In J. E. Coulson (Editor) *Programmed learning and computer-based instruction.* New York: John Wiley and Sons, 13–24. *56*

Skinner, B. F. (1958) Teaching machines. *Science, 128,* 969–977. *146*

Skinner, B. F. (1961) Teaching machines. *Scientific American, 205* (November): 90–102. *147*

Skinner, B. F. (1968) *The technology of teaching.* New York: Appleton-Century-Crofts. *151*

Smith, W. I., and Moore, J. W. (Editors) (1962) *Programmed learning.* Princeton. D. Van Nostrand, 57–80. *97*

Stolurow, L. M., and Lippert, H. T. (1964) Prompting, confirmation and over-learning in the automated teaching of a sight vocabulary. In J. P. DeCecco (Editor) *Educational technology.* New York: Holt, Rinehart, and Winston. *54*

Weisman, R. G. *See* Krumboltz and Weisman (1962).

Woods, P. M. *See* Hartley and Woods (1968).

Zeaman, D. *See* Kaess and Zeaman (1960).

Subject Index

*All items prefaced with an asterisk are defined at length in the Glossary.

Summary and Recommendations

The earliest studies of programmed instruction (PI) compared programmed to nonprogrammed material, or they compared various PI techniques, linear to branching being the most popular comparison. A natural reaction set in against this type of research, and PI researchers narrowed their attention to such specific, definable, and describable program properties as overt *versus* covert responding and immediate *versus* delayed redundancy. In turn, this trend proved too atomistic and neglected the interactional effects these program properties can have upon one another. The value of small-step size, for example, cannot be stated. The contribution made by small-step size is questionable in the presence of heavy, formal prompting, but can be significant in the presence of thematic prompting.

The present studies attempted to incorporate both the old and the new looks in PI research. Relative figures of merit were assigned to techniques, not just the popular techniques of Skinner, Crowder, and Pressey, but to new combinations of the familiar PI principles of overt responding, immediate feedback, and small steps. The PI principles themselves were also studied, but in a configurative framework and for specified classes of learners. These studies led to the following recommendations:

1. Certain PI principles should be considered as mandatory. These are the principle of objective specification (or behavior analysis) and the principle of empirical testing. Also, included is the principle of self-pacing as long as self-pacing is interpreted to mean that the rate of progress through a program is mainly established by

the individual learner, not by the entire class. But the principle of self-pacing should not rule out such refinements as:

(*a*) speeded presentations by computer, and,
(*b*) on frames having long latencies, such supplementary prompts as leading questions or analogies.

(See Chaps. 1 and 12)

2. Certain PI principles should be considered as optional. These are the principles of overt responding, immediate feedback, and small steps. Of the three optional PI principles, small steps is the riskiest to delete from a format. Those formats containing small steps are those that most reliably give acceptable large learning yields and acceptably small program times. The next riskiest principle to delete is the immediate-feedback principle, particularly, if either overt or covert responding is present and if small steps are absent. In effect, this is tantamount to saying that pure confirmation should be replaced by some form of prompting. (See Chaps. 1, 5, 6, 8, 10, 11, and 12)

3. As instructional formats include a greater number of the optional principles and features of programmed instruction, the learning yield tends to increase. However, the yield from any two or more features acting in combination will usually make a lesser contribution toward learning than would be expected from the separate contribution of each feature. (See Chaps. 5, 6, 10, and 11)

4. There are a minority of training and educational situations where the criterion of near-perfect performance must be attained. To compare techniques for instruction in such situations, the instructional technologist should set the criterion of success as high as indicated and compare the times required by various instructional techniques to achieve the criterion. However, the vast preponderance of training and educational situations require only that instruction bring about substantial improvement. To compare techniques for instructing the bulk of the population, more use should be made of the efficiency index: posttest gain/program time. It must be recognized that the relationship between posttest gain and program time is nonlinear, in practical terms, only if an extremely high criterion of performance is adopted and the entire learning curve is used. Based upon pilot studies, research designers must anticipate the scores on both dimensions: posttest gain and program time. The plotted value for each technique investigated must fall upon the "reasonably flat" portion, i.e., the initial portion, of its negatively accelerated curve. (See Chap. 6)

5. In designing programs for efficiency, greater stress should be placed upon the differences in time required by various instructional formats because differences in time often play a greater role in

determining efficiency than do differences in learning yields. The importance of time is too frequently discounted, although for many comparisons the minor differences in learning yield lead to a situation where a format which required half as much time could cover twice as much scope if time were held constant. (See Chaps. 5, 6, 7, 10, and 11)

6. Generally prompting is to be preferred over confirmation, particularly in the early stages of learning where most PI materials are employed. But where prompting is used heavily, programs should also contain some redundant frames with prompting gradually faded to the point of absence. Thus, some pure confirmation is utilized in the terminal stages of instruction in order to consolidate learning and insure retention when the additional stimulus support supplied by the program is no longer present. (See Chaps. 5, 6, 8, and 11)

7. While both thematic and formal prompting generally yield more learning, formal prompting requires significantly less time. The use of formal prompting can benefit where it cannot adversely affect attentiveness in reading the text. An example of appropriate use would be to establish a particular set of responses. But for purposes of associative learning, formal prompts should be used with caution, particularly on small-step programs, since they may hinder the establishment of desired stimulus control. (See Chaps. 5, 6, 8, and 11)

8. Program time tends to increase with the addition of:

(*a*) overt responding
(*b*) immediate feedback (knowledge of correct response or remediation)

Program time tends to decrease with the addition of:

(*a*) small steps
(*b*) option to review text prior to responding
(*c*) prompting (thematic or formal)
(See Chaps. 5, 6, 10, and 11)

9. In practice, the use of small steps automatically supplies thematic prompting and the opportunity to review text after viewing a test item. All of these three PI features engender less errors and are thus desirable. Because the three features are confounded in actuality among existing PI techniques, little is known of their separate contributions. In the recommendations below, whenever small steps are used, all three features will be understood. (See Chaps. 5 and 6)

10. While small steps tend to increase learning yield as well as to decrease program time, it is probably the latter phenomenon that accounts primarily for the greater efficiency of small step programs. (See Chaps. 5 and 6)

11. Where a program has small steps, prompting, and the opportunity to review text after viewing a test item, the learning yield from either overt responding or immediate feedback does not seem to be commensurate with the cost in program time. (See Chaps. 5 and 6)

12. The simplest form of immediate feedback is to indicate to the learner whether or not a particular response is correct. This form of feedback is referred to as KCR (knowledge of correct response). When feedback is postresponse, as in a program using the confirmation mode, KCR is about as efficient as more elaborate forms of feedback, such as the remediation used in branching programs. (See Chaps. 5, 6, 10, and 11)

13. Wherever overt responding is used, it should be accompanied either by immediate feedback or, preferably, by small steps, or both. That is to say, responses should always be either prompted, or confirmed, or both. For most instructional objectives, confirmation could be deleted more readily than prompting. (See Chaps. 5, 6, 8, 10, and 11)

14. For learners who are likely to make many errors whether due to low ability or questionable motivation, the above recommendation is underscored. If an instructional technologist does incur the time penalty of overt responding, he had better also introduce feedback and/or small steps. It would not be a sound practice to encourage or permit learners in the lower half of the ability range or with low motivation levels to make mistakes because, through the use of small steps, mistakes can be efficiently reduced to one quarter or one third. If for some reason large-step size must be used, immediate feedback should be present so that the mistakes can be promptly corrected. The conventional workbook accompanying many contemporary texts may hamper, rather than help learning. (See Chaps. 5, 6, 10, and 11)

15. Where poor motivation among learners is present, the novelty value of PI techniques that utilize immediate feedback and small steps are helpful *per se*. In addition, where small steps are present, the thematic prompting and opportunity to review text are helpful in reducing error rate and enhancing motivation. Where immediate feedback is also present, it has the merit of bringing to the attention of the learner his erroneous responses and furthermore causes him to emit the correct response eventually. He also spends more time in contact with the materials and probably takes more time before emitting his initial response to most test items. (See Chap. 10)

16. Program noise (irrelevant information in the text) is to be avoided, but its harmful effects can be somewhat reduced by overt

responding and appreciably reduced by overt responding plus immediate feedback. (See Chap. 9)

17. Programmers should elicit relevant responses. And when they do, they should elicit all the relevant responses. If some text information is elicited, some nonelicited, and some miselicited, the nonelicited and miselicted material may be learned less well than from a conventional book. Miselicitation appears to be particularly detrimental to the high-ability learner. It directs his attention to trivia when his ordinary disposition is to apprehend the key points in the text. (See Chap. 9)

18. Programmers must be careful to elicit relevant responses, especially when the program is small step and so permits the reading or rereading of the text to be influenced by the nature of an accompanying test item. The detrimental effects of miselicitation and nonelicitation of relevant responses are particularly severe in such circumstances. (See Chap. 9)

19. In program development, improvements first should be made by revising the inadequate text, and then remediation should be introduced only after repeated efforts at communication have failed. (See Chaps. 5, 6, and 12)

20. Where multiple-choice test items are used, as on branching and auto-elucidative programs, the number of distractors should be kept to a minimum except in certain special circumstances, as in the terminal stages of discrimination training. (See Chap. 7)

21. For efficiency in instructing learners in the top octile of ability, there is little justification for replacing a plain text with either an auto-elucidative or a book-presented branching program. Per unit time, the high-ability learner may learn about as well or better from plain text, and the latter is cheaper to produce and print. (See Chaps. 5, 6, and 11)

22. If branching programs are to be used, machine presentation is less time-consuming and more efficient than book presentation. Machine presentation without the typical remediation found in branching programs may be as efficient as machine presentation with remediation. It might not teach as much content, but it might teach as much per unit time while not requiring as complicated a presentation apparatus. Moreover, a machine-presented branching program without remediation appears to be more efficient than either a book-presented branching program with remediation or an auto-elucidative program. (See Chaps. 5, 6, 10, and 11)

23. There exist gadgets and gimmicks that are designed to convert instructional material into programmed form but that actually distract the learner's attention from the software intelligence. Included among the gadgets are Pressey's "trainer-tester response

cards," which, like some of the complicated response languages demanded of the learner by the more primitive CAI (computer-assisted-instruction) programs, require the learner to direct his attention away from the text. It is doubtful if the presumed benefits derived from any such gadget offset the negative consequences. (See Chaps. 5, 6, 10, and 11)

24. The foregoing recommendations are general guidelines that help avoid mistakes in program design. However, all program formats should be empirically checked for both instructional effectiveness and efficiency, particularly, where the learning task or the learner population is known to differ from the tasks or populations upon which similar formats have been tested. (See Chaps. 5, 6, 10, and 11)